Colonel John Hewson:
Cromwell's Enforcer

John F. Barry

Published by

MELROSE BOOKS

An Imprint of Melrose Press Limited
St Thomas Place, Ely
Cambridgeshire
CB7 4GG, UK
www.melrosebooks.co.uk

FIRST EDITION

Cover designed by Melrose Books

ISBN 978-1-908645-07-4

Printed and bound in Great Britain by:
TJ International Ltd, Padstow, Cornwall

MIX
Paper from
responsible sources
FSC
www.fsc.org FSC® C013056

For Mairi

BATTLES AND SIEGES
IN THE FIRST CIVIL WAR

YORK

MARSDEN □
MOOR

LINCOLN

□ NASEBY

EDGEHILL □

GLOUCESTER

BRISTOL

BRIDGEWATER □ NEWBURY (2)

EXETER

BASING HOUSE

CORFE CASTLE

LOSTWITHIEL

□ BATTLE

● SIEGE

CONTENTS

Oliver Cromwell

PREFACE AND ACKNOWLEDGEMENTS

Originally this record of the life of Colonel Hewson was compiled as an aid to students of the Civil Wars period, a "sign post" towards further research, possibly at postgraduate level.

It became clear that Hewson's involvement in so many key events identified him as a figure of unexpected interest. To produce a biography appealing beyond the requirements of the formal historian, I have sought to paint in a political, military and social background to these momentous years. Many of the views expressed are my own, and I accept responsibility for factual errors that may have been made.

The information presented has been gleaned from a wide ranging trawl through numerous books and articles published during the last four centuries. This work rests on the shoulders of others.

The initial enquiries into Hewson's life were made by my sister Elizabeth, and I am deeply appreciative of her original work, and continuing support.

I am grateful to Dr Glenn Foard for allowing me to refer to his definitive book, "Colonel Pickering's Regiment of Foot 1644–1645", for details of Hewson's military career.

Also I would like to acknowledge the assistance of the Drogheda historian, Brendon Matthews, who has thrown fresh light on events in the siege of that town.

My deep thanks extend to my daughter Caroline for assistance in preparing the manuscript. Particular gratitude is due to Jenny Barwell of Arena Personnel Ltd. of Letchworth, for ever cheerful secretarial help.

The striking cover illustration is by Chris Collingwood. All reasonable efforts to contact the copyright holder have been without success.

INTRODUCTION

The proud banner of England was held high. Through London's streets the funeral procession wound its way to the Abbey Church of Westminster. It was the 23 November 1658, and the funeral was that of Oliver Cromwell. The people were marking the passing of the Protector, the man who had brought their King to the scaffold, and had then tried to impose his vision of a better England upon a divided nation. He had died before his task was completed, yet (whatever their private opinion of Godly rule) all recognised that the towering figure of the age was leaving them.

As the multitude watched his regiments streaming through the narrow streets, they saw that the Banner of England, accorded precedence even over the Protector's family, and the great men of state, had been entrusted to the Lords Tomlinson and Hewson. This book is the story of John Hewson.

CHAPTER I

"From the lowest situation"

Who was John Hewson? He was a London tradesman who emerged from obscurity to be a senior officer in Cromwell's army, played a leading part in the politics of the Commonwealth, and on the Restoration of the Monarchy in 1660, disappeared from public view. His earliest biographer, the Reverend Mark Noble, wrote in the following century... "John Hewson, Esq., was soldier of fortune, and rose from the lowest situation, having originally, it is thought, been a cobbler; at the time of the death of King Charles I he was a colonel".[1]

Possibly on account of the opprobrium in which the regicides were subsequently held, little evidence of his origins is now to be found. According to Barbara Taft,[2] quoted by Brian Manning in *The Crisis of the English Revolution,*[3] Hewson was usually described as .... "of mean parentage and brought up to the trade of a shoemaker, may have been a cadet of a landed family in Kent".

However valuable research by Robert Temple[4] suggests that he was a son of John and Margery Hewson. This John Hewson was also a shoemaker, and may have founded the family business. The *Dictionary of National Biography*[5] states that ... "On 26 February 1628 the Massachusetts Company agreed to purchase of John Hewson eight pairs of shoes ..." but the date suggests that the John Hewson mentioned was the father rather than the son. Professor Temple refers to the work of a family historian[6] who claims that these Hewsons were connected with the Husons of Tenterden, in Kent. Certainly this ties in with Barbara Taft's supposition, as well as heraldry evidence.

It is interesting to note that the Will of a John Hewson, described as a citizen and merchant tailor of London, appears in the Calendar of Wills recorded by the Prerogative Court of Canterbury, Year 1653, folio 334. Whether he was related to the Hewsons we are concerned with has not been established. And whether the John and Symon Hewson, both of Bell Yard, City of London, admitted to the Cordwainer's (leather workers) Company around 1640[7] are of the Hewson shoemaking family, again, has not been established.

John Hewson (son) first appeared in the public domain as a thunderous preacher of radical views – anathema to the Established Church – and regarded as politically subversive. His was an Old Testament doctrine, exhorting his hearers to smite the enemies of the Lord, rather than to follow Christ's message of love. Perhaps it was fitting therefore that Hewson's way in life was made with the sword.

He would have been acquainted with the firebrand John Lilburne, who ... "was a young apprentice in the puritan household of Thomas Hewson, a clothier at London Stone who was a friend of the Winthrop family, of Henry Jessey, and of Rosier".[8]

A leader of the small London Puritan community, whose critical preachings so irritated Archbishop Laud and the other prelates of the Established Church, was John Winthrop of this family, who ... "worked in London for many years prior to his departure for Massachusetts in 1630".[8] It is possible that Thomas Hewson was an uncle or cousin, whose religious convictions influenced the youthful John Hewson.

Many writers of the time, disparaging the humble beginnings of Colonel John Hewson, refer to him as a 'cobbler'. In fact the family business was shoemaking in Westminster, possibly located in Tothill Street. This was close to Parliament and the Royal Court, and doubtless catered for a fashionably well-heeled clientele. Certainly (as previously noted) orders were obtained from the newly founded Colony of Massachusetts. The 1921 Edition of the *Dictionary of National Biography* gives 1628 as the date. However other editions give 1632. If this latter date is correct, is it too fanciful to suggest that this was at the recommendation of the Governor, John Winthrop? The business seems to have been substantial, and continued even after John Hewson joined the Parliamentary cause in 1642, since it is recorded that it supplied shoes to the Army.[9] This is supported by C. V. Wedgwood in his essay, "Trial of Charles I", where he writes … "Colonel Hewson, who was called a shoemaker by the Cavaliers but seems to have been a manufacturer on a relatively large scale …".[10]

Nothing is known of John Hewson's upbringing. However his writings mark him as a man of some education: received, no doubt, in a Puritan establishment.

In 1642 the rift between Charles I, and Parliament, became irreconcilable. For many years Parliament had distrusted the King's intentions, being opposed to his associations with the Catholic nations of France and Spain, and his marriage to the French princess, Henrietta Maria.

Furthermore the King's attempts to improve the Royal finances by dubious, and often unlawful, taxation measures antagonised the increasingly influential English middle classes. For his part, the King regarded Parliament's opposition as a challenge to his divine right to rule and he endeavoured to reduce its constitutional role. His attempts to rule without Parliament failed; alone, he simply could not raise sufficient revenue to pay for his religious wars with Scotland.

Matters were brought to a head by the rising in 1641 of the Catholic Irish, and the massacre of hundreds of Ulster Protestants. The reports reaching England were grossly exaggerated, but served to inflame public opinion. King and Parliament agreed on the necessity of raising an army to crush the Irish rebels, but neither would trust the other with its control.

Parliament continued its efforts to weaken the King's position, and in exasperation the King attempted to use force to arrest five of his leading tormentors. He failed, and with the populace of London turning against him, left his palace at Whitehall for Hampton Court.

Parliament fell more and more under the influence of extremist members, and in response the King made preparations to secure his position by arms.

Queen Henrietta took the Crown Jewels to Holland to raise money for military supplies, and on the 22nd August 1642 the King raised his standard at Nottingham, and declared Parliament and its servants, traitors. War was enjoined.

Charles I

CHAPTER 2

"The First Civil War"

Quite when John Hewson first smelt powder, and heard the cries of battle, is not known. Most probably it was as a member of the Earl of Essex's regiment at the battle of Edgehill.

How England slid into civil war remains the subject of debate amongst historians. It was the cruellest of conflicts, divided the nation, setting Parliament against its King, town against country, and father against son. As the Parliamentary General, Sir William Waller, famously observed, this was indeed a "…war without an enemy". Though many areas remained loyal to the King, London staunchly supported Parliament; in particular, the King's arbitrary tax demands, and his refusal to accept religious observances other than those he approved, aroused the antagonism of most of its inhabitants. John Hewson, a "radical independent and a famous lay preacher",[1] must have been incensed by the King's high church views. Perhaps he was influenced by the popular fear that, under the influence of his Catholic Queen, Henrietta Maria, the King might seek to restore popery.

Relations between King Charles and Parliament deteriorated during the summer of 1642, both sides coming to the conclusion that peaceful resolution was impossible, and consequently making military preparations. On 15 July, the Earl of Essex was appointed Captain General of Parliament's army. He set about forming his own regiments, which would include many Londoners. John Hewson joined, his education and standing in the city enabling him to obtain a commission as a captain in the Earl of Essex's Regiment of Foot.

Formal hostilities were announced by the raising of the King's Royal Standard at Nottingham on 22 August, 1642. A Parliamentary military force left London on 7 September. Two days later, to the cheers of the citizens, the Earl of Essex, in person, followed. Clearly he did not take an altogether hopeful view of this endeavour since it is recorded that he left "… carrying with him his coffin and winding sheet, together with his escutcheon, which would be needed at his funeral". His contingent probably included the Earl's own foot regiment, whilst the artillery train and baggage moved out on the 12th. The whole force assembled for a review at Coventry on 20 September. "The first two months of its campaign were spent mainly in the Midlands, marching hither and thither as the Royalists seemed to threaten one centre and now another."[2]

Essex followed the King's army, heading towards Worcester. Prince Rupert, the King's nephew, who had occupied the town, withdrew. On 23 September, Rupert's covering force clashed with Parliamentary horsemen, including Essex's own bodyguard, at Powick Bridge. The surprised Parliamentarian troopers "… fled so confusedly that some broke their horses' necks, others their own; some were taken, others slain; and scarce half of them escaped".[3]

Captain Hewson was not in this action, being with the foot soldiers who entered Worcester the same day. There Essex concentrated on serious military training, though not without incident, for some days later a soldier inadvertently discharged his musket loaded with two balls, killing one of his comrades.

Hearing on 12 October that the King had left his base at Shrewsbury with the intention of marching on London, Essex hurried to intercept. The two armies met on 23 October, 1642, at the foot of Edgehill, south of Warwick. Essex's foot regiment formed part of the Parliamentary centre. Not only did the centre hold its ground, even though both wings were routed, but prevailed, at "push of pike", over the Royalist centre. The King's standard-bearer was killed, and the standard taken. But the fall of night, and the return of the Royalist horse, saved the King's army. Both armies were in chaos, and disengaged in the darkness.

BATTLE OF EDGEHILL - 23 OCTOBER 1642

ACTIONS

1. RUPERT'S HORSE CHARGE - ROUTING RAMSAY.
2. WILMOT SCATTERS PARLIAMENTARY CAVALRY.
3. FOOT SOLDIERS ADVANCE - SEVERE FIGHTING.
4. BALFOUR'S REGIMENT ATTACKS KING'S LEFT WING.

RAMSAY'S TROOPS

RUPERT'S HORSE

RADWAY VILLAGE

RESERVE
KING'S HEADQUARTERS

ESSEX'S INFANTRY

BALFOUR

KING'S INFANTRY

WILMOT'S HORSE

FIELDING'S
REGIMENT

PARLIAMENTARY
CAVALRY

PARLIAMENTARY
FOOT SOLDIERS

ROYALIST
CAVALRY

ROYALIST
FOOT SOLDIERS

There was a sharp frost that night, many injured lying on the battle-field surviving only because the cold congealed bleeding wounds. Next morning both sides withdrew, allowing the King to resume his advance towards London.

Essex also headed for the capital but, pursuing a more direct route, arrived first, entering to a hero's welcome. The slower Royalist army approached London from the west. On 12 November, Prince Rupert's advance guard attacked Brentford, overwhelming the Parliamentary garrison, and inflicting great loss of life. After this success the Royal army edged closer to London.

Parliament organised a formidable defence. The disciplined, and fully equipped, London trained bands mustered, and on the following day, led by the Earl of Northumberland, marched out to meet the threat. The Parliamentary field army, recovered from the experience of Edgehill, marched separately under the Earl of Essex. No doubt Captain Hewson of the Earl's foot regiment was there in this resolute show of strength. The fighting men were supported by the women of London carrying baskets of vittles. The combined forces took position at Turnham Green. Faced with the massed ranks of Parliament's troops, the now tired and heavily outnumbered Royalist army chose not to provoke an unwinnable conflict, and retired from the field. Charles had lost his best opportunity to reclaim his capital.

The campaigning season over, both sides went into winter quarters. With the money of the City to call on, the Parliamentary field army re-equipped, and it is interesting to note that in December a warrant was issued for the supply of 400 sets of coats, shoes, snapsacks and shirts to Captains Gawler, Smith, Hewson and Scaltick of the Earl of Essex's Regiment of Foot. Perhaps to raise morale, the colour chosen for the coats was a cheerful, tawny orange![4]

The events of the autumn had taught both sides that a quick and easy conclusion to hostilities was not possible. Both desired a negotiated settlement. However, meaningful discussions did not take place, and with the early arrival of spring, military operations resumed.

The Earl of Essex planned to take Oxford, the King's temporary

DECEMBER 1642

ROYALIST AREAS SHADED.

AT THIS STAGE OF THE CONFLICT MANY AREAS WERE DISPUTED.

LONDON AND SURROUNDING COUNTIES STRONGLY SUPPORTED PARLIAMENT.

capital. In a series of leisurely moves, Essex secured the surrender of Reading and reached Thame, only some thirteen miles east of Oxford. His army became widely dispersed, and suffered from harassing attacks by Rupert's horsemen. Indeed, these so dispirited Essex that he abandoned his advance, and offered to resign his command. Parliament declined to accept.

The war was also going badly for Parliament in the west. At the end of July, 1643, Bristol, then the second port of England and gateway to Ireland, was stormed by the Royalists. Rupert and the King followed up this success by laying siege to the strategically important city of Gloucester. Parliament woke up to the seriousness of the threat, swiftly organising relief. Essex's army marched, strengthened by five regiments of London's trained bands (encouraged by the provision of a generous supply of bread, cheese and beer). This powerful force approached Gloucester. The King, fearful of being trapped between it and the newly heartened garrison, withdrew. On 8 September, 1643, Essex entered the city gates, to the great joy of its people. His arrival was indeed timely; food had run out, and the defending garrison had but three barrels of powder left. However, with the trained bands largely drawn from the City's work force, it was incumbent on Essex to return to London as soon as possible.

Prince Rupert persuaded the King that the war would be won if Essex could be cut off from London, then defeated in a decisive battle. The Royalist army pursued Essex, and, near Newbury, succeeded in barring the road back to London.

The clash came on the morning of 20 September, 1643. The Royalists were supremely confident, and had some advantage in numbers. However, Essex had deployed his troops carefully, whilst the experienced commander of the London regiments, Skippon, took the initiative to occupy Roundhill. This natural feature overlooked the battlefield and, from here, Parliamentary cannon was able to blunt the charges of the Royalist horse. The Royalist charges were also impeded by the numerous hedgerows criss-crossing the area, and by the steadfast courage of the London trained bands. The battle raged all day. By nightfall, the King's powder was largely spent, and, disheartened by the loss of some of his most trusted officers, he ordered withdrawal under cover of darkness. The first battle of Newbury must be regarded as a serious setback to the King's cause.

Next day, Essex's army was able to resume its march to London. On arrival, the battered army was welcomed with bell-ringing and celebrations, for the citizens recognised that defeat would have resulted in occupation by the King's army. The war would have been lost.

No contemporary evidence has been found to confirm that Captain Hewson took part in this campaign. Nevertheless, it was almost certainly the case, for his regiment would have been with Essex in all his major engagements.

The year 1643 ended with the King having secured the west, and from his base at Oxford, he remained a threat to London itself. He planned to increase his forces by recruiting in Wales, and by bringing back English troops previously employed fighting rebels in Ireland.

For its part, Parliament realised that only a wholehearted effort would avoid defeat. Negotiations had been opened with the Scots earlier in the year, and in September, Parliament had entered into the Solemn League and Covenant. Scotland would provide military assistance in return for an English Church reformed on Presbyterian lines. To counter the King's increasing military strength, Parliament formed two additional armies; that of the South Eastern Association, led by Sir William Waller, and that of the Eastern Association, under the command of the Earl of Manchester.

The Army of the Eastern Association had developed from an assortment of troops raised by the counties of East Anglia. Lieutenant Colonel Oliver Cromwell had, during 1643, brought together contingents from Essex, Norfolk, Suffolk, Cambridgeshire and Hertfordshire. Later in the year, those of Huntingdon and Lincolnshire were added, to form a cohesive, well organised army. The Earl of Manchester was appointed its commander in August, 1643, with Cromwell in charge of the horse, and second-in-command overall.

From the first, Cromwell determined that newly formed regiments

DECEMBER 1643

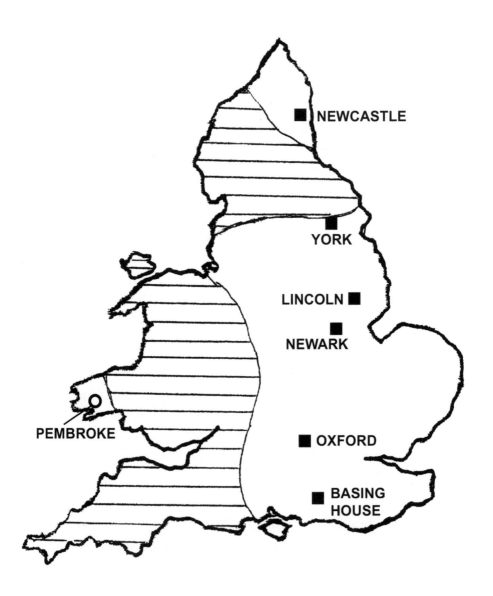

ROYALIST CONTROLLED AREAS SHADED.

■ ROYAL GARRISONS IN PARLIAMENTARY AREAS

○ PARLIAMENTARY GARRISONS IN ROYALIST AREAS

should be officered by professionals, or suitable persons with military experience. He sought to advance "honest, godly" soldiers, regardless of social class, claiming that he wanted "a plain russet-coated captain that knows what he fights for and loves what he knows". Many of the newly appointed officers were not Presbyterians, and included a wide spectrum of believers, e.g. the radical John Lilburne, who transferred from Essex's army. So also did John Hewson, by now a hardened infantry captain. Hewson took his opportunity to secure promotion, becoming lieutenant colonel in Colonel John Pickering's newly recruited regiment of foot. Hewson, who appears to have had recurring financial difficulties, no doubt welcomed his pay increase from fifteen shillings a day as a captain, to one pound ten shillings a day! He was formally appointed on the 26 March, 1644.

As Lieutenant Colonel, the day to day running of the regiment fell to Hewson, his Colonel often being absent on staff duties. Clearly he took up his responsibilities energetically – the new regiment was ready for action within weeks. Both he and Pickering were deeply religious men, and quickly infused the regiment with a Biblical fervour. A similar regiment of foot was formed by Pickering's friend, and relation by marriage, Edward Montague (later the first Earl of Sandwich). Montague was described as one of "those two valiant religious colonels".[5] The other was Francis Russell, who commanded another of the new foot regiments.

Ken Bradley[6] advances the suggestion that Pickering's regiment, together with those of Montague and Russell, were always selected for particularly difficult operations, e.g. assaults on strong fortifications, or forming the exposed front line in major set-piece battles, chosen because their puritan zeal made them the most resolute of Parliament's infantry.

The army commander, Manchester, grouped the regiments of Pickering, Montague and Russell, into a brigade under Major General Laurence Crawford, an experienced and courageous soldier. The fourth regiment in the brigade was Crawford's own.

The regiments were soon to be blooded. On the 20 April, 1644 Manchester's army assembled at Huntingdon, then marched north to Lincoln. The city was in the hands of the Royalists, and well prepared to withstand an assault. This was launched on the 6 May, with Montague's and Russell's regiments taking the lead. The outer defences were quickly overrun, forcing the Royalists to retire to the strongly held castle and cathedral area. The whole of Crawford's brigade took part in a final and successful onslaught – Colonel Pickering winning admiration for his personal gallantry.

Stone walls of York

Manchester led his regiments further north to join the large Scottish army (which had crossed the Border in January), and the Yorkshire Parliamentary forces under the Fairfaxes. These three armies combined to tighten the noose around York. York was the Royalist capital in the north of England, protected by formidable stone walls, and ably defended by the Earl of Newcastle. It had been holding out since April. On 6 June Manchester's regiments took the outlying defences, and advanced up to the medieval city walls. In a rash attack on the 16 June, around 600 men from Crawford's brigade broke into the city through a breach opened by cannon fire. They were quickly surrounded by some 2,000 of Newcastle's finest soldiers, and badly mauled, hundreds surrendering. Some of Pickering's men were apparently involved in the fiasco, but to what extent cannot now be established.

Lincoln Castle

On 28 June, the Parliamentarian leaders learned that Prince Rupert was on his way to relieve York. Two days later they abandoned the siege, and prepared to confront him.

The battle took place on the 2 July, 1644, at Marston Moor, eight miles west of York. The leaders of both armies were anxious to fight. Rupert was determined to secure a decisive victory – confident that his dashing cavalry would, yet again, scatter the opposing horse.

For his part, the canny Scots Earl of Leven, Commander-in-Chief of the combined parliamentary armies, believed that his numerical superiority, some 27,000 men against an estimated 17,500 Royalists, provided the opportunity to crush the King's forces in the north.

All that summer's day, both sides made troop dispositions, both adopting the conventional formation of massed foot soldiers in the centre, flanked by protective regiments of cavalry. Rupert had the advantage of being first on the field, enabling him to secure the better tactical position. However he was infuriated by the delay, until late afternoon, of vital reinforcements from the York garrison.

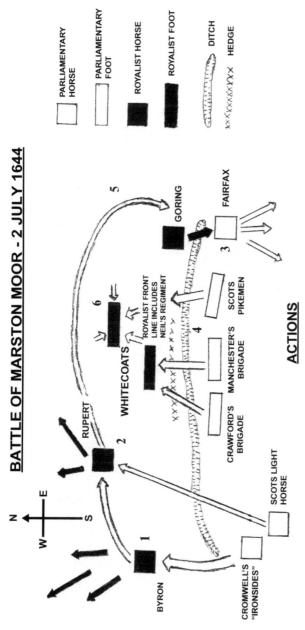

BATTLE OF MARSTON MOOR - 2 JULY 1644

PARLIAMENTARY HORSE

PARLIAMENTARY FOOT

ROYALIST HORSE

ROYALIST FOOT

DITCH

HEDGE

ACTIONS

1. CROMWELL'S "IRONSIDES" SCATTER BYRON'S HORSE.

2. RUPERT'S RESERVE CONFRONTS CROMWELL, BUT IS OVERRUN WHEN SCOTS LIGHT HORSE ATTACK HIS FLANK.

3. GORING ROUTS FAIRFAX'S HORSE.

4. PARLIAMENT'S FOOT ADVANCE SLOWLY IN HEAVY FIGHTING.

5. CROMWELL REGROUPS "IRONSIDES", THEN FALLS ON GORING'S NOW DISORGANISED TROOPS.

6. SURROUNDED "WHITECOATS" EVENTUALLY OVERWHELMED.

Prince Rupert decided that it was now too late in the day to open hostilities. Despite the misgivings of some of his senior officers, he stood down his troops from immediate readiness, and allowed them to make themselves comfortable for the night. Fires were lit to cook the evening meal, and horses ungirthed.

The Earl of Leven let the Royalists assume that the battle would not commence until the following morning, after all only a few hours of daylight remained. He waited until around seven in the evening before suddenly launching the "Ironsides", Cromwell's famed psalm-singing, highly disciplined regiments of horse, against Rupert's cavaliers. Though taken by surprise, the Royalist horse fought manfully, trading blow for blow with Cromwell's troopers, until dispersed by the flank attack of a force of fresh Scottish horsemen.

At the heart of the battle, the massed ranks of foot soldiers on both sides faced each other. Crawford's brigade was in the left forefront of the Parliamentary army, Pickering's regiment standing alongside Montague's and Russell's. "In the centre of the battle-line, Manchester's foot also surged forward valiantly and after eliminating the 'forlorn hope' of the Royalists ahead of their battalia, managed to capture their guns ..."[7] They encountered fierce opposition, first overcoming O'Neill's regiment. "Upon the advancing of the Earle of Manchester's foot, after short firing on both sides, we caused the enemy to quit the hedge in a disorderly manner."[8] Their advance brought them against Newcastle's own regiment of "Whitecoats" (which had wreaked such execution at York). A contemporary news sheet reported "... how the Brigade consisting of Colonel Russell, Colonel Montague and Colonel Pickering's regiments behaved themselves most gallantly".[9]

Meanwhile, following their success against Prince Rupert's cavaliers, Cromwell's horse cleared the remaining Royalist cavalry from the field. Still maintaining their good order the "Ironsides" were then free to surround the royalist foot. Some regiments melted away, but the "Whitecoats" resisted valiantly to the end, few being taken alive. Prince Rupert himself escaped by hiding in a bean field!

It was a comprehensive victory, with thousands of Royalists slain.

The King's power in the north was irretrievably lost.

However the war had taken a different course in the south. Since the Scots had entered the conflict on the side of Parliament, its conduct was directed by "The Committee of Both Kingdoms". This body was made up of senior parliamentarians, Scottish representatives, and army leaders. It had no outstanding personality to establish a coherent policy, whilst its decisions were weakened by factionalism. Against the instructions of the Committee, the Earl of Essex led his army into the south-west – his intention being to deprive the King of support from the fiercely loyal counties of Devon and Cornwall. The Royalist commanders were quick to seize their opportunity, and by August, 1644, had no less than four armies in Devon. Essex found his extended supply line from London cut, and he was herded deeper into hostile Cornwall. Short of food and ammunition, and with no hope of sea-borne assistance, Essex was in an impossible situation. A small body of his horse managed to evade the encircling Royalist forces, breaking out under cover of a mist. Essex himself escaped by sea, and, on the 2 September, his abandoned foot soldiers laid down their arms at Lostwithiel. Of the 6,000 foot soldiers of Essex's army who surrendered, only about 1,000 eventually returned to London. The rest were murdered, or perished from cold and hunger on the road. Hewson was indeed fortunate in having transferred to Manchester's army!

Essex sought to cast the blame for this disaster on everyone but himself, and succeeded in persuading the Committee of Both Kingdoms to appoint him to command a reconstituted army incorporating the survivors of Lostwithiel.

Following their success at Marston Moor, the Parliamentary armies in the north separated; Fairfax remained in Yorkshire, whilst the Scots marched north to besiege Newcastle. Manchester took the Army of the Eastern Association south. However, the lesson that decisive battles could be won by uniting separate armies to achieve numerical superiority on the day had been learned. Waller's forces linked up with Manchester's army at Basingstoke, and both joined up with Essex's new army on the 21 October, 1644. Characteristically, the Committee shirked appointing an overall commander for the combined armies, leaving it to a local council of war to conduct the campaign.

The King, buoyed up by his triumph in Cornwall, had brought back his main force to the Oxford area, and looked to confront the Parliamentary armies. Taken together, the three Parliamentary armies amounted to some 19,000 men, including 8,000 horse, greatly outnumbering the Royalists. For his part, the King had only 9,000 men, and lacked his experienced cavalry regiments, which had been detached under Prince Rupert. The King chose to take up position a little to the north of Newbury, in an area where the enemy could not easily attack his flanks, thus mitigating his numerical inferiority. Close by stood Royalist held Donnington Castle.

The Parliamentary council of war, without the Earl of Essex who had stayed behind in Reading pleading a heavy cold, came up with a daring plan – a fifteen mile night march, to circle around the Royalist position and surprise the King's army in the rear. This difficult operation, involving more than half the combined army, was led by Waller, Skippon and Cromwell.

Fighting commenced at dawn on the 27 October, with Manchester's troops making a frontal assault on the King's position. This was repulsed, and little further action took place until three o'clock in the afternoon, when the striking force overran the King's rearguard. The plan previously agreed was that Manchester's regiments would then simultaneously make a frontal attack. However, Manchester delayed his advance until about four o'clock, by which time the King had seen the danger of encirclement. Manchester subsequently attempted to explain that his inaction was due to his failure to recognise the agreed signal, the sound of Waller's cannon firing on the King's rear guard. Manchester claimed that he could not distinguish these guns from the general noise of battle.

Pickering's regiment was in the forefront of Manchester's eventual assault, attempting to capture the stoutly defended Shaw House. The Royalist garrison replied with a hail of gunfire, driving back the regiment. As Glenn Foard notes, this was "the only significant defeat in which Pickering's were ever involved".[10]

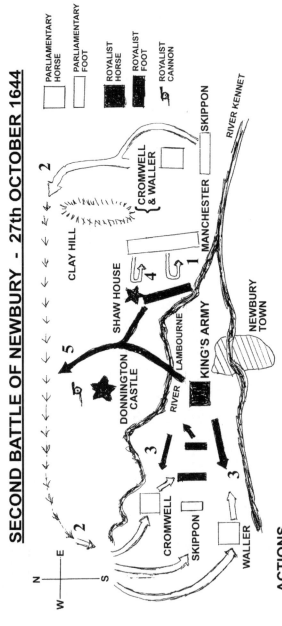

SECOND BATTLE OF NEWBURY - 27th OCTOBER 1644

Key:
- PARLIAMENTARY HORSE
- PARLIAMENTARY FOOT
- ROYALIST HORSE
- ROYALIST FOOT
- ROYALIST CANNON

CLAY HILL

SHAW HOUSE

DONNINGTON CASTLE

RIVER LAMBOURNE

CROMWELL & WALLER

MANCHESTER

SKIPPON

KING'S ARMY

NEWBURY TOWN

RIVER KENNET

CROMWELL

SKIPPON

WALLER

ACTIONS

1. MANCHESTER'S DAWN ATTACK REPULSED.
2. WALLER, CROMWELL AND SKIPPON'S LONG OVERNIGHT MARCH TO SURPRISE KING'S REARGUARD.
3. KING'S RESERVES COUNTER ATTACK.
4. MANCHESTER'S LATE ASSAULT ON SHAW HOUSE BEATEN BACK.
5. UNDER COVER OF DARKNESS, KING'S ARMY ESCAPES THE PARLIAMENTARY PINCER.

DECEMBER 1644

ROYALIST CONTROLLED AREAS SHADED

■ ROYALIST GARRISONS IN PARLIAMENTARY AREAS

○ PARLIAMENTARY GARRISONS

<u>NOTE:</u>

FOLLOWING THE BATTLE OF MARSTON MOOR IN JULY 1644,
THE ROYALISTS HAD LOST CONTROL OF THE NORTH OF THE COUNTRY.

Darkness began to fall, and the King, fearing that his army would be cut in two, reluctantly ordered his troops to retire. They made their escape from the jaws of the trap in the increasing gloom, covering fire from the guns of Donnington Castle deterring organised pursuit.

This second battle of Newbury was a severe rebuff for King Charles, but Manchester (as the most senior of Parliament's army leaders) failed to follow up his success. Had he been able to catch and finish off the King's weakened army, the outcome of the war would have been settled. As it was another year of conflict had to follow. Pickering's regiment had been campaigning virtually since being formed in March 1644. It had taken part in two major set-piece battles, and a number of intensely fought minor actions. Although actual battle casualties had not been severe, regimental strength had fallen dramatically – from a maximum of 738 men in May to only 243 by the end of the year.[11] Throughout this period, the regiment, like its sister regiments, suffered intermittent visitations from serious infectious diseases. Poor food, and hardship in the field, brought on a variety of illnesses. Pay was often in arrears: many soldiers, especially pressed men, deserted when opportunity arose. But it must be said that the regiment, due to the superior organisation of the Army of the Eastern Association, undoubtedly fared better than foot regiments in other armies.

As might be expected, the year ended in an atmosphere of frustration and recrimination amongst Parliament's supporters. Cromwell and Waller blamed Manchester for the poor outcome of the campaign, citing his failure to keep to the agreed plan at the second Battle of Newbury, and his apparent reluctance to inflict a decisive defeat on the King. There was an acrimonious difference of opinion between the party of Manchester, Essex, and senior Presbyterian members of Parliament, (who favoured a negotiated settlement); and Cromwell, Waller and the more aggressive army leaders (who argued that the King's military strength must first be broken before any negotiations). This dispute mirrored the emerging religious tensions between a largely Presbyterian Parliament, and an increasingly independently thinking army.

People in the seventeenth century held deep religious beliefs which governed day to day living, and influenced the course of public affairs. The developing antagonism between Presbyterians and the various Protestant sects gathered under the banner of Independents, played a major part in the discord between Parliament and the Army. Basically the Presbyterians wanted a state-regulated, structured church, although rejecting bishops. The Independents rejected both central authority and bishops. The Independents stood for freedom of choice and individual belief – though not, of course, for Catholics. These differences came to a head in Parliament. In November, Cromwell returned to the Commons, and made a damning speech, highlighting Manchester's "slowness in all things", and his repeated failures to take advantage of military success. It was clear to all that, if the war was to be prosecuted successfully, a fresh start with new leaders was required. Parliament set out to reorganise the military. The disintegrating patchwork of regional armies was to be replaced by a single national army under Parliament's control and financed by it. On the 21 January, 1645, Parliament passed the Ordinance authorising establishment of the New Model Army, with a target strength of 22,000 men. The new army commander was to be Thomas Fairfax, who had been a successful commander of Parliament's Yorkshire forces, and was associated with neither faction.

Thomas Fairfax

"The nucleus of the cavalry was provided from what had been the Earl of Manchester's army, which had been largely trained by Cromwell. That was (apart from his political activities) Cromwell's only contribution to the creation of the new army. This was Fairfax's responsibility. Over 8,000 men had to be pressed to join the infantry."[12]

Pickering's regiment was transferred to the New Model Army from the Army of the Eastern Association, being brought up to strength with men from the now disbanded foot regiment of Colonel Ayloffe.

Senior military appointments had to be approved by Parliament. Fairfax submitted a list of his preferred officers, including John Hewson to remain as lieutenant colonel of Pickering's regiment. The

Lords challenged no fewer than 58 of Fairfax's nominations; 34 had served in the Army of the Eastern Association. This high proportion reflected that army's reputation for radicalism. Those objected to included Colonel Pickering, Hewson, and the regiment's major, John Jubbs. It appears that the objections raised were on religious or political grounds. In Hewson's case one may assume that the Lords took exception to his history of fiery preaching in London. It was not until the 1 April 1645, that Fairfax's list was finally approved by the Lords – and then only by a single vote.

It was remarked at the time that a good third of the senior officers of the new army could not be described as gentlemen, and the Royalists singled out for scorn Colonel Pride, the former drayman, Okey the ship chandler, and Hewson "the cobbler". The fact was that Hewson had managed to keep his shoe manufacturing business running, and indeed had successfully contracted to supply shoes to the army.

The new army formed up on Windsor Meads, and on the 3 April 1645, its new commander, Fairfax, "called a general rendezvous of the army and there he remained until the end of the month 'busie in modelling his Army'".[13]

Hewson had been appointed the regiment's lieutenant colonel by the Commons on the 18 March, and was responsible for incorporating the foot soldiers from Ayloffe's disbanded regiment. His letter to the Treasurer of the Army, undated but presumably written in April, confirms this addition to strength, and (unsurprisingly) requests funds to meet pay arrears![14]

Pickering's reinvigorated regiment was soon in action. On 29 April 1645, Cromwell ordered an assault on Royalist held Farringdon Castle, an outpost of the defences around Oxford. The regiment formed the main part of the attacking force, but without cannon in support, failed. Cromwell received fresh orders from Fairfax, and withdrew his troops without a further attempt.

Fairfax, in May, moved to surround Oxford, the King's headquarters. It is recorded that Hewson was detached to assist the delivery of arms and medical supplies to the besieging forces.[15] However, Fairfax lacked heavy guns and no attempt to take the city could be considered.

The Royalists sought to draw Fairfax away from Oxford, and decided to "fall upon some place possessed by Parliament". On the 29 May Rupert surrounded Leicester. His cannon breached the walls, and on the 31st the town was overrun. The indiscriminate slaughter that followed was one of the worst atrocities of the war.

Rupert's cynical action had the desired result. Fairfax gathered his forces, and left Oxford intending to confront the King's Army. Rupert and the King, though they affected to despise the "New Noddle Army", were anxious to avoid battle, at least until strengthened by the return of Lord Goring's experienced horsemen from operations in the south-west. However, Fairfax and Cromwell caught up with the King's army at the village of Naseby, near Market Harborough, before this could happen.

When the Parliamentary advance guard rode into the village they surprised a Royalist rearguard ensconced in the local hostelry, drinking and playing quoits! Apprised of his peril, the King called a midnight council of war; and on the following morning, the 14 June 1645, ordered his army to make a stand near the village. Clarendon states that his strength was about 7,400 men, but this estimate is generally regarded as low, more probably it was nearer 9,000. For his part Fairfax had around 13,000. The Parliament horse was formidable, largely made up of Cromwell's well disciplined and well equipped "Ironsides". However, Parliament's foot regiments were generally below strength, whilst many of the rank and file were raw and unwilling recruits.

On Cromwell's advice, Fairfax moved part of his army back. Prince Rupert saw this taking place and assumed that the Parliamentarians were withdrawing. Just as Cromwell had hoped, Rupert was encouraged to take the offensive, and the two armies closed.

As at the battle of Marston Moor a year earlier, both sides adopted the conventional deployment of their troops – massed infantry in the centre, protected on their flanks by regiments of cavalry.

Both sides carefully chose their positions, with the Parliamentary centre on (or just behind), a ridge known as Red Hill. Cromwell was

BATTLE OF NASEBY - 14 JUNE 1645

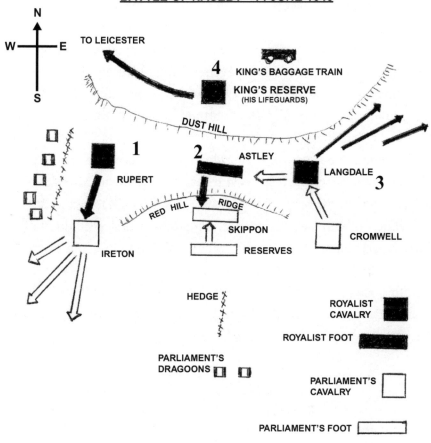

ACTIONS

1. PRINCE RUPERT'S CHARGE SCATTERS IRETON'S CAVALRY, BUT HE DELAYS RETURNING TO THE MAIN BATTLE.

2. ASTLEY'S FOOT ADVANCE, DRIVING BACK PARLIAMENT'S FRONTLINE REGIMENTS. HOWEVER, RESERVES STAND FIRM, AND IN HEAVY FIGHTING, THE ROYALISTS ARE EVENTUALLY REPULSED.

3. CROMWELL DRIVES LANGDALE'S HORSE FROM THE FIELD, THEN RETURNS TO SURROUND ASTLEY'S WEAKENING FOOT SOLDIERS.

4. THE KING'S RESERVE HORSE CHARGE - BUT IN WRONG DIRECTION. BY THE TIME THE CHARGE IS RECALLED THE BATTLE HAS BEEN LOST. THE KING AND SURVIVING ROYALISTS ESCAPE TO LEICESTER.

in broken ground on the right wing. His brother-in-law Ireton, on the left, faced Rupert's cavaliers.

Rupert's horse scattered Ireton's regiments in a vicious charge, but swept on too far, and lost any semblance of order. When they did return to the scene of the main action they were too disorganised to mount any serious threat. Meanwhile, on the other wing, Cromwell's "Ironsides" easily drove the already dispirited and outnumbered Northern Horse of Langdale from the field.

In the centre, the Royalist infantry launched a determined assault on the Parliamentary foot regiments. Pickering's regiment, Montague's, and Waller's took the brunt of the attack. As a Royalist report tells "… ours falling on with Sword and Butt end of the Musquet did notable execution; so much as I saw their colours fall, and their foot in great disorder …".[16] This was indeed the case – the three regiments breaking and falling back in headlong retreat. Though Pickering and the other officers attempted to halt their fleeing soldiers, they were forced to retire to the protection of the reserves.

> "The Colonels and Officers, doing the duty of very gallant men, in endeavouring to keep their men from disorder, and finding their attempts fruitless therein, fell into the reserves with their colours, choosing rather there to fight and die, than to quit the ground they stood on."[17]

Their resolution stemmed the rout; and, reformed, the broken regiments were led by their officers back into the fray.

The King, realising that the battle now hung in the balance, decided to throw in his reserves to support his valiant foot soldiers. Resplendent in full armour, His Majesty took his place at the head of his waiting horsemen. But just as Charles dug in his spurs, his aide, the Earl of Carnwarth, turned the King's horse's head, so that the whole Royalist charge thundered off in the wrong direction! By the time the charge had been recalled, reformed, and augmented by Rupert's returning cavaliers, it was all too late.

Attacked on both sides by Parliamentary horsemen, the outnumbered

Royalist foot soldiers were overwhelmed. Hundreds were killed, and over 5,000 taken prisoner. The King and Rupert, seeing that the day was lost, made their escape to Leicester.

Although the King did not appreciate it at the time, Naseby was the graveyard of his hopes. His main field army had been destroyed by the despised New Model Army; and with it, any belief in the King's eventual military victory.

Just as crippling for the Royal cause was the capture at Naseby of the King's baggage wagons. The Parliamentary soldiers discovered Charles' private papers, including correspondence showing underhand dealings with Irish papists, and attempts to elicit aid from the French. The King's enemies lost no time in publishing this damning material. Many of his supporters were turned against him, whilst the influence of those political leaders who sought a peaceful accommodation with the King was fatally undermined.

The victorious Fairfax now turned his attention to the Royalist heartland in the south-west. After retaking Leicester (and with it most of the King's remaining store of arms), the New Model Army force-marched through Dorset into Somerset, intending to break Goring's siege of Taunton. Goring had a small but competent army, around which the King still hoped he could rebuild a force to counter the New Model Army, by strengthening it with new Welsh recruits and experienced troops received from Ireland. This fantasy was quickly destroyed at Langport. On 10 July, Fairfax and Cromwell's brave and well disciplined horse overran a strong position held by Goring's best. The surviving Royalists took refuge in the nearby town of Bridgwater.

Bridgwater town was militarily important, controlling the lowest crossing of the River Parrett, as it flowed into the Bristol Channel. The river ran through the town, which had been fortified since the Middle Ages. The Royalists had added additional defences, and had recut a medieval tidal ditch. The fortifications were strongest on the west side, crowned by a massive stone castle and a 30-foot wide moat. It is said that the

Royalists had 40 cannon to provide defensive fire power.

Fairfax decided to attack both sides of the town simultaneously. Half of the army, under General Massey, was detached to assault the west part, while his best foot regiments, including Pickering's, Montague's, Skippon's and Waller's, were detailed to take the fortifications on the north-east side.

In the early hours of the 21 July:

> "About two of the clock in the morning, the storm began accordingly on this side of the town, (the forces on the other side only alarming the enemy...). Our forlorn hope was manfully led on by Lieutenant Colonel Hewson."[18]

He was supported by Major Dove with 600 chosen men. As described by Ian Gentles:

> "... Hewson's men quickly crossed the temporary bridges that Army had thrown across the moat, clambered over the walls in the teeth of furious musket fire, beat the defenders from their cannon and then turned the cannon against them, and let down the drawbridge. As soon as the cavalry had entered, many of the enemy surrendered, but the others retreated across the river to the western part of the town, raising the drawbridge behind them."[19]

The western part of the town remained in Royalist hands, the planned assault by Massey not being attempted. The Governor, Sir Edmund Wyndham, deliberately set fire to the captured eastern side by raining red hot shot on to the thatched and wooden houses, so that only three or four escaped the conflagration.

The next day, the 22nd, Fairfax prepared to attack the remaining defenders, commencing with a heavy cannonade. The Royalist Governor accepted the inevitable, and surrendered the following day.

Hewson's leading role in this action was widely applauded, and this is perhaps the first time we have opportunity to see the man. To the many congratulations he received, he simply replied with outward humility, "we are unprofitable servants, we can do nothing ...".[20]

Following the fall of Bridgewater, Fairfax's policy was to clear the area of Royalist garrisons. On 27 July 1645, Colonel Pickering, with some 2,000 foot, was dispatched to take the castle at Sherborne, which stood near the main road to the south-west. The Royalist garrison commander was defiant, and it was not until heavy guns were brought by sea from Portsmouth, and the thick walls of the medieval castle breached, that a successful assault could be mounted. Though Pickering's regiment was present, it is not known what part it played in taking the castle.

His communications now secure, Fairfax decided to recover Bristol; and, in late August moved the New Model Army into positions around the city. Prince Rupert himself took charge of its defence, as apart from the King's headquarters at Oxford, it was the last major city remaining in Royalist hands.

Fairfax was not confident that, so late in the year, his army could sustain a lengthy siege. Accordingly the decision was taken on the 9 September to embark on an all out assault.

This was launched on the following day. Montague's Brigade, led by Pickering's regiment, made a decisive attack on the city defences, quickly taking Lawford's Gate,

> "... with great resolution [it] beat the enemy from their works and possessed their cannon. Their expedition was such that they forced the enemy from their advantages, without any considerable loss to themselves. They laid down the bridges for the horse to enter ... Then our foot advanced into the Castle Street: whereinto were put a hundred men: who made it good." [21]

Prince Rupert realised that he lacked sufficient troops to man the extended city fortifications, and requested negotiations. He formally surrendered on the 11 September, much to the chagrin of the King, who dismissed him from his service for a "mean action".

Following the capture of Bristol, Fairfax set out eliminating the remaining centres of Royalist resistance. Pickering's regiment took part in the seizure of Devizes Castle, Laycock House, and in early October, Winchester. The great fortified Royalist stronghold of Basing House, in Hampshire, was a harder nut to crack.

Basing House controlled one of the main roads to the south-west, and had already withstood earlier sieges by Parliamentary forces. Operations were commenced on the 20 August 1645, under the direction of the professional Dutch engineer, Colonel John Dalbeir, using heavy cannon, approach trenches and even primitive chemical warfare (arsenic and sulphur smoke!). Cromwell arrived on the 8 October, bringing his finest foot regiments, and powerful siege cannon. Dalbeir's guns had earlier made a serious breach in the fortifications, and on the 14th, a general assault was undertaken. Pickering's regiment stormed through this breach, but ran into determined resistance. According to one account the regiment suffered heavily,[22] but pressed home the attack.

> "At the gatehouse of the Old House, the garrison still resisted hopelessly but fiercely. Pickering, at the head of his storming party, shouting "... Fall on, fall on, all is ours! ..."[23]), took the gateway, and when a wave of Waller's and Montague's men came over the wall, all resistance was at an end." [24]

A few days later, Hewson and a Major Kelsey were sent to treat with the governor of Langford House, a local Royalist stronghold. The governor, Sir Bartholomew Pell, had a garrison of only 100 men, and, sensibly, capitulated.

Exeter remained in Royalist hands, so Fairfax now took the New Model Army into Devon; to recover it, and to dispose of the small Royalist army of Hopton, still operating in Cornwall. On the way he detached Pickering's regiment to support the Parliamentarian governor of Poole, Colonel Bingham, who had earlier laid siege to Corfe Castle.

Corfe Castle

This formidable Royalist stronghold could not be taken easily. It occupied a commanding position, and its massive medieval stone fortifications could defy all but the heaviest bombardment. In events, Fairfax left sufficient forces for Bingham to maintain the blockade, but instructed Pickering to join him for operations against Exeter. Fairfax invested the city, setting up the army headquarters at Ottery St Mary, a village ten miles to the east. He attempted to negotiate terms for the Royalist surrender of the city, inviting Ireton, John Pickering and the Judge Advocate to take part in the discussions.

Conditions for the besieging army were severe; the winter of 1645–6 came early, whilst the exhausted army was inadequately supplied. In addition it was ravaged by illness. By early November 1645, the army was beset by the "new disease". Some authorities claim that this was a form of influenza, typhus is also a possibility. Colonel Pickering fell ill at Ottery St Mary, and died on 24 November. He had been a brave and honourable soldier, and the whole army grieved his passing. His firm religious belief moulded his regiment, and was the driving force behind its success in battle.

John Hewson assumed command of the regiment; he was experienced, and had always acted when Pickering was absent on other duties. However he was forced to wait for confirmation in his new rank. In June 1646 Hewson was still recorded as Lieutenant Colonel.[25]

The pace of military events slowed. Corfe Castle finally surrendered on the morning of 27 February 1646, and Exeter followed on 16 April. The King had returned to his headquarters at Oxford in November. The succession of defeats convinced him that he could not overcome Parliament by force of arms, but he determined to pursue his cause by political means, by deviousness, by delaying tactics, and, hopefully, by setting his opponents against each other.

In the spring of 1646, King Charles escaped from Oxford in disguise; and on 5 May, calmly surrendered to the Scottish army, encamped near Newark. Oxford asked for negotiations, and on the 24 June its garrison marched out on generous terms. The First Civil War was over.

CHAPTER 3

"Soldiers' Grievances"

The conflict had ended with the New Model Army military master of England, and King Charles in the hands of his enemies, the Scots.

A murky period of negotiations followed. Charles sought to divide his opponents. He made secret offers. To some of the army leaders he implied a future of religious tolerance, to the Scots he hinted at acceptance of their intolerant form of Presbyterianism. The majority group of Presbyterian politicians running the country sought to negotiate a peace settlement with the King. His Majesty ignored the fact that he had just lost the war, and argued for effective retention of his constitutional powers.

Whilst the Presbyterian group in Parliament struggled to reach a constitutional agreement, some independent members, and the radical soldiers, feared that too many concessions were being made to the King. Moreover the soldiers were pressing for payment of their longstanding arrears of pay, and distrusted the intentions of Parliament. Charles was well aware of the developing tension between Parliament and its Army, and stalled discussions, hoping to play one off against the other.

In the summer of 1646, Hewson was with his regiment, part of Fairfax's army surrounding around Oxford. Bridgewater had established his military reputation, and though Hewson was officially still only Lieutenant Colonel, he was invited to become a member of the Army Council of War.

In June Oxford surrendered, and the regiments were freed from the pressures of war. There were many instances of the victorious soldiers, in the belief that the God of Battles was with them, occupying pulpits in village churches, to the fury of the ousted clergy. This was in defiance of an Order passed by Parliament on 25 April 1645, sent to Fairfax when the New Model Army was established, that no person should be permitted to preach who was not an ordained minister.

> "At Steeple Aston, Lieutenant Webb interrupted the sermon in the morning, and seized the pulpit himself in the afternoon. Webb finally in a rage went out of the church calling Mr Skinner, the preacher, 'the black frog of Revelation'. Next Sunday his Colonel (Hewson) occupied the pulpit both morning and afternoon, proving in his sermon the lawful minister of the parish to be Antichrist by the thirteen marks of a false prophet."[1]

> "The previous Sunday Hewson had been with his major, Daniel Axtell, at Wallington Church, where they elbowed out the incumbent and took turns preaching in the morning and afternoon."[2]

News of these exploits reached London, and duly appeared in the newspapers of the day.[3]

In the autumn, the regiments of foot were dispersed, being variously quartered in Oxfordshire, Worcestershire, and Staffordshire for some six months. During this period the troops were paid irregularly. They had to wait until August to receive 49 days arrears. Then there was a further delay until the next payment in the last week in November – some 86 days.[4]

A remarkable and revealing event took place on the 12 November 1646. As described in Ian Gentles' *The New Model Army in England, Ireland and Scotland*:

> The soldier's intervention in the religious and intellectual life of Oxford was formalized in a public disputation between several officers and six Presbyterian ministers in November 1646. The conference, which lasted from three in the afternoon till

nine at night, was dedicated to resolving whether only the ordained could be permitted to preach. A leading participant was Colonel Hewson, ".... A most categorical disputant, yet so rude... we wondered [at] so much true logic and false English ...." Many other "gifted officers" also took part, as well as the chaplain William Erbery... [The disputation came to no conclusion, indeed the clergy failed to attend the next meeting on the following Thursday.] Unabashed, the officers then threw out a public challenge to the university as a whole to prove that their calling was from Christ.[5]

Meanwhile, on the larger stage, the Scots had seen through the duplicities of their uninvited guest, eventually realising that the King had no intention of agreeing to their demand to impose a Presbyterian church on England. Accordingly a deal was struck with Parliament, whereby King Charles was handed over to Parliamentary Commissioners, in return for payment of the first instalment of the substantial war debt owed to the Scots. This was in January 1647.

At the beginning of that year therefore, the Presbyterian leaders in Parliament must have felt secure. The King was in their hands, and the Scots were marching home. The Army, however, needed to be put in its place, and vengeance needed to be visited upon the Papist rebels in Ireland. The massacre of the Ulster Protestants in 1641 had not been forgotten.

The army issue was promptly mishandled. Most of the Presbyterian majority instinctively disliked and distrusted the Army – they feared the increasing influence of the radical political and religious ideas sweeping through the regiments. Claiming the need to reduce Government expenditure, Parliament decreed a substantial reduction in Army strength. However the soldiers had been looking forward to settlement of their arrears of pay – the foot was owed for eighteen weeks, the horse for forty-three. Parliament's proposal was six weeks' pay. This derisory offer sparked anger in the ranks, and a determination to stand up for their rights. The soldiers also pressed for pensions for the widows and orphans of dead comrades, and a pardon for actions carried out in the course of the war. The soldiers feared that, once disbanded, their just claims would be ignored.

Parliament persisted in a heavy-handed approach. To forestall any plans for organised resistance it determined that half the Army should be disbanded, that the remainder should be sent for service in Ireland or dispersed throughout England, and that (apart from General Fairfax) all senior officers be reduced to the rank of Colonel.

The Presbyterian majority in Parliament, headed by the influential Denzil Holles, was confident that it would prevail. It had the backing of most Londoners (who resented being taxed to pay for idle and free thinking soldiers), and it knew that it could rely on the proven military strength of London's Trained Bands.

Confident of carrying out its plans, Parliament sent commissioners to the Army headquarters at Saffron Walden in Essex. At this meeting on the 21 March 1647, they found that the officers were unwilling to discuss disbandment, and instead were demanding to hear Parliament's proposals concerning service in Ireland, and the other issues in dispute.

It was nearly a month before the Commissioners returned to Saffron Walden. On the 15th April, they faced the assembled senior officers in the ancient parish church – the only building in the village capable of accommodating the two hundred officers attending. The Commissioners explained that the Irish expedition would be led by Skippon (a capable soldier, but very much a Londoner) and General Massey (who had not impressed the Army by his curious inaction at Bridgwater).

The officers had other ideas. Five representatives, Lieutenant General Hammond and Colonels Lambert, Rich, Lilburne, and Hewson, (who had just returned from a visit to Ireland) were elected to present counter-proposals. The Army wanted its own trusted leaders, Fairfax and Cromwell, to head the Irish operation. A document was quickly drawn up, and signed by most of the officers, to impress Parliament with the strength of its feelings.

Two days later, Fairfax convened a meeting of some one hundred officers, to discuss Parliament's Irish plans. They elected a working Committee (being the same members as the Committee of Officers elected two days previously). The working Committee reluctantly undertook to encourage their rank and file to volunteer for the operation, but also sought their support for the concerns expressed to the Parliamentary Commissioners on their first visit.

The Committee's attempt to raise troops did not win much support. On the 25 April it is recorded that, "None of Colonel Hewson's can be persuaded to go for the service upon those terms tendered …".[6] This is hardly surprising – Hewson was prominent in leading the Army's demand for early settlement of its grievances.[7]

The officers decided to take the initiative, and put their case directly to Parliament. "A Vindication of the Officers of the Army", a heartfelt rebuttal both of Parliament's attempts to weaken the Army, and denying malicious rumours currently sweeping London, was drawn up. No time was wasted; and, to quote Ian Gentles, "Openly defying the recent prohibition against petitions from the army, a high-level delegation consisting of Colonels Okey and Hewson, Lieutenant-Colonels Reade and Pride, Majors Wroth and Rogers, and Captains Reynolds and Goffe, laid it before the Commons on 27th April."[8] Not surprisingly, members took offence at such insubordination, and refused to allow the officers' statement to be read.

The increasingly frustrated regiments provided a receptive audience for radical troublemakers. Originating amongst London's poor, and puritan in tone, subversive ideas of the equality of man, and the dream of a democratic republic, were being spread by a group of radical activists, commonly nicknamed "Levellers".

To express their grievances, each regiment was allowed to elect spokesmen, somewhat misleadingly called "Agitators". In Hewson's regiment two officers, Captain John Carter and Captain Alexander Brayfield, were elected. Two rank and file representatives were also chosen, Richard Nixon and Edmund Garner (or Garne). Garner's election did no harm to his career – he was a Lieutenant in the regiment by November![9] No doubt this was an indication by Colonel

Hewson of support for his men's demands.

On the 28 April, "The Apology of Interest", a pamphlet published by the Levellers, appeared on London's streets. It set out the concerns of the Levellers in the Army, primarily the need for an amnesty for wartime acts. It argued also that Parliament's plan for an Irish expedition was simply a ploy to divide the Army.[10]

The jitters that existed in the New Model Army at this time gave rise to a curious incident. Ian Gentles' description paints the picture:

> "In Essex on Sunday 2nd May the general officers at headquarters returned from the afternoon sermon to meet a panicky Lieutenant-Colonel Jubbes of Hewson's regiment. He had just received intelligence that the Essex trained bands were preparing to attack and disarm them that night. In self-defence the regiment had crowded into a church with their arms. When no attack materialised, Hewson's men sheepishly filed out of the church the next day, conceding that it had been a false alarm."[11]

According to a newsletter sent on 3 May from Saffron Walden, Jubbes had informed Cromwell and Ireton that Colonel Middleton planned an action against the Army that night. Jubbes had alerted his regiment and moved it to a secure location. The soldiers in the town "were much nettled at the news of Colonell Hewson's Regiment, and every man provided powder and bullett and kept guards with their swords drawne at the street corners, and durst not be knowne what was the reason they stood there".[12] Colonel Hewson could hardly have been pleased at the ridicule brought on his regiment: by April the following year, Jubbes had left the regiment.

By now the Presbyterian majority in Parliament began to appreciate the depth of discontent in the Army. Four members were nominated as Commissioners to ascertain the real situation. The four included Skippon, Cromwell and Ireton, who naturally had maintained close links with the regiments. The Commissioners instructed the regiments' Colonels to submit reports detailing the complaints of their regiments. Colonel Hewson's report is stated to have been prepared in collaboration with that of Fairfax's regiment, and emanated from the elected representatives of the rank and file. Settlement of outstanding pay arrears, and the need for an act of indemnity, headed the list of grievances.

The Commissioners faced the officers on Saturday 15 May 1647 in the church at Saffron Walden. Colonel Lambert spoke for the officers and soldiers, and explained that a declaration of grievances was being drawn up on behalf of the whole Army. General Skippon agreed to defer the formal meeting until the following day, even though a Sunday. After the Commissioners had left the church, the various regimental reports were heard. Colonel Hewson spoke, explaining that the regiments desired that one of the senior officers at the conference should collect the grievances "into one particular summe and present them to you".[13] However the assembled officers preferred to appoint an ad hoc committee (which included Hewson), to collate the reports into one document for presentation to the Commissioners. This was quickly done and the statement completed by the following day. In the few hours available the committee could hardly go through the reports in proper detail and it seems that their formal statement was based on the report received from Rich's regiment, with suitable modifications.

The feeling in the Army against service in Ireland was conveyed in Hewson's own report to the Commissioners on that Sunday. He explained that he had read the decisions of Parliament to his men: "Truly I found them in noe distemper, but very quiett; only I find that there was some grievances lay upon them... I moved about the Irish affaire; they seemed to be utterly unwilling for to stirre in that untill such time as they had some satisfaction."[14]

Faced with this intransigence, Parliament adopted a hard line – either volunteer for service in Ireland or disband. On 25 May Parliament approved a motion by Denzil Holles calling for the disbandment of certain regiments; not surprisingly, Hewson's was one. "Colonel Hughson's Regiment is at Bishops Stortford, and the order comes for its being disbanded on the next market day, Thursday, 3rd

June, and further that those who are prepared to engage for Ireland are to march to Puckeridge to receive orders."[15] The regiment did not disband as ordered, and not a man marched to Puckeridge. The army was standing out for cash payment of its arrears, proper discharge from service, and indemnity for acts done in the war.

The Army now was in open defiance of Parliament. On the 4 and 5 June the regiments (including Hewson's) gathered in a "General Rendezvous of the Army", at Newmarket. As described by Antonia Fraser:

> "On 5th June the Army at Newmarket issued a declaration of which the basic theme was the stirring up of war by the Presbyterian leaders – it asked for the names of all those who had evolved Holle's resolution – but which ended with two more potentially helpful clauses, put in at Cromwell's instigation. The first of these established an Army Council of Generals and senior officers, also to include two commissioned officers and two other representatives from each regiment. Cromwell would therefore be a member as would Fairfax and Ireton. The second clause denied that the Army intended to overthrow Presbyterianism: it merely wanted liberty of conscience for its members."[16]

One of the notable characteristics of the New Model Army was its cohesion – religion being a leading factor. During the early part of the war, most of its senior commanders were Presbyterians, but their influence had waned, and by 1647 the officers were mostly Independents – a term, of course, covering a variety of beliefs from Anabaptist to strict Puritan.

In June of that year, perhaps influenced by revulsion against the Presbyterians in Parliament, or inspired by the spreading of Leveller ideas, the rank and file turned on many of the remaining Presbyterian officers, driving them from their regiments. In all more than 167 officers were forced out, sometimes by violence.

Colonel Hewson, as we know from his outbursts the previous year at Steeple Aston, was a fiery preacher. A number of his officers were also radical sectarians, most noticeably Daniel Axtel, his major, and Captain Alexander Brayfield. The strength of religious feeling in the regiment has attracted comment. Ian Gentles writes, "In 1647 for example, a soldier from Hewson's regiment, writing of the manifest presence of God among them, exclaimed, 'the sweet union we had with God doth endear us together in love.'".[17] Their record of military success was viewed as confirmation that they were the chosen instruments of the Lord of Hosts.

Parliament's clumsy attempts to force disbandment of its Army had effectively forced it into mutiny. Predictable results followed. Firstly, all ranks of the Army, and all the regiments, drew together in resentment; secondly, Parliament, rather than the King, came to represent the enemy. And now the Army was prepared to use its might. On 10 June, 1647, the whole army, some 21,000 men, assembled in a general rendezvous at Triploe Heath in Hertfordshire. This show of force was intended to send a message to Parliament.

More dramatically, on 3 June, the Army took possession of the King's person from Parliament's representatives. Though the seizure was carried out by an armed force led by a very junior officer, a Cornet Joyce, there can be no doubt that he was acting with the connivance of senior officers – most probably Cromwell himself was privy to the abduction. The Army now was in a position to negotiate its own settlement with the King.

Freed from any sense of loyalty to Parliament, the Army moved. By the 12 June, it advanced to St Albans - on the old Watling Street – an obvious threat to London. A new declaration was put forward by the Army containing the first suggestions for the removal from Parliament of members it disapproved of.

A delegation of officers, including Colonel Hewson, presented to Parliament a complaint against Denzil Holles and ten other prominent Presbyterian members. The officers contended that the eleven should be impeached, not only for plotting to disband the Kingdom's army, but also for creating the potential for a new civil war by setting up its own armed forces. This was a well-founded assertion – the

Presbyterian members had the backing of the formidable London Trained Bands, and had been recruiting former soldiers, known as "Reformadoes".

The King had remained in the close custody of the Army since his abduction. Realising that he was a wily customer, Cromwell and Hewson wrote on the 25 June to Colonel Whalley, then in charge of the troops guarding the King, to ensure that he did not escape: "Prethee be carefull of the King's securing... we hold you free of all further charge, save to looke to your Guards that his Majestie make noe escape, and therein you must be carefull and more now than ever."[18]

The Army leaders decided to press for formal impeachment of the eleven Presbyterian members. On 5 July, a group of senior officers, including Cromwell and Hewson, was instructed to meet lawyers to draw up charges; and to make arrangements to present them to Parliament. No time was wasted, and on the following day... "The twelve officers and soldiers duly attended at the House of Commons,... when Colonel Scrope delivered the charge and impeachment against the eleven members '...in the name of his Excellency Sir Thomas Fairfax, and the Army under his Command,...' and desired the House '...to take it into speedy Consideration'. The gist of the charges against these eleven was that they were intriguing with the Royalists, and with the Scots, were 'listing and engaging men for a new war'; and had made false statements as to the willingness of certain officers to serve in Ireland. After the House had heard their answers to the charges, the eleven members were given six months leave of absence".[19]

This response by Parliament was regarded by the regiments as inadequate. On the 16 and 17 July, 1647, a full Council of the Army, including the Agitators and over a hundred officers, was convened at Reading under General Fairfax. He and his second in command, Cromwell, faced urgent demands that they lead a march into London, and seize control of Parliament. Fairfax remained unwilling to take such unlawful action.

Events were moving elsewhere. Presbyterian London was in uproar, and on the 26 July, rioting apprentices forced the Speakers of both Houses, and the prominent Independent members, to seek protection with the Army.

Enough was enough, and on the 1 August Fairfax and Cromwell bowed to pressure from the rank and file, and agreed to march on London. Four regiments, Hewson's being one, occupied Southwark on the 4th. London Bridge was forced, and the City occupied on 6 August. The next day, Fairfax ordered a march of the main strength of the Army, 18,000 men, through London. Rainborowe's regiment brought up the rear of the foot – a novel formation more suited for battle![20] Not surprisingly, the eleven members were nowhere to be found. After this show of force, Fairfax ordered his Army to quarters around Croydon, though leaving contingents to secure the City and Parliament.

However little progress was being made to meet the most pressing concern of the Army. In early September,

> "Fairfax ... sent a tough letter to the Lord Mayor, demanding £50,000 towards the arrears, and adding that 'Delay will be equal to a Denial'. The General Council of the Army authorized him to collect this amount himself if it was not forthcoming. The Commons decided to meet this by selling what was left of the bishops' lands, and those belonging to deans and chapters. Fairfax kept up the pressure and threatened to send Colonel Hewson's regiment into the City to collect the money."[21]

Discontent amongst the rank and file was fuelled by the propaganda of the Levellers, and the "new agents". Whilst the officers sought a settlement with Charles to protect the rights of men of property, the radical elements pressed for government by a Commons elected by all the people, rich and poor equally. The King and the House of Lords would be swept away.

Alarmed by this developing republican sentiment, the Army leaders convened a meeting at Putney, at the end of October 1647, of senior officers and army radicals, to agree on a future political settlement. Held in the chancel of the fifteenth century church of St Mary the Virgin, the Putney debates must rank as a milestone in the evolution of western democracy. Cromwell took the chair, and allowed free speaking. Colonel Hewson expressed forthright opinions, opposing the populist political reforms demanded by the Leveller-influenced agitators. On the other hand, he argued for reduction in the Royal powers. Under the Coronation Oath, the limit and extent of the King's part in the legislative process was "a power" to withhold assent to bills submitted by Parliament, i.e. his "negative voice". In discussing a future constitution, Hewson addressed the representatives, "The Scots have no negative voice among them, and why should not we make the same provision with them?"[22]

Other speakers were also from Hewson's regiment. Lieutenant Colonel Jubbes called for a limited form of monarchy, and saw a conflict between the use of armed might and Christian peace. Resentment against the King was bitter, Captain John Carter said he now had no intention to pray for the King.

To demonstrate the regiment's commitment to the Army leadership, a declaration of loyalty, "The Humble Remonstrance and Desires of Divers Officers and Souldiers in the Army under Colonel Hewson", dated the 4 November 1647, was prepared. This tract denounced both disbandment and service in Ireland. It was submitted to General Fairfax... "from Colonel Hewson's regiment, which asked him to communicate it to both Houses of Parliament. Hewson himself signed it, along with Lieutenant-Colonel Jubbes, Major Axtell, twenty six other officers, and ten 'agents' of the soldiery – presumably an 'agent' for each company. They had hoped, they said, to enjoy the fruits of peace after God had scattered their enemies, but now they grieved to see ... 'a dismal cloud again arising over our heads from divisions and discontents.' They affirmed their resolution to obey Fairfax constantly, and to serve him in the suppression of all incendiaries who '...raised divisions and distempers in the army.'[23] The last phrase was condemnation of '...the forces of division, which everyone understood to mean the "new agents" and their Leveller backers.'"[24]

The Putney debates achieved no agreement, and served only to bring into sharp focus the determination of the army grandees to protect their property rights, and the demands of the rank and file for the common people to have equal say in government. To prevent the split in the army deepening, Cromwell called a halt to further discussion; and secured undisputed control of the Army by ordering the agitators back to their regiments.

Ian Gentles describes the final act in the Putney Debates:

> "Before adjourning, the General Council nominated a committee to draft the text of a Remonstrance to be offered to the regiments for their approval. The eighteen-man committee included only two agitators, Allen and Lockyer, as well as two radical officers, Major William Rainborowe and Commissary Cowling. The others were all hard-nosed conservatives such as Cromwell, Ireton, Hewson, and Stane, or moderates such as Tichborne, Captain Deane and Lieutenant-Colonel Cowell."[25]

It is interesting to observe Hewson's apparent change of stance over the course of some six months. In April and May he was an outspoken supporter of the just demands of his men – even risking unpopularity with the Army leadership. Yet by November he is described as "a hard-nosed conservative", now very much one of the grandees.

One can only speculate on the causes of this change of heart. Perhaps he saw the movement for soldiers' rights being hijacked by extremists for political ends, anathema to him. Or the soldier in him saw that the disorder provoked in the regiments by Leveller-influenced agitators, and in particular the breakdown in military discipline involved in the expulsion of the 167 Presbyterian officers, as seriously weakening the Army. However a less worthy motive may be postulated. By August the Army had rendered Parliament impotent, and the energetic Army leaders, Cromwell and Ireton, became the most powerful men in the Kingdom. Self-interest would lead

Hewson to throw his lot in with them.

While the Army had been agonising over the form that a peace settlement might take, the King (still in Army custody) had not been idle, being in secret negotiations with the Scots.

On the 11 November, the news broke that he had escaped, and gone, no man knew where. The King hoped to secure military intervention by the Scots to restore him to his throne, in return for his undertaking to promote Presbyterianism in England. Rumours of these negotiations filtered through into the Army, and although Charles was soon back in Army hands, safely lodged in Carisbrooke Castle, on the Isle of Wight, the possibility of fresh hostilities drew the regiments together. Leveller influence declined, while a threatened mutiny by two regiments at Corkbush Field, near Ware, was put down firmly.

Fairfax called a rendezvous of a large part of the Army on the 18 November at Hare Warren, near Kingston. The conduct of Hewson's regiment at this review was described as "exemplary".[26]

The funds to pay the Army arrears, promised by the City fathers in September after Fairfax had marched his troops through London's streets, had failed to materialise. The General determined on decisive action, deciding to carry out his threat to employ Colonel Hewson's regiment to enforce due payment. His choice of Hewson's regiment may well have been influenced by its recent demonstrations of loyalty and efficiency. On the 19 November, Hewson was ordered to enter "the City with a thousand men ... to billet them on those citizens who were withholding payment. The Lord Mayor and Corporation protested to Fairfax; the Commons took umbrage too, and directed Cromwell, as the senior military officer in the House, to countermand Hewson's march. Fairfax gave way, but sent a tart reply to the Lord Mayor, making it clear that Hewson's orders might be reactivated if the City did not pay up."[27] ... "As a result of this intense activity the crisis was averted for the time being. Colonel Hewson's regiment drew up in Hyde Park, the City sent a delegation to Fairfax at Windsor, promising to do better with its overdue payments, and as a sign of goodwill, the Merchant Adventurers offered a £10,000 loan to tide the Army over."[28]

Around mid-November, the Army established its headquarters at Windsor Castle. On the 7 December, Sir Thomas Fairfax and the General Council of the Army presented proposals to the Commons, ideas for raising money to pay army arrears, suggesting that specific counties should be responsible for maintaining allotted regiments. Provision was suggested for the settlement of sums due to disbanded soldiers, and larger financial powers were sought for the Committee of the Army. Members were warned to give approval to these proposals (or alternative arrangements satisfactory to the army) by the end of the week.

> "The General Council, furious with the way in which the Londoners were withholding their contributions, was evidently dissatisfied that Fairfax had countermanded Hewson's occupying force; for it finally requested not only that a substantial body of troops should be quartered on the defaulting citizens until they paid up but that the City should be made to pay £100,000 in reparations, partly to the army for what the soldiers had suffered and partly to the neighbouring counties where they had been quartered in order to keep the pressure up."[29]

The Army Council held further meetings at Windsor Castle. Usually the officers commenced their discussions by prayer; on the 21 December it is recorded that Colonel Hewson led the prayers. This particular meeting was noteworthy for considering the idea of a trial for Charles. Details were secretly passed to the King by Watson, the Quartermaster-General of the Army.[30] It is interesting to speculate on the King's reaction to this information!

The following day was devoted by the Army Council to religion:

"…Wednesday, December 22nd, was according to appointment kept as a general fast by the General and officers; the duties of the day were performed by divers of the officers, amongst whom there was a sweet harmony, the Lieutenant-General, Commissary General Ireton, Col. Tichborne, Col. Hewson, Mr Peters and other officers prayed very fervently and pathetically; this continued from nine in the morning till seven at night."[31]

Yet whilst the officers prayed, and the army rank and file schemed to extract money from Parliament, few realised that a fresh storm was about to break.

CHAPTER 4

"The Second Civil War"

Whilst King Charles had no choice but to bow to the military might of Parliament, and accept imprisonment, he steadfastly believed in his god-given duty to recover his throne, and return the country to sacred forms of worship. Originally he hoped that he might re-establish his position by playing off Parliament against the Army, but in late 1647 decided to seek help from the Scots. Following protracted wrangling, in December of that year, he signed the Engagement, under which agreement the Scottish leaders promised to send an army to restore him to the throne in return for his acceptance of their religious demands. Rumours of these negotiations circulated around London, the threat of the King's return leading initially to some reduction in the ill feeling between the Levellers and the Army leaders, and between the Army and Parliament.

However the cessation of actual warfare had not restored peace and prosperity across the country. Indeed general discontent was rising. Resentment was widespread against the censorious attitude of the Presbytarian influenced Government, whilst the intrusive and increasingly dictatorial County Committees enraged local populations. In the areas affected, the continuance of free quartering of soldiers after Parliament's Ordinance of the 24 December 1647, was supposed to have ended this imposition, caused great anger. In Kent, in particular, moderates who had supported Parliament against the King now saw the new regime as even more oppressive. In London many citizens had been grievously offended by the Army's forcible occupation in August 1647, by its repeated demands for money, and by the religious extremism of its leaders. Nor had the well-being of the ordinary people improved. A series of bad harvests led to a serious rise in food prices, with the doubling of the price of bread.

Trouble first flared in Canterbury:

> "Parliament had passed an ordinance against the recognition of fast days and religious festivals, regarding them as 'vain and superstitious observances'. Christmas Day of 1647 saw the citizens of Canterbury gathered together in St. Andrew's church celebrating the birth of the Lord. The Mayor had a duty to enforce the ordinance and this he did by insisting that the merchants and tradesmen open up their shops and continue business as usual. One irate individual, incensed by the peremptory manner of the official, was abusive. The Mayor sent the man sprawling with a well directed right hook and within minutes a hostile mob had gathered around him. Someone produced a firearm and shots were fired, the Mayor was punched, kicked, and then held in confinement. As unrest spread throughout Canterbury the mob placed guards on all the main city gates."

A different explanation for the riot was that the unfortunate Mayor had attempted to stop the football match traditionally played in the market place on Christmas Day.

The local Justices of the Peace persuaded the rioters to keep quiet; all arms were laid down, and calm restored:

> "… In the meantime, however, the affronted Mayor communicated with the Parliamentary authorities, and Colonel Hewson came with his regiment of foot, or, according to another account, the County Committee sent 3,000 of the Trained Bands. The force broke in the City gates, breached part of the walls … and seized the ring leaders of the uprising."[1]

Certainly Hewson's regiment was stationed in Kent, for around mid-January 1648 it was ordered to move nearer London.[2]

Seeing the storm clouds gathering, the Army leaders were consolidating their hold on power. Later in the same month the new

Committee of Safety (known widely as the Derby House Committee) had its first working session. It replaced the old Committee of Both Kingdoms, Presbyterians being replaced by hardliners. To counter the threat posed by the Scots, the Army of the Northern Association was amalgamated with the New Model Army to form the Standing Army, with Fairfax in command.

It seems that Hewson was still finding difficulty in adjusting to his newly elevated position amongst the Army grandees. He provoked much mirth by an unfortunate slip at a meeting in March of the General Council of the Army. "Colonel Hewson then made a learned speech and instead of addressing himself to his Excellency (i.e. Fairfax) said; 'an't please your Majesty...'."[3]

The spring of 1648 saw the outbreak of rebellion. On the 23 March, Colonel Poyer, Governor of Pembroke Castle, dissatisfied with Parliament's handling of his claim for arrears of pay, formally declared for the King. Chepstow Castle in Gwent followed suit. London was in turmoil in early April following the Lord Mayor's sending a troop of militia to stop boys at Moorfields playing tip-cat on the Sabbath day. To quell the growing disturbance, Cromwell personally sent in cavalry, further alienating the citizens. Serious fighting broke out in the north when the former Royalist leader Langdale captured Berwick on the 28 April; and on the following day, Sir Phillip Musgrave took Carlisle for the King. These successes left England wide open to an invasion by the Scottish army.

Nearer to London, Kent was now in open revolt. Sir Anthony Weldon, the bitter and bigoted leader of the Kent County Committee, had antagonised the people, effectively provoking the rising. As Everitt points out, "It was the last, in fact, of the great local insurrections of English history."[4]

> "At local musters defaulters became so numerous that the Committee asked Parliament for authority to levy a 'pecuniary mullet ... with a power of levy thereof by distress and sale. Reinforced by troops sent from Parliament under Colonel Hewson, the committee men made an official progress through

the county in order to set matters at peace. Everywhere they came, however, they now began to find ... themselves laughed at and by mean people affronted.'"[5]

In Surrey, too, there was general dissatisfaction with the government. A petition was brought to London and presented to the Commons by a crowd of some 3,000. They waited three hours for an answer, but as none was forthcoming they became restive. They abused the guards, and attempted to enter the building. Colonel Barkstead then acted on his own initiative and used 500 soldiers to disperse the crowd. Following this disturbance, one Gilbert Mabbott, an assistant to John Rushworth, the Secretary to General Fairfax, was impelled to pen an urgent letter on the 16 May to the General, "I am commanded by Colonell Hewson, and some other officers of your Excellencies here in towne, to desire your excellencie forthwith to give speedie orders for some considerable force that lies quartered neare this place, to advance hither, or neare Westminster [6]..." to restore order.

East Anglia had also risen. On 18 May, Fairfax told the Committee of Both Houses that he had no foot to spare for operations against the rebels in Kent and East Anglia other than his own regiment and half of Hewson's.[7] The situation in Kent deteriorated – Rochester, Dartford and Deptford were quickly taken by the Royalists. Worse, the Parliamentary fleet stationed in the Downs mutinied, and declared for the King. This meant that the Royalists might blockade London, or even bring assistance from the Continent.

To what extent these widely scattered revolts represented genuine protest by ordinary people against an unpopular government, or were instigated by Royalist strategists abroad, remains unclear. No doubt in every area there remained Royalist sympathisers waiting for an opportunity to whip up popular anger against a distant and intolerant government in London.

It must be said that, in this crisis, the Army leaders kept their nerve, and acted decisively. By the 11 May Cromwell had already joined the local Parliamentary commander, Horton, to commence action to suppress the South Wales rebellion. On the 21 May, Fairfax assembled on Blackheath a force to put down the Kentish Royalists. This included the regiments of Hewson, Rich and Whalley, all first class troops. In support a supply train was moving from Surrey into West Kent. However, by this time the rebels had also seized the Channel ports of Dover and Deal, as well as Walmer Castle, which protected the strategically important anchorage at the Downs.

Knowing that the Kentish rebels now far outnumbered his troops, and expecting a further 3,000 rebels to rise in Surrey, Fairfax wrote on the 26 May from Army headquarters at Windsor to the Derby House Committee, requesting that the regiments at Whitehall, and the Tower, be sent out tomorrow to rendezvous with him on Hounslow Heath. Fairfax sent Colonel Hewson "To attend Your Lordshippes for that purpose ..." (to consult with the Committee, and receive instructions on behalf of Fairfax) "... having noe other whome I could att present spare; and there being likewise much neede of his speedy returne, I desire hee may receive a dispatch from your Lordshippes as soone as may be."[8] In answer to his request, certainly Barkstead's regiment joined Fairfax.

The Parliamentary force struck into the heart of Royalist held Kent. Gravesend was reached on the 31st. Next day Fairfax advanced towards Maidstone, an important town on the far side of the Medway River. The Earl of Norwich, the Royalist commander, expected Fairfax to attempt the crossing at the Aylesford Bridge, some way to the north of the town, and had stationed the bulk of his forces to oppose this. However Fairfax's plan was to attack the town by making the crossing at Farleigh Bridge, higher up the river, i.e. to the south.

Although it was now late afternoon, he ordered Hewson's regiment to lead the way, to secure a good position to launch a full assault on the town the following day. At first there was little opposition, but once across the river, and into the southern approaches to the town, his men came under brisk fire. Moving determinedly, they soon forced a way into the town itself. By then the defenders had organised, and blocked the streets with barricades of furniture dragged out of the houses. Royalist musketeers lined the upper windows, and inflicted heavy casualties on Hewson's men. However their blood was now up, and storming the barricades, they rushed forward. Bloody hand-to-had fighting ensued. As was written by an eyewitness, "… though I have been a member of this army ever since the first going out, and have seen desperate service in several stormings, I have not seen before; for every street in the town was got by inches".[9] For a while little success was achieved:

> "… till Colonel Hewson with his regiment opened a passage into one of the streets, where the dispute growing hot, he was knocked down with a musquet; but recovering himself, he pressed the enemy so hard that they were forced to retreat to their main guard, and falling in with them at the same time, so disordered them that they all began to shift for themselves; wherein they were favoured by the advantage of the night: yet many of them were made prisoners, and many killed; many horses and all their artillery fell into the hands of ours."[10]

Once the town was secured, Fairfax's men advanced on Norwich's main force, which, discouraged, retreated towards Rochester.

Hewson's conduct in the action was commended in his commander's report to Parliament. Fairfax wrote, "I cannot but take notice of the valour and resolution of Col. Hewson, whose Regiment had the hardest task (Major Carter, his major, being hurt and Captaine Price, a deserving and faithfull officer, slain)".[11]

Whilst Fairfax with the main army pursued Norwich, Colonel Nathaniel Rich's regiment of horse, together with Hewson's foot, was detached to clear the rest of Kent. The most pressing need was to relieve Dover Castle, then under siege by some 2,000 Royalists. Troops led by Lieutenant Colonel Axtell (Hewson's second-in-command) and Sir Michael Livesey reached the castle on the 6 June. The Royalists hastily retreated to Canterbury:

"There they were joined by those who had refused to follow Norwich (into Essex, and eventually Colchester) and had marched eastward under Sir Richard Hardres. The city of Canterbury thus became 'the seat of the whole action' in Kent. Colonels Rich and Hewson approached it from the south, and Fairfax himself from the west. Within the town, there was time neither to replace the gates removed and burnt in the previous December, following the Christmas rising, nor to repair the breaches then made in the city walls. Money and provisions were scarce."[12]

In fact, there were not above 1,300 fighting men to man the walls. Neither garrison nor townsmen were anxious to mount a hopeless defence, and after brief negotiations, Canterbury surrendered.

Colonels Rich and Hewson then marched to recapture Walmer Castle from the Royalists. They had 2,000 horse and foot, though no guns.

The fortifications at Walmer and Deal, popularly referred to as castles, were really coastal forts, specifically designed to defend against seaborne invasions. Built by King Henry VIII to the latest theories of warfare, they had been funded from the spoils of the religious houses suppressed following his break with Rome. With carefully planned arcs of fire, and protected by moats, they were difficult to overrun. However they were intended for short sharp engagements, not to withstand prolonged sieges.

Lacking cannon, the Colonels attempted a frontal assault on Walmer Castle. This failed. A Royalist Paper, "Mercurius Melancholius", of 26 June 1648, reported the action: "Rich and Hewson ... had under mined the ground as far as the Ditch, but could go no further, so they for madness fell to storming but had as ill-success ..."

In their turn the Royalists made repeated attempts to break the siege, both by land and sea, but were unable to bring in supplies. With all hope of relief gone, and provisions rapidly dwindling, the disheartened garrison surrendered. The exact date is not known but it was between the 9 and 12 July 1648.

Although the main body of Royalists in Kent had given up at Canterbury, and Walmer Castle had been retaken, the two other fortifications commanding The Downs still held out.

Colonel Rich moved against Deal Castle. This was the most powerful of the three coastal artillery forts which defended The Downs, the name given to the important fleet anchorage near the Goodwin Sands, and which gave control of the English Channel. Like Walmer Castle, it had been completed by Henry VIII in 1540, but was larger, having no fewer than 145 gun ports and embrasures. With thick walls, and all exposed surfaces rounded to deflect shot, it was immensely strong.

Although Colonel Rich had failed in an earlier attempt to occupy Deal Castle, a second attempt was made with the force that had secured Walmer Castle. His regiment, and Hewson's foot, took up positions around the castle on the 15 July. This expeditious move was well timed, since on the following day thirty Flemish ships appeared in The Downs to furnish support for the garrison.

The Royalists in Deal Castle were full of spirit, and launched a determined attack on their besiegers. As graphically described in a contemporary Parliamentary account, "That very morning also the enemy sallied out … and intended to surprise our forlorn guard., which was between three and four hundred yards of the castle; but they were soon discovered, and by a Reserve guard … they were gallantly refused, and driven back to the very gates of the castle."

It soon became obvious that recapture of such a stoutly defended fortification without siege artillery might be a lengthy business. On the 21 July, Colonel Rich sent an urgent demand to Parliament's fleet commander, the Earl of Warwick, for Navy cannon; specifically requesting guns from the man-of-war Sovereign, then lying at Tower Wharf. Two cannon and two demi-cannon were hurried from London, as well as powder and shot. However he had to send again for the services of a master gunner before they could be used effectively.

Rather leisurely, the Royalist fleet riding in The Downs landed troops. On the 13 August, their leader, Prince Charles, put ashore 800 men under cover of darkness, intending to surprise the Parliamentary positions from the rear. Fortunately, about 2 a.m. Colonel Rich was alerted to the imminent threat by a Royalist deserter. Reacting promptly, he despatched 300 musketeers commanded by Colonel Hewson and his second-in-command, Axtell, supported by 100 horse from his own regiment under Major Husbands. In the morning light, Hewson's force fell on the Royalist flank. The lightly armed seamen were no match for his experienced troopers, and were quickly scattered. Hewson lost a horse in the engagement – possibly it was the one that Lieutenant Colonel Axtell had killed under him, since Hewson often preferred to fight on foot alongside his men.

Colonel Rich reported the victory to the Speaker of Parliament, writing from Deal the same day. He claimed that the Prince had lost 80 men killed, and that he had taken 100 prisoners. Hewson's force lost no officers, and only seven other ranks. His letter went on, "Colonel Hewson ... going up (to London) to solicit the necessary supply of his regiment, and guns, and many other things we want here requisite to these castles' reducement ..." and it promised that he would bring to Parliament an exact list of the prisoners taken.

The letter was brought by Major Husbands to the Commons personally. It received his report enthusiastically, voting £300 to replace the horses lost by Major Husbands (the shot that killed Husbands' horse actually removed the heel of his boot though leaving him unhurt), and Colonel Hewson, in the action.

The attempt to relieve Deal Castle having failed, and with big guns in place to pound it, the Royalists accepted that further resistance was futile. On 25 August they surrendered, the garrison being permitted to march out honourably.

Colonel Rich again wrote to the Speaker, this letter being entrusted to Axtell. "In reporting to the Speaker the surrender of Deal, Colonel Rich praised the bearer of his despatch, Lieutenant Colonel Axtell, as ..."Extraordinary active and diligent" ... both then and at the siege of Walmer and the House voted him a reward of £100." [13]. Rushworth writes that Axtell ... " and Hewson also distinguished themselves in the defeat of a force landed by the fleet of the Prince of Wales to relieve Deal, and Hewson was voted £150." [14]. (Presumably this is the payment to replace his dead horse).

The last of the three castles covering The Downs, held by the Royalists, was Sandown (Sandowne) castle. Like Walmer and Deal it had been built by Henry VIII in 1539–1540 to protect shipping, and defeat possible landings by Continental invaders on the adjoining sandy beaches.

Following the destruction of his landing force outside Deal, Prince Charles had sailed first for the Thames estuary, then north to East Anglia. This left the way clear for Warwick to bring the Parliamentary fleet into The Downs on 2 September. Here it linked up with ships from Portsmouth. The Sandown garrison knew that relief was now impossible, and parleyed with Colonel Rich and Hewson. Surrender followed on the 5 September, 1648, thus ending the Kentish rebellion.[15]

By early September, Parliament had effectively won the war. Cromwell had crushed the rising in South Wales, and then marched north to join the Parliamentary forces under Lambert. Cromwell advanced to meet a large invading Scottish army, and in a running battle near Preston, destroyed it. The rebellion in East Anglia collapsed with the surrender of Colchester on 27 August.

The victorious Cromwell concluded an agreement with the new Scottish leader, Argyll. Only Pontefract Castle in Yorkshire remained holding out for the King. Cromwell was reluctant to incur the loss of life inevitable in a frontal assault, and commenced a prolonged siege.

The Second Civil War ended, men's thoughts turned again to the vexed question of Government.

CHAPTER 5

"That man of blood"

The Second Civil War in 1648 had hardened attitudes. The condition of the ordinary people became, if anything, worse. A rainy summer was followed by an even wetter autumn; the harvest rotted in the fields. People longed for a return to normality – and that required some sort of accommodation with the King. Parliament's increasingly influential peace faction, led by Denzil Holles, made contact with Charles in September 1648. Negotiations between the King and a commission of moderate members took place at Newport, on the Isle of Wight, but ended in deadlock in mid-November. The King could not be persuaded to agree to a Presbyterian format for the English Church.

Having beaten the Royalists for a second time, the Army claimed a voice in the political settlement. Senior officers were divided, some preferring to work with like-minded members of Parliament. Others blamed Charles for plunging the country into bitter conflict, not once, but twice; and considered that he had thereby forfeited any part in the peace process. The regiments sent a stream of letters and petitions to Fairfax, many expressing agreement with Leveller policies. The petition from Hewson's regiment supported establishing a republic, urging "that the government of Venice, Holland, Switzerland and other parts may be examined, that we may not idolize any one creature, nor never be any more at this charge".[1]

The peace faction, who were in the majority in Parliament, once again sought to weaken the army. During the early months of 1648 pay for the troops had been forthcoming, but once it was clear that the

Army would prevail over the Royalists, that ceased. The unpaid rank and file were in desperate straits; while most officers advanced funds out of their own pockets there is no indication that Colonel Hewson did so. Regimental discipline broke down, and it is recorded that "Hewson's and Ewer's men vented their impatience at lack of pay by terrorizing the inhabitants of north Middlesex and St. Albans."[2]

Fairfax responded to this situation by convening a Council of Officers, meeting on the 7 November in the abbey church of St Alban. Only twenty officers attended, including but two colonels, Hewson and Whalley; the Lieutenant Colonels present included Hewson's Axtell. The proceedings opened with prayers and a sermon. Then the officers considered various regimental petitions. The agents of several regiments stationed in the west requested that in prosecuting those responsible for starting the recent war " there should be no exemption for either king or subject".[3]

Ireton (who worked closely with his father-in-law, Cromwell) was convinced that decisive action against Parliament had to be taken quickly. He feared that the parliamentary delegation negotiating with the King would allow Charles to resume his authority, and all the sacrifices of the two wars would be wasted. Ireton needed support, and appears to have won over Hewson and Whalley, and later more revolutionary Colonels including Ewer, Harrison, Pride and Tomlinson. Under Ireton's guidance, the Council of officers commenced drafting a petition to Parliament setting out the Army's position. To widen support, he negotiated with the Levellers; unsurprisingly, the revised version incorporated most of their constitutional demands.

The final form of the petition, known as "The Remonstrance of the Army", was approved by the Council of Officers. It was presented to Parliament by a delegation of officers on the 20 November, 1648. The petition bluntly called for the King to be put on trial for treason against his people; and for a new, more equitable, constitution. The reaction of the moderate majority in Parliament was predictable – the officers were accused of "insubordination", and their proposals contemptuously sidelined for later debate, possibly in a week's time. Obviously members hoped that by then a settlement would have been agreed with the King. The angry and frustrated officers took matters into their own hands.

Fearing a return of the King to London to popular acclaim, Colonel Ewer was dispatched to the Isle of Wight to ensure that he remained in the Army's custody. On the 25 November the Army moved its headquarters from St Albans to Windsor Castle, a tactically superior situation. Though Fairfax remained Army commander, it was Ireton and the group of radical colonels who were now forcing events. It was remarked that these were of a lower social class than the Parliamentarian leaders who took up arms six long years before. Colonel Harrison was the son of a grazier, Colonel Okey a tallow-chandler, Goffe a salter, Barkstead was variously described as a goldsmith or thimble maker, Kelsey a button maker, and the decisive Colonel Pride had been a brewer's drayman. Only Colonel Hewson had any claims to being a gentleman. Cromwell chose to watch events from a distance, preferring to occupy himself in the personal direction of siege operations against Pontefract Castle in Yorkshire, by now the last outpost of Royalist resistance.

All London feared the Army's next move. The General Council of the Army, meeting at Army Headquarters at Windsor, decided on the 28 November to occupy the capital. Ireton, Constable, Harrison and Hewson were entrusted with the task of drafting a formal Declaration to justify such action. On Friday, 1 December, 1648, the army moved. Troops, including Hewson's regiment, marched in heavy rain from their morning rendezvous at Hounslow Heath to Hyde Park.[4] Around noon the following day, still in pouring rain, the troops advanced into Westminster. They were generally well behaved: "Thanks to Fairfax's orders and the efforts of zealous colonels like Hewson, only a few minor incidents of misbehaviour, such as soldiers jeering at passers-by as they marched, were reported."[5] Hewson's regiment took over the Royal Palace of Whitehall (which now became Army headquarters), while Pride's regiment occupied St James' Palace, the other royal residence in London.

Matters came to a head three days later. Despite all the evidence of King Charles' duplicity, the majority Presbyterian members of

Parliament still believed that an honourable constitutional settlement might be agreed, and on the 5 December voted by 129 votes to 83 to continue negotiations. This was the final straw. The furious Army officers, and radical members of the Commons, gathered in a private meeting later in the day. They appointed a small committee, which was charged with the task of determining which members of Parliament should continue to sit, and which members should be excluded from future Commons sittings. Next morning, Wednesday, 6 December, at 7 am, soldiers from Colonel Pride's regiment gathered around the doorway of the House of Commons. Aided by one of the doorkeepers who knew their faces, and by Lord Groby, Colonel Pride stopped all members on the committee's exclusion list attempting to enter. Some 240 Presbyterian members were shut out; 41 members who protested were arrested. The admitted members protested feebly to Fairfax, as Army commander, at the affront to the dignity of the House, but accepted the fait accompli. Any second thoughts were settled later in the day by Cromwell's arrival from the north. He approved of the action, saying "he had not been acquainted with this design; yet since it was done, he was glad of it, and would endeavour to maintain it".[6]

"On 6th December Pride's Purge made the Colonel famous. Colonel Hewson and Sir Hardress Waller shared the work, but Pride was most prominent. Waller and the others (presumably including Hewson)" were "… putting him (William Prynne, a leading Presbyterian member) down forcibly behind."[7] Prynne was manhandled to the Court of Requests, and detained. Having weighed up the new situation, Cromwell appeared the following morning before the "purged" Commons, now reduced to some 50 or 60 members. Tight security was still maintained: "As on the Wednesday, the place was surrounded by soldiers; this time men of the regiments of Deane and Hewson."[8]

Hewson's men were busied the next day, 8 December, in a more congenial task. Fairfax had been pressing the City for £40,000 promised to Parliament for pay arrears. Perhaps because they were the most reliable: "A force drawn mainly from Hewson's regiment went to secure the Parliament's [sic] main treasuries."[8] Occupying Haberdasher's

Hall, Weaver's Hall (where they found £2,000 in cash), and threatening the Committee for Compounding at Goldsmith's Hall, the City Fathers were left to understand that the Army was in no mood to be trifled with.

On the 12th, Major General Browne, a Presbyterian officer on the Army's wanted list, was taken. His trial before the Council of Officers at Whitehall lasted until the 19 December. He protested vehemently against the proceedings. Finding his language, as Colonel Hewson put it, "too peremptory", the officers confined him in St James prison without the creature comforts of "hangings or bedding".[9]

However the main business of the Council of Officers (which had replaced the General Council of the Army) between December and the end of January, 1649, was an attempt to devise a new constitution. Both senior and junior officers were members, and various civilians (mostly radical clergy), took part in its discussions. A Royalist, the diarist John Evelyn, managed to disguise himself, and trick his way into the officers' meeting room.[10] Before the Council was a document, a draft "Agreement of the People", largely based on Leveller ideas for the future governance of the country. It assumed that the monarchy and House of Lords would be swept away, and that the now purged Commons, derisively termed "the Rump", would obligingly vote itself out of existence on 30 April, 1649. A replacement, more representative, Parliament would elect an executive Council of State to run the country. Most of these proposals were agreed by the officers, but the issue of religious tolerance provoked fierce discussion. On the 14 December, the proposition debated was "How far the civil magistrate (the State authority) had power from God (in matters of religion)?" Colonel Hewson spoke:

> "No man hath said that in this Agreement nothing hath been expressed. The main thing is not whether he should be entrusted, but what should be reserved. I think that's sufficient. For to trust him, if they have a power in themselves either to bind or not to bind, I think that will be a thing questionable still."[11]

Hewson's contribution was cut short by Colonel Rich for straying from the question as put, i.e. whether the civil magistrate has or has not to have any compulsive or restrictive powers in matters of religion.[12]

Two days later, the Council was embroiled in discussion about what powers the state should have concerning military conscription. The question put was "Wether wee shall propound in this Agreement any reserve from the power of the Representatives (the name to be given to the planned new Parliament) in point of impresting men for the Warre." Ireton led a minority of officers, including Hewson, against the reserve.[13] A vote permitting exemption from impressments for service in foreign wars on grounds of conscience was passed by the Council, only Colonel Hewson and Scoutmaster Roe objecting.[14] Perhaps the soldier in Colonel Hewson had no time for pacifists.

On the 18 December the Council of Officers formally debated the question "That the Representatives intermeddle not with the execution of laws, nor give judgment … where no law hath been before provided". The senior officers, led by Ireton, constituted a more conservative and authoritative group, whilst the junior officers tended towards the views of the preachers and civilians. Ireton opposed this proposition, perhaps fearing that at some point it might be used to undermine the legality of a trial of the King. However the proposition stood, the junior officers winning a close vote by 18 to 16. Whilst Hewson voted with Ireton and the senior officers, his lieutenant colonel, Axtell, joined with the more radical junior officers. It is interesting – in five recorded divisions, Axtell always voted against his regimental commander. There is no evidence of personal animosity between the two men – it will be remembered that some months earlier Hewson had been willing to lend Axtell his own horse – so the divergence must have been only on political grounds. It appears that the army leaders had no intention of exerting pressure on their junior officers to secure the results that they wanted.[15]

The Council of Officers had not settled the religious question. Following the debate on the 14th, a special Committee was set up to make recommendations to the Council. It included the prominent Leveller leader, John Wildman, some preachers, and officers. Hewson was appointed to the Committee on the 18th. Basically the issue was whether "to entrust the civil government with positive power" in religious matters. Ireton thought that the government should have such authority. The Leveller view was that "matters of religion and worship are not 'trustable' to any civil power: liberty of conscience is a birthright which cannot be constrained."[16] The Committee met again on the 21 December – though Colonel Hewson was present, it is not known how he voted.

The most pressing issue of the day was how to bring the King to account for his misdeeds. Whilst the Army had no doubt that Charles deserved to die – he had betrayed his duty to protect his people by taking up arms against them – Cromwell was concerned that, as far as possible, the King's trial should be conducted openly, and in accordance with the laws of England. The purged Commons bowed to Cromwell's demands, agreeing to set up a so-called High Court of a hundred and thirty-five persons, under the Presidency of John Bradshaw, an undistinguished London barrister. Cromwell had also found difficulty in finding a suitable lawyer to lead the prosecution. He was forced to give the task to John Cook, a member of Gray's Inn, a Republican already noted for his virulent hatred of the King. Although Cromwell and the army leaders had now decided that Charles was to die, an appearance of justice was expedient.

Charles, meanwhile, remained under close guard at Windsor Castle, having been escorted there from the Isle of Wight by Colonel Ewer in early December.

On the 22 December Colonel Hewson is recorded as being at Windsor Castle, attending a meeting of the General Council of the Army. It was marked as a day of religious observance, with fasting and prayers from the morning until night. Colonel Hewson is described as praying "very fervently".[17] Cromwell and Ireton were anxious to prevent any possibility of a Royalist attempt to rescue the King: "… Captain Brayfield of Colonel Hewson's regiment with his own and two other companies of foot was ordered to Windsor Castle to secure it and the King's person therein."[18] The troops had to be quartered in the town and nearby Eton, due to lack of accommodation in the castle itself.

Windsor Castle

Colonel Hewson was back in London by the 26th, attending a meeting of the Council of Officers discussing the powers of the Representatives, the body that under the proposed new constitution would replace Parliament. Clearly by this time the officers took it for granted that the Monarchy would be eliminated.

On a happier note, sometime after this month, Colonel Hewson's daughter, Agnes, became the second wife of Captain Richard Lawrence, younger brother of the respected politician, Henry Lawrence.

At Westminster, preparations for the King's trial were pressed forward. The High Court of Justice was to sit in the Hall of the ancient Palace of Westminster. This historic chamber had to be converted into a dignified Court room, with access for the public, yet providing for the security of the Court officers and for the prisoner. The fear of a desperate Royalist rescue action was ever-present. To guard against an assassin's bullet it is recorded that the Lord President of the Court, Bradshaw, took the unusual precaution of having his hat lined with steel plates. This curious hat may yet be seen in the Ashmolean Museum in Oxford.

In early January 1649, the High Court was convened. Colonel Hewson was named as a Commissioner, and nominated as a judge. On the 15 January, a Committee (including Hewson) was formed to manage the trial arrangements. He was also a member of a separate Committee set up to examine witnesses against the King.

Saturday 20 January was the first day of the King's trial. The Court assembled in Westminster Hall shortly after two o'clock and awaited the arrival of the Royal prisoner. Charles was led in, surrounded by soldiers, to take his solitary position facing his judges. Partly for security, and partly to keep the thronging onlookers at a distance, the area behind the King was packed with armed soldiers drawn from Hewson's regiment. They were commanded by his impetuous lieutenant colonel, Axtell. Hewson himself, as one of the judges, sat on the bench next to the fanatical Colonel Pride.[19]

Westminster Hall

Barely had the proceedings begun than there was disturbance in the Hall. This was blamed, in the official reports, on the noisy influx of further spectators, pushing forward to get a better view. However, many years later, Lady Anna de Lyle made the bizarre claim that she had raised her voice on behalf of the King, and for her pains, had been branded in open Court by Colonel Hewson.[20] Whilst this story is undoubtedly fabrication, it does suggest that by 1666 Colonel Hewson had acquired the status of a mythological hate figure.

For his part, the King, with cold dignity, denied that this Court had authority over him, and repeatedly refused to enter a plea. Angry and frustrated, Bradshaw ordered that the prisoner be taken away.

Proceedings resumed on the following Monday. Again the King challenged the jurisdiction of the Court, indeed asserting that in so doing he was defending the liberty of his people against usurped authority. The prosecutor, John Cook, threatened him; saying that if he did not plead, his silence would be taken as an admission of guilt. The King was not to be bullied, and reiterated that, in standing up to an unlawful authority, he was defending the rights of all his subjects. Impasse had been reached.

The King's defiance was all too much for Colonel Hewson watching from the judge's bench. In a fury, he rushed forward and spat in the King's face, calling out to his men, "… justice! justice upon the traitor!" The King drew out his handkerchief, wiped his cheek, and with compelling dignity replied, "Well, Sir!, God hath justice in store both for you and me."[21] At that, Charles was removed from the Court.

The Commissioners decided to continue pressure on the King to plead, and thereby acknowledge the authority of the Court. Brought before the Court on the third day, the King insisted that his was the rightful authority, "… I am your King …", and that his duty was "to uphold justice, to maintain the old laws".[22] The Clerk of the Court interrupted the King, calling on him to answer the charges against him. Charles again denied the legality of the Court, and amid uproar, was again taken away.

From the Commissioners' point of view the trial, was turning into a disaster. Without the production of evidence, it was impossible to demonstrate the King's guilt, and thereby justify his execution. Moreover his lucid and dignified stance in the face of a hostile Court, was winning respect and sympathy amongst the onlookers. This could not go on. The Commissioners decided to take evidence in private for future publication. This was done.

Meeting in private on the 26 January, the baffled Commissioners decided that, unless the Royal prisoner finally bowed to the Court's jurisdiction, he should be declared guilty of all charges, and sentenced to death.

Colonel Hewson was present on the final day of the trial, Saturday 27 January. That dark afternoon, the King was brought before the assembled Court. Barely had the President, Bradshaw, commenced his opening address, when there was commotion in the public gallery. A lady, her face masked, rose to declare loudly Oliver Cromwell a traitor. An infuriated Lieutenant Colonel Axtell, standing amongst the guard from Hewson's regiment surrounding the King, completely lost his head, and shouted at his men to aim their muskets at her. Some say that he wildly ordered them to fire. If he did, the men had more sense than to obey. The onlookers in the gallery, no doubt realising that they were in the line of fire, hastily bundled the lady out of the gallery, and by the time Axtell's soldiers reached it, she had made good her escape. The lady's identity was at first a mystery, but doubtless Cromwell had recognised her voice – she was none other than Lady Fairfax, wife of his army commander.

Not to be deflected, Bradshaw continued with his address. The proceeding dragged on through the afternoon in a tense atmosphere. Bradshaw emphasised that the King was undoubtedly guilty – had he not waged war on his own subjects? He finished speaking and abruptly ordered the Clerk of the Court to read out the sentence of death. Bradshaw denied the King a final opportunity to speak, and had him escorted from the Hall. The soldiers took King Charles to nearby Whitehall, and kept him under close guard to await execution.

Meanwhile the Commissioners had adjourned to the Painted Chamber to discuss the public beheading. Detailed arrangements were entrusted to a small group of senior Army officers. Difficulty arose in securing a headsman. The official Public Hangman was a professional, Richard Brandon, whose skill and steady nerve were widely regarded. Understandably, however, he was unwilling to take on this particular duty. He lived in the City, near the Tower of London, and many of his neighbours had great sympathy for the King. He and his family would be targets for revenge. It was rumoured that Brandon had gone into hiding. At all events, Colonel Hewson was ordered to find an executioner. According to a sergeant called Richard Gittens, who gave evidence at the post-restoration trial of Colonel Hacker, Colonel Hewson summoned about 38 of his sergeants, made them take an oath of secrecy, and then offered a reward of £100 to the man who would behead the King. But, according to Gittens, no one then was prepared to do it.

The historic beheading of King Charles was carried out three days later, on the afternoon of Tuesday 30 January 1649, on a scaffold built against the Banqueting Hall, Westminster Palace. The small platform was crowded. Colonel Hacker supervised the execution whilst the King was guarded by Colonel Tomlinson and several soldiers. The King made a short calm statement (which was taken down by shorthand writers), laid his head on the block, and died, as he had lived, with dignity.

The beheading was achieved with one, clean, fall of the axe. This was not the work of a bumbling amateur. It suggests that Colonel Hewson had prevailed on Brandon. This cannot be known for certain, since both the executioner and his assistant were unrecognisable. In addition to the traditional black facemasks, both men wore beards and hairpieces, clearly not their own.

Public curiosity about the identity of the headsmen was intense, and various names were bandied about. Much speculation centred on Colonel Peter Stubbers as being the actual executioner. Certainly this most unpleasant individual was unexpectedly advanced by Cromwell, being subsequently appointed Military Governor of Galway. Another name was Henry Walker, scathingly nicknamed "Pious Harvey". Walker was well known as the publisher of *Perfect Occurrences*, a popular news tract, though why it was rumoured that he might be the disguised executioner is now unknown. However suspicion would hardly have been allayed by the fact that he was an intimate of Colonel Hewson – indeed one of his few real friends.

The issue was examined in J G Muddiman's "Trial of King Charles the First", published in 1928. He records that a sergeant in Hewsons's regiment named Hulet, alias Howlet, was accused of being the executioner, or at least his assistant. This was widely believed in the army, his subsequent promotion to captain might have significance. Hulet may well have been assistant to Brandon.

As might have been foreseen, the King's death did not extinguish the Royalist cause; loyalty was now focused on the young Charles II, safely protected in Holland. Cromwell, however, was more concerned with putting in place the new regime. Within a week of Charles' execution, Parliament abolished the Monarchy, establishing the Commonwealth. The King's executive role would be taken by a newly appointed Council of State, composed of the ablest men in the Army, Parliament and the Law. It was often chaired by Cromwell himself. Apart from also abolishing the House of Lords, Cromwell sought to rebuild the machinery of government on the traditional lines. This disappointed the Levellers, their supporters in the lower ranks of the Army, and in London. This vocal and well-organised movement had hoped for real constitutional advance, calling for an extended franchise, reform of Parliament, and improvements in the legal system. They thought that their demands had been accepted in the main at the meetings with the Council of Officers in December, and felt betrayed when they realised that the new Government had no intention of implementing them. Indeed they distrusted Cromwell, suspecting him of seeking to be a military despot.

About the middle of February, 1649, the Army leaders discovered that the Levellers were interfering with the Army "….by urging the soldiers to demand the reappointment of Agitators, and to revive the disused General Council of the Army in order that these Agitators might again have an equal voice with the officers in determining the political action of the Army." As might have been expected, the officers took offence at the suggestion. At a Council of Officers held on the 22nd February, where there was discussion on a petition from Fairfax's regiment in which the views of the Levellers were embodied, heated language was used. Hewson recommended that those who drew up such petitions should be tried by military courts martial, whether or not they were soldiers. In a typically violent outburst: "....we have had tryal enough of Civil Courts, we can hang twenty before they will hang one."[23] His attitude was similar to that of Cromwell, who later remarked angrily about the Levellers "....you have no other way to deal with these men but to break them or they will break you...."[24] In the end, the Council decided to ask Parliament to pass an Act for the punishment of civilians stirring up discontent in the Army. Colonels Hewson and Whaller were asked to work with Cromwell and Ireton on this approach.[25]

At the same meeting, the Council also appointed Hewson to a Committee of Officers to make preparations for the abolition of the hugely unpopular free quartering system.[26]

Leveller dissatisfaction increased, and at the meeting of the Council of Officers on the 1 March, Fairfax produced a petition from eight Leveller troopers basically calling for democratisation of the Army. The officers ordered their court martial for conduct tending to disunite the Army. Their trial was held two days later, on 3 March, and the five troopers charged were found guilty. The sentence of riding the wooden horse, and cashiering, was carried out on the 6 March in the Palace Yard, Westminster.

"A fortnight later the five cashiered men published their defiant answer to their tormentors. Entitled the 'Hunting of the Foxes', the pamphlet exposes the extreme animosity to the Levellers harboured by Colonels Hewson, and Barkstead, the latter having been the president of the court martial that had tried them."[27] It was apparent that the pamphlet had been written by a far sharper mind than any of the troopers, and therefore the officers called them in for questioning. One trooper asked for time to write his explanation, and to this request Colonel Hewson retorted, "Yes – and then he that wrote the other can write that too!"[28]

A new topic was discussed at the meeting of the General Council of Officers on the 23 March – Ireland. The Irish Catholics had to be punished for their barbaric massacres of the Ulster Protestants in the uprising in 1641. This had long been the avowed intention of both the King and Parliament. Since 1641 it had been envisaged that the costs of the punitive expedition would be advanced by private investors, to be repaid handsomely by grants of sequestrated Irish land. Cromwell is known to have been one of these investors, the "Adventurers". Hewson was not.

The Irish issue had acquired urgency. The new King, Charles II, saw that his best opportunity of recovering his throne was an invasion of England mounted from Ireland. Events were moving his way. The Royalist Lord-Lieutenant in Ireland, his faithful Marquess of Ormonde, had secured the support of the native Irish at the beginning of the year. He had signed the treaty of Kilkenny, which allowed the practice of the Catholic faith. Combining the various Irish armies with his experienced Royalist, largely English, troops tipped the balance of military advantage against Parliament. Parliament still held Dublin and the surrounding area, and had influence in Ulster, and parts of Munster. However Ormonde now had substantial numerical superiority, and was poised to take over the whole country.

By mid-April 1649 plans for an Irish expedition were well advanced. Cromwell had agreed, albeit reluctantly, to lead the force, since it was clear that the troops would follow only him. Initially his own regiment of horse and two others were nominated. On the 20 April other regiments were drawn by lots, the names being picked out of a hat by a child. In this way the Lord was being invited to show his Will. His choice of foot regiments was those of Ewer, Cook, Deane and Hewson. One may well ask whether the selection of Hewson's regiment – so valued by Cromwell and Fairfax – truly was the unassisted work of the Almighty.

The men were told that no one would be compelled to go to Ireland, though any who elected to stay in England would not be permitted to remain in the Army. On hearing this, many soldiers who had resolved not to leave England until the demands of the Levellers had been granted – 300 in Hewson's regiment alone – threw down their arms. They were promptly cashiered, and received each of them a small sum sufficient to return them to their homes. That disaffection was not general was shown by the alacrity with which volunteers came forward to fill their places from those regiments not picked for Irish service.[29] However many refuseniks felt they had been treated unfairly, that the sum was insufficient, and indeed some had even received harsh treatment. It was said that in Hewson's regiment they were even stripped of their coats.

As for the officers in the chosen regiments, outwardly at least, they "expressed much cheerfulness at the selection".[30] Hewson's officers were willing to go with the regiment. Daniel Axtell remained as his lieutenant colonel, John Carter as major, and his company captains included George Jenkins, Alexander Brayfield, Sam Axtell, Smith, Thomas Atkinson, Grimes (or Graime) and Gale. Two former agitators remained on the regiment's payroll, Edmund Gardner (or Garne) as a lieutenant, and Daniel Hincksman (or Hinchman) as a quartermaster.[31]

Leveller discontent continued to simmer in the army. On the 26 April, one Robert Lockyer, who had been the leader of a minor mutiny in Waller's regiments, was shot following court martial. The sentence was carried out in St Paul's churchyard by six musketeers of Hewson's regiment, the execution supervised by Colonel Okey, and Hewson's major, John Carter. The latter "was much troubled at the thought that they were killing one of the saints".[32] Clearly the army leaders were determined to stamp out any Leveller inspired disaffection in the normally reliable regiments trusted to be stationed in London.

To secure the Tower of London (and its armoury) from any Leveller action, 400 reliable infantry from Pride's and Hewson's regiments, now known for their anti-radical sentiments, were marched in on the night of the 8 May. "As they entered the gates they railed against Lilburne as the source of all their troubles … and promised him fire and faggot for his pains if they live to see all quiet". Lilburne had by that time been confined to the Tower, and the Lieutenant of the Tower was ordered to keep him "under strict surveillance ... and to deny him pen, ink, or paper".[33]

Militarily and politically, matters were hastening to a crisis. During April the Leveller leaders, particularly Lilburne and Overton, had been attempting to turn the army rank and file against their officers, to overthrow the purged Parliament and to support the Leveller's radical constitutional aspirations. Agents had been sent around the country seeking to foment unrest both amongst the soldiers and the long-suffering poor. The response was sporadic, but various troops in Essex and in the Oxford area mutinied. If they united, there was a serious risk that they could occupy Oxford itself, as the garrison had been infected by Leveller propaganda, and could not be relied upon.

Fairfax and Cromwell acted decisively. To quote Ian Gentles:

> "...Having ensured that London was under control, the grandees decided to move a large force to the locus of the discontent around Bristol. On the 9th May they mustered five of the best regiments in Hyde Park. Fairfax's and Cromwell's horse were joined by Fairfax's, Hewson's and Ewer's foot. While Fairfax listened, Cromwell assured the troops that Parliament was looking out for the best interest of both nation and army."[34]

Although there was some sullen muttering in the ranks, the troops heard him out. The total force of some 2,500 then marched west to confront the growing numbers of Levellers.

In event no conflict took place. During the early hours of 14 May, Cromwell's horse surprised the sleeping Leveller troops quartered in the little town of Burford. Some 340 were captured, and secured in the local church. Three leaders were shot the following day, but the rest released. After that, the few remaining bands of mutinous soldiers were quickly dispersed.

The city of Oxford had hosted King Charles' government during the First Civil War, the University, in particular, providing enthusiastic support. It was now time to win favour with the new rulers.

Taking advantage of the presence in the area of the army leaders, flushed with their success in quelling the Leveller uprising with so little bloodshed, the University authorities invited them to accept academic honours.

> "On the 19th [May, 1649] the now puritan University gave to the successful soldiers the highest honours it could bestow. Fairfax and Cromwell donned the scarlet gowns of Doctors of Civil Law, whilst Harrison, Hewson, Okey, and other martial figures were decked in the soberer costume which designate a Master of Arts."[35]

As Colonel Hewson had not received higher education, this award must have been gratifying. Doubly pleasing, being from the hands of his erstwhile enemies.

The army leaders could now turn attention to the Irish operation. It is probable that Colonel Hewson first returned to London to make final preparations. The Venetian Ambassador, writing to his masters on the 24 May 1649, reported: "The regiment of Colonel Hewson has left Whitehall for Brentford, on its way to Ireland, following the regiment of General Fairfax."

On the 5 June, the formal action was taken: "The Council of State gave orders for Flemish ships to transport the horses into Ireland, and for the regiments to march to Chester and other ports."[36] This date was adopted as the commencement of Irish service in calculating arrears of pay of the troops in Ireland. The Venetian Ambassador further commented, "The regiments destined for Ireland by Parliament do not show much desire to go there; indeed they seem to contemplate joining the other side." This latter assertion strains credulity, though there is evidence that many of the rank and file of the designated regiments entertained resentments.

However the City clearly wanted the expedition to leave. No doubt their motives were largely mercenary – many of the City fathers had funds invested in the Irish Adventure. They stood to reap great profit should Cromwell's army successfully expropriate Irish lands. Moreover the city Presbyterians believed grossly exaggerated tales of barbarities inflicted in 1641 by the Irish Catholics on defenceless Ulster Protestants, and felt retribution long overdue. The improved relations between the City and the Army were marked by "A magnificent banquet given by the City of London authorities on 7th June as an official thanksgiving to the Government for the ending of the Leveller troubles". No doubt Colonel Hewson enjoyed the City's hospitality, for Antonia Fraser writes, "At the banquet itself, which included all officers above the rank of Lieutenant ..."[37]

The Venetian Ambassador's information that many soldiers in the regiments picked for service in Ireland remained unhappy was not ill founded. The *Moderate*, a London newsletter of 6 July, 1649, stated that a petition was presented to General Fairfax by Captain Jubbs, in the name of Colonel Hewson's regiment "...expressing many grievances that lay upon their spirits in relation to the public".[38] The mood of apprehension in the ranks led to the forthcoming campaign being dubbed "the cut-throat war", and the soldiers feared it would be their throats.

Needless to say, the manifold preparations required to dispatch Cromwell's expedition did not pass unobserved by the Royalists' information service. One agent in London wrote on the 14 July 1649, warning Ormonde of Cromwell's intentions: "Hee hath drawen towards the West 7 regiments of foote, which hee intends to carry with him from thence, viz his owne regiment, Jextons who is gone with him, Coll. Cookes, Coll. Ferris, Coll. Stubbes, Coll. Hustons, and Coll. Owens." The agent suggested that the force totalled 5000 foot and 2000 horse.[39] This intelligence may also have suggested to Ormonde that Cromwell would land in the south of Ireland – which, of course, he would have had to do, should the port of Dublin fall to Ormonde. Not surprisingly, the communication was unsigned!

In fact Cromwell had moved faster than the agent reported. By then, an advance guard of 2,000 men was on its way to Dublin, being quickly incorporated into the forces commanded by the

Parliamentary General, Michael Jones, holding that city against the threatening Ormonde.

Cromwell left London for Milford Haven on the 9 July. He had refused to move until he had assurances that the expeditionary force would be fully equipped, and importantly, fully funded. He foresaw that the campaign would involve siege operations, and insisted on having a powerful artillery train. The new Commonwealth navy ensured command of the seas, thus enabling cannon and supplies to be transported as required. The agent had underestimated the strength of Cromwell's Army – in fact it amounted to 10,000 men with 4,000 horses. In all, 130 ships in three fleets set sail for Ireland.

CHAPTER 6

"Cromwell's campaign in Ireland"

Cromwell's first sight of Ireland was the purple outline of the Wicklow Mountains, soon to be replaced by the softer hills around Dublin Bay. He had never been to sea before, and contemporaries commented that never had they seen anyone suffer such sea-sickness. Colonel Hewson, however, may well have been to Dublin in more peaceful times, on visits to obtain quality hides for his shoe-making business. Apparently, he visited the country in the spring of 1647.

The first fleet of some thirty-five ships sailed into Dublin Bay on the 14 August 1649, Cromwell landing at the little harbour of Ringsend.

Once on dry land Cromwell quickly recovered his cheerfulness and authority. He found the military position vastly improved. During July, the combined Irish and Royalist forces, under the experienced Ormonde, had surrounded Dublin City, the last significant outpost of Parliamentary government in the country. Its defender, Major General Michael Jones, was a resolute soldier. His troops, including four regiments recently sent from England, repeatedly made spirited sallies to disrupt the besiegers. On 2 August his army surprised Ormonde near Rathmines with a full-scale attack, scattered his superior force, and captured his guns. The defeated Royalist and Irish contingents dispersed, leaving no coherent army capable of opposing Cromwell in pitched battle. Cromwell rewarded Jones by promoting him Lieutenant General, and appointing him as his second-in-command.

Cromwell was welcomed into Dublin. Thomas Coonan writes "… Cromwell was greeted by the roar of cannon from the walls of Dublin and he was received in the city with acclaim by a great crowd of people. Jones had been careful beforehand to banish the Catholics from the city under pain of death. Cromwell addressed the crowd in a '…most sweet and reasonable speech…' in which he promised favour and reward to all who helped '…against the barbarous and bloodthirsty Irish…', for the propagation of the Gospel, the establishment of truth and peace, and the restoration of '…this bleeding nation of Ireland to its former happiness and tranquility.'"[1] Unlike the opposing Royalist and native Irish forces, Cromwell had a full Treasury, and ample supplies. In his capacity as Lord Lieutenant of Ireland, he ordered that troops under his command should refrain from troubling or molesting the inhabitants of the country, and that all provisions obtained should be paid for. He hoped that the good conduct of his soldiers would win, if not the support of the people, at least their passive acceptance of the situation.

As further ships brought in more and more troops and provisions, Cromwell prepared for his campaign of conquest. His regiments were drawn out of plague ridden Dublin, and given field training in the surrounding countryside. The English regiments already in Dublin under Jones were reorganised, and brought up to strength. Cromwell's plan for the conquest of Ireland was simple. Jones' defeat of Ormonde at Rathmines had eliminated the possibility of any immediate effective Royalist opposition in the field. Cromwell was anxious to secure the seaports in the south and east of the country before the arrival of winter to deny Ormonde receiving assistance from the Continent. However before he could advance south, Cromwell needed to protect his rear, and also his base in Dublin. He decided therefore that first he would strike north, to take the vital town of Drogheda.

The advance guard, led by Jones, marched on 31 August, followed by the main force under Cromwell. In all, the army might have amounted to some 12,000 men. Although the distance was only some 30 miles, Cromwell's troops did not reach the outskirts of Drogheda until 3 September.

The town of Drogheda was strategically important, commanding the road to Ulster, and a strong military position in its own right. It straddled the River Boyne; the two parts connected by a bridge. The smaller part was on the south bank, containing a small hill crowned by a wooden palisade enclosing a small fortification. This was Millmount. Both parts of the town were surrounded by high walls, strengthened by defensive towers. Below the eastern wall around this south part, ran a deep natural ravine. Ormonde had garrisoned the town with his best troops, mainly English Royalists, which included some of those defeated at Rathmines. Command was entrusted to Sir Arthur Aston, known for his uncompromising support for the Royalist cause. He had lost a leg during the First Civil War in England, but remained a deter-mined soldier. Despite being severely short of ammunition, Aston and his officers were in good heart, and confident that the town could hold out against Cromwell until Ormonde rebuilt his field army. Further, Aston hoped that a prolonged siege would lead to Cromwell's force being severely weakened by exposure to the Irish weather, disease, and shortage of food.

Cromwell took his position facing the south part of the town, and dispatched cavalry across the river to surround the north part, to pre-vent military support reaching Aston. However stormy seas delayed the arrival of the ships carrying Cromwell's heavy cannon, and it was several days before they sailed up the Boyne. Cromwell decided to attack the south part of the town, and sited his guns in two batteries. The first was on high ground opposite its east wall, firing over the ravine. The second was on flatter ground facing the southern wall and towers.

As was the military usage of the time, Cromwell offered Aston the chance to surrender the town before commencing bombardment. Confident of the strength of his defences, Aston refused. He was aware that, if Drogheda fell, he and his men could then expect no quarter.

Firing began on the morning of 9 September. Soon the air was thick with gunpowder smoke. The ancient city walls, built of soft lime-stone, crumbled under the impact of Cromwell's huge cannon balls, some weighing up to two stone. The guns were employed in pounding selected stretches of the wall. Some two or three hundred rounds opened up two breaches, and brought down the tower near the southern city gate. Inside, the defenders prepared to meet the anticipated assault by digging trenches behind the city walls.

By late afternoon of the following day, Cromwell was ready to assault both breaches. Hewson's regiment advanced down into the ravine, then clambered up the opposite slope to attempt the gap in the eastern wall. Colonel Castle, supported by Ewer's regiment, led his men through the opening in the southern wall. Both assaults were thrown back. Colonel Castle was killed. As Cromwell's men ran forward they had lost formation, and were cut down by the lines of waiting musketeers, and by charges of Royalist horse.

In a letter written shortly after the event, Colonel Hewson described what happened at the eastern wall: "We entered the breach, but not so orderly as was appointed; we were stoutly resisted, and after a short dispute, did retreat disorderly, tumbling over the breach and down a steep hill that ascends up to the wall."[2]

Tom Reilly explains in his definitive study of this action how some Parliamentary regiments were beaten back, rallied, and attacked again. Their second assault was also repelled.[3] This probably occurred at the southern breach, where the attacking regiments had to advance across a large open space under fire.

In this moment of crisis, Cromwell displayed his true mettle. As Ian Gentle writes:

> "Cromwell then unleashed a cannonade of half-pound shot to clear the Royalist horse from the breaches. Augmenting the three regiments with reserves from Venable's and Farre's [Phayres], he ... accompanied the men on foot..." for a determined assault. "As the last daylight ebbed away they overran the enemy's entrenchments, took possession of St. Mary's Church, and opened the nearby gate to their own cavalry."[4]

Colonel Hewson's own account of his separate action at the eastern breach explains:

"Col. Venable's regiment and Col Phayre's being both upon
guard ... did come down another hill (into the ravine) ... so that
before our men got half way down the hill upon their retreat,
we got them faced about ... that they fell on again, entered the
breach, beat off the enemy, pursued him".[2]

Cromwell's men broke into the south part of the town, pouring through
the breaches in an unstoppable rush. The hastily prepared Royalist
defences were overwhelmed, and the soldiers ran for their lives. Many,
including Aston, took refuge in the fortification at Millmount. What
happened next is clouded with uncertainty. One contemporary account
suggests that Lieutenant Colonel Axtell of Hewson's regiment, with
some twelve of his men, went up to the top of the mount, and persuaded the Royalists to surrender; once disarmed, quarter was denied,
and they were slaughtered. Amongst them was Sir Arthur Aston. The
Parliamentarian Ludlow wrote in his Memoirs: "A great dispute there
was amongst the souldiers for his artificial leg, which was reported to
be of gold, but it proved to be of wood."[5] Legend has it that the disappointed soldiers then beat Aston to death with his own leg.

Meanwhile other fleeing Royalists made for the bridge over the
Boyne, seeking safety in the north part of the town. Ludlow claims
that Cromwell's men "followed them so close that they overtook them
at the bridge preventing them from drawing up the bridge, entered
pell-mell with them into the place where they put all they met to the
sword, having positive orders from the Lieutenant-General to give no
quarter to any souldier".[6] (The Lieutenant General referred to was, of
course, Cromwell, not Michael Jones.)

Ludlow was not present at Drogheda, and his reference to "drawing
up the bridge" appears fanciful. Brendon Matthews, a local historian
attached to the Millmount Museum, has recently established that, by
1649, the original wooden bridge had been replaced by a substantial
two arch stone construction. He claims that Cromwell's troopers had
quickly seized the bridge, thereby trapping most of the fleeing Royalist
soldiers on the southern side of the river. Few, if any, were spared.

SIEGE OF DROGHEDA - SEPTEMBER 1649

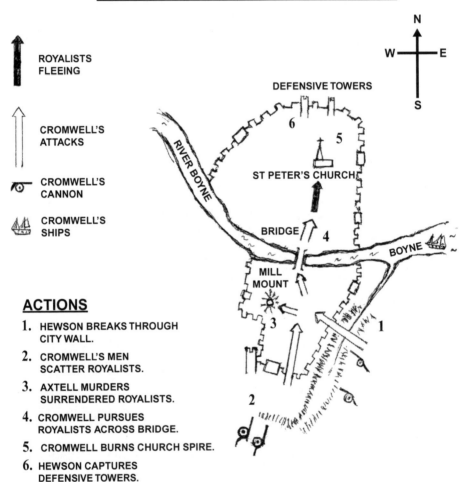

ROYALISTS
FLEEING

CROMWELL'S
ATTACKS

CROMWELL'S
CANNON

CROMWELL'S
SHIPS

DEFENSIVE TOWERS

RIVER BOYNE

ST PETER'S CHURCH

BRIDGE

BOYNE

MILL
MOUNT

ACTIONS

1. HEWSON BREAKS THROUGH
   CITY WALL.

2. CROMWELL'S MEN
   SCATTER ROYALISTS.

3. AXTELL MURDERS
   SURRENDERED ROYALISTS.

4. CROMWELL PURSUES
   ROYALISTS ACROSS BRIDGE.

5. CROMWELL BURNS CHURCH SPIRE.

6. HEWSON CAPTURES
   DEFENSIVE TOWERS.

What subsequently followed was a night of horror that has forever stained Cromwell's good name. His order was to slay all who "were in arms in the town", and in this he was justified by the rules of war of the period. Aston had been offered the opportunity to surrender, and had refused, costing the lives of many of Cromwell's men. However Cromwell did not rescind his order, and thousands of helpless Royalists were hunted down and killed. Escape to the north was impossible because of the cordon of Parliamentary cavalry encircling the town.

Perhaps the worst incident took place at St Peter's Church, in the centre of the northern part of the town. Here some 100 fugitives sought sanctuary. This has been described by a Dr Bernard, who was then the preacher at St Peter's, and lived close by. In his account, he records what happened in the church that night: "Not long afterwards," he says, "came Colonel Hewson, and told the Doctor he had orders to blow up the steeple (which stood between the choir and the body of the church), where about three score men were run up for refuge, but the three barrels of powder which he had caused to be put under it for that end, blew up only the body of the church, and the next night" – this should have been the "same" night – "Hewson caused the seats of the church to be broken up, and made a great pile of them under the steeple, which, firing it, took the lofts wherein five great bells hung, and from thence it flamed up to the top, and so at once men and bells and roof came all down together, the most hideous sight and terrible cry that ever he was a witness of at one." In fairness to Hewson, it has to be said that the order to set the steeple on fire was given personally by Cromwell.

During the rest of that night the slaughter of Royalist and native Irish soldiers continued. No Catholic priests were spared, and an unknown number of civilians also perished. Many of those who survived were shipped out to Barbados, to work in slavery in the sugar plantations. On the following morning, 12 September, operations commenced against two towers still holding out, for their garrisons had no trust in Cromwell's offer of quarter. Hewson was in charge of this work, which ended in their capture.

Siege of Drogheda

St Peter's Church

That night's events changed the Irish perception of Cromwell, and destroyed his preferred policy of seeking to win the hearts and minds of the ordinary people.

Cromwell determined to exploit his success. A strong force was dispatched north into Ulster to prevent any threat to his Dublin base arising from that direction. Colonel Hewson, with his regiment, remained in Drogheda to secure the town. Being in the forefront of the assaults, his regiment had suffered heavier casualties than some of the others, and a period of recovery was advisable. Cromwell's other regiments conducted operations in the area, while the General himself was back in Dublin by the 16 September. According to John Hewetson, on that day he promulgated the appointment of Hewson as Governor of Dublin.[7]

On 22 September, Colonel Hewson wrote to his friend Henry Walker. This letter was published in the latter's London news sheet *Perfect Occurrences*, issued on Friday 5 October 1649, and gives Hewson's account of the storming of Drogheda, the events at St Peter's church, and the taking of the last two towers.

Cromwell was now making preparations to occupy the main ports along the east and south coasts of Ireland. Their capture would not only deny Ormonde any possibility of assistance from the Continent, but would enable Cromwell to supply his army from the sea. Furthermore he looked forward to using captured towns as winter quarters for his troops.

The English army commenced its march south from Dublin on 23 September. Colonel Hewson was sick, and remained in the city. Quick progress was made, and within a week the army was threatening the important port of Wexford. That city fell to Cromwell after an eight-day siege, on 11 October. Once again success was tainted by widespread slaughter. Although Cromwell's reputation was blackened (primarily by nationalistic writers in the nineteenth century) by allegations of massacres of civilians at Drogheda and Wexford, modern research suggests that in fact few civilians were wantonly killed. Cromwell's proclaimed policy of severe consequences for towns that refused to surrender paid dividends in the short term (by shortening the campaign, and reducing casualties amongst his men), in the long term it proved counter-productive by sowing the seeds of a hatred that persists even to this day.

As indicated, Cromwell's seventeenth century version of "shock and awe" produced quick successes. Six days after taking Wexford, Cromwell was encamped in front of the town of Ross, or New Ross, which guarded the most important crossing of the river Barrow. He wrote a courteous note to that town's governor summoning him to surrender "… to avoid the effusion of blood". The governor, Major Lucas Taffe, was well aware that Cromwell was not to be trifled with, and on 19 October thankfully signed generous terms of capitulation.

For over a month, Cromwell remained in the town, resting his troops and planning his next move. The arduous campaign, and wet weather, had weakened his men's resistance, and many hundreds were seriously ill. Even Cromwell himself fell victim, and was confined to bed. However he could reflect that events were moving his way. Much of Ulster and Leinster were now under his control, and defections from the Royalist cause had handed him all the main ports in Munster, save only the thriving city of Waterford. Before he had occupied New Ross, its bridge had been destroyed and so Cromwell employed his men in constructing an impressive replacement bridge of boats.

Meanwhile the new Governor of Dublin, Hewson, had not been idle. Cromwell had left behind many sick men in that city when he advanced south. While Cromwell lay at New Ross he sent for reinforcements from Dublin. Hewson rounded up all available men, to the number of 1,200, many far from fully recovered, and ordered them to march down the coast to Wexford. They were to be escorted by a force coming up to meet them. However, before the arrival of the supporting troops, the Royalist, Inchiquin, fell on the soldiers marching from Dublin, with far superior numbers. The weak and tired English fought manfully and succeeded in driving Inchiquin from the field. This encounter greatly raised the morale of the Parliamentary army.

It was late in November before Cromwell was ready to leave New Ross. His army crossed the new bridge, and turned south, intending to capture Waterford. This time his plans went awry. The advance force failed to take "Passage Fort" guarding the seaward approach to the city. His transport ships, carrying the indispensable siege artillery, dared not attempt to enter the harbour. Without his cannon, and with his troops shivering in persistent downpours, Cromwell was not prepared to assault this strongly defended city. Rather than risk a costly repulse, Cromwell withdrew his army from Waterford, and marched in appalling weather west to Youghal. From here the troops were dispersed to winter quarters in various friendly towns, mainly in Co. Cork.

Down the east coast of Ireland, between Dublin and Wexford lies the small port of Arklow. It had surrendered to Cromwell, without resistance, in September:

> "Three months later, the town was besieged by the O'Tooles and O'Byrnes (fierce Irish clans from the Wicklow mountains rising behind Arklow). Hewson set out from Dublin with 1000 horse and foot to relieve it; at his approach the besiegers retired. When he had supplied it plentifully with provisions and powder he returned to Dublin."[8]

As far as is known, this operation was carried out on Colonel Hewson's own initiative, and represented his first independent military action.

Always aware of the larger picture, Cromwell must have been concerned that he had no direct communications with his Dublin base. He had secured Munster but to do this his army had followed a circuitous route around the southeastern coastline. True, this had allowed continuous support from his fleet, whilst the sea protected one flank from surprise enemy assault, but to pursue large-scale military operations, a shorter, direct road link was required. Although Ormonde had not the resources to attack Dublin, nevertheless the City was uncomfortably hemmed in to the south and west by a network of Royalist held strong points. Furthermore the limited safe area outside the City inevitably restricted the amount of food, and fodder for the horses, that could be grown.

A weakened Royalist grip on the surrounding countryside was essential if a secure overland route to the south was to be established.

To this end, Colonel Hewson mounted a series of energetic forays out of Dublin, to capture or destroy Royalist strongholds. Whether this was on his own initiative, or under orders from Cromwell, is unknown. In December, he ordered his troops to occupy the local town of Naas, south-west of Dublin. His letter to the Parliamentary Speaker in London, written on 10 January 1650, goes on:

"I sent a party three weeks ago to …take…,the Black Ditch [probably modern day Nurney] by surprise, which by storm was unfeasible. The latter was effected upon a stormy night, a place that twenty men might easily keep against twenty thousand. I have placed twenty four of my men there under Lieutenant Moore …"

The letter continues: "… and the same party took Castlemartin a considerable place …" Though his troops had been able to capture Black Ditch by surprise, Castlemartin required an onslaught. This place, a seat of the Royalist Fitz-Eustaces, was well sited on the south bank of the River Liffey, west of Dublin. However the fortress of Ballysonan was too strong to attack, and had to be left.

The new year saw Colonel Hewson undertaking more formidable military operations. In his letter he mentions that after Black Ditch, he also took Rathred (otherwise known at Rathbride, or Rothdrid), a strongpoint beyond the Liffey, in Co. Kildare, where he left a strong garrison. This place is some three miles north-east of the town of Kildare, and was owned by a junior branch of the Fitzgeralds. In the same operation, Hewson also occupied Panser's Grange (otherwise known as Pangers Grandge, or Punch's Grange), some five miles north of Kildare. The town of Kildare itself fell to Hewson's troops, apparently without a fight. He described it as a useful garrison.

In his letter of the 10 January 1650 to Speaker Lenthall, and his follow-up letter from Dublin of 3 March, Hewson describes a less successful expedition into the Bog of Allen, in Co. Kildare. Entirely surrounded by marsh was the Island of Allen, defended by the castle of Kilmagog (Kilmore). According to the latter letter he "marched with a party of 1000 horse and foot into the Island of Allen, and summoned Kilmagog therein; but finding it not feasible to storm without guns", he seems to have retired. The chronology of these various activities is unclear but according to Paragraph 78 of the English *Official Chronicle of Irish Wars*, the Bog of Allen rebuff was on 1 January 1650.

Around the same time, Colonel Hewson's men also captured the strong point of Hertwell (Hartwell); and Cotlingstowne (Cotlandstown), which had been defended by Ormonde's troops.

Following these successes, Colonel Hewson withdrew to Dublin for reprovisioning. Furthermore he had realised the necessity of using cannon to overawe recalcitrant fortresses.

The improved weather in January encouraged Cromwell into making an early start to his 1650 military campaign in the south of Ireland. He planned to strike at the city of Kilkenny, then the capital of the Catholic and Royalist confederation. Sometime during the month, Cromwell wrote to Hewson in Dublin, ordering him " to march speedily to him with all the forces he could conveniently draw together".[9]

Cromwell's strategy was to threaten Kilkenny, Ormonde's main centre, and the largest inland town in the country, with two columns approaching from the south, while Hewson would march to cut it off from the north east. Between Hewson and Kilkenny lurked Lord Castlehaven's field force of some 3,000 to 4,000 Royalists.

Colonel Hewson spent most of February 1650, preparing his forces, and making arrangements for the governance of Dublin during his absences. On 25 February he issued a Proclamation holding the Irish living in occupied areas responsible for any attack made against the lives or property of Protestants, and stipulated financial penalties to be charged on the district's baronies in which the outrage took place. He referred to the 1647 Proclamation issued by his predecessor, Colonel Michael Jones, and declared "that such was the neglect and contempt of the former Proclamation by the protected Irish that there were daily murders, robberies, and other most cruel outrages committed by the Tories (Irish outlaws) and rebels coming into the English quarters without control or pursuit of the Papist inhabitants..." of the areas through which they had passed. For a Cromwellian Lieutenant Colonel, Major or Captain murdered, the fine on a barony was £100, for other persons £20.[10] Instructions to put these sanctions into force were issued by the Commissioners of Revenue, and Commissioners for the Administration of Justice. These punishment levies on the unfortunate Irish received the scathing description of "Prey Monies".

The garrison of Ballysonan (today called Ballyshannon), a Royalist held stronghold, some 5 miles south-south-east of Kildare, sought to

surrender it to Parliament – but on its own terms. Apparently emboldened by Hewson's inability to take it at the end of December, its commander, Captain Donnogh O'Kelly, wrote in early February to Hewson
in Dublin setting out his propositions for surrender. These included
employment of the garrison as a separate regiment in Parliament's
army with religious freedom (and its own priests), promotion for the
officers, and settlement of arrears of pay. Unsurprisingly, Colonel
Hewson dismissed this out of hand.

Colonel Hewson's response was to lead a force of some 2,000 foot
and 1,000 horse against Ballysonan. On Tuesday, 26 February, 1650,
he marched out of Dublin. This time he brought cannon; a powerful artillery train of one culverin, one demi-culverin, and one mortar
piece. He made rapid progress, and the next day reached the town of
Naas. Two days after leaving Dublin, Hewson's column approached
the fortress of Ballysonan. In his December operation Hewson had
been unable to surprise it, or lacking artillery, to storm it. Now he
intended to punish the garrison's presumption.

The action is best described in Hewson's letter of 3 March 1650 to
Lenthall, the Speaker of the House of Commons:

> "… and about four a clock with the Van of the party, I came to
> Bellisonan a strong Garrison, double works, and double moted,
> full of water one within another, and a mount with a fort upon
> it, most of the officers with me esteeming the taking of it to be
> unfeazable, it being late, and I unwilling to lose time, did sent in
> a summons …"

This was refused. Hewson brought up his guns, placing them in position
to pound the fortress on the mound. Conscious of the threat of attack by
Castlehaven's cavalry, the battery had defensive protection to its rear.[11] By
the next day the cannon had inflicted significant damage. He addressed
a last summons to the Royalist garrison commander, "Sir , Blood I doe
not thirst after yet so far a souldier, as not to neglect present opportunity…", offered to discuss a negotiated surrender. He undertook to send a
Captain Hewson into the fortress as security for the safety of one or two

HEWSON'S OPERATIONS
DECEMBER 1649 - JANUARY 1650

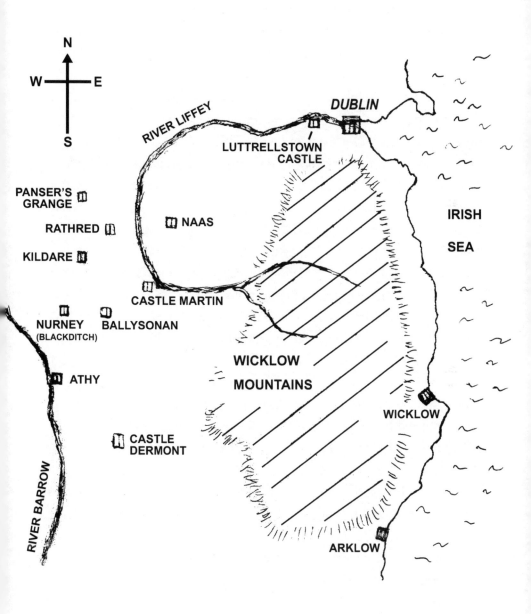

SCALE: 6 MILES TO 1 INCH

defenders authorised to agree terms. This Captain Hewson may well have been a son of Colonel Hewson. Honourable terms were agreed, allowing the defenders to march out "with their colours flying, and drums beating".

Hewson continued his policy of taking fortifications from the enemy. This process was clearing the road to Carlow, and then south to Kilkenny. He also hoped to tempt Castlehaven into battle, since the Royalist army represented a threat to Parliamentary supply lines. Hewson took Lea Castle, but decided to dismantle it. Similarly he took the fortress of Dunamaise, and blew it up. He also took the castles at Kilkea (whose Governor Talbot surrendered cravenly), Maryborough (now known as Port Laoise), and Athy. This latter had been abandoned by the Royalists, who had partly demolished its defences and broken down the bridge. However, because of its military value, guarding a crossing of the river Barrow, Hewson decided to retain it. Leaving a strong garrison, with considerable quantities of ammunition, he moved against the town of Castledermot (Castle Dormount), taking Harristown on the way. Castledermot was a small walled town some seven miles from Athy, and was notorious as being the chief residence of the aggressive Irish clan, the O'Tooles (with whom Hewson had earlier clashed at Arklow). The commander of the Royalist forces in Leinster, Lord Castlehaven, was unable to defend the town and had abandoned it, but only after pulling down its walls, and burning a great part of the castle. Some of the residents had taken refuge in a strong tower, but the frustrated Hewson caused a great quantity of straw and other combustible materials to be piled against the door and set on fire. Those inside quickly surrendered.

By now Hewson's force was exhausted by this vigorous campaign, and reduced in numbers by the various garrisons left behind. Accordingly he ordered a return to Dublin.

Meanwhile Cromwell, far to the south, had not attempted a direct assault on Kilkenny. This, the second city of Ireland, was the capital of the Confederation, the disparate alliance of Catholic Irish and Royalists (both Catholic and Protestant), opposing him. He was aware that the plague had broken out in the city, and perhaps he preferred to

let it ravage the garrison. As it was, he contented himself by capturing a string of nearby towns, Fethard, Cashel, and Callan. He wrote to
Colonel Hewson in Dublin, requiring him to bring his troops towards
Kilkenny. As Cromwell explained in a letter to Speaker Lenthall, that
having heard of Hewson's successes "we thought fit to express to
him, to march up to us for a conjunction: And because we doubted
the sufficiency of his party to march with that security which were to
be wished, Colonel Shilbourn was ordered to go with some troops of
horse out of the County of Wexford (which was his station) to meet
him".[12] In fact Colonel Shilbourn prudently decided to join Hewson in
Dublin, rather than attempt to cut across hostile territory.

In Dublin, Colonel Hewson had administrative concerns as well as
resting and strengthening his force. Parliament exercised control from
London:

> "Influenced by the representations made by John Owen in his
> famous sermon with respect to the lamentable state of reli-
> gion in Dublin, and the great need for preachers, the English
> Parliament further advised in March 1650 that Colonel Hewson,
> the Governor, should fit out and set apart certain of the churches
> in that city as public meeting places for such ministers as they
> should appoint to "dispense the gospel" there."[13]

Colonel Hewson acted with his usual energy. According to James Scott
Wheeler, he was ready to march out of Dublin within three days of his return.

We now have an eyewitness account of events. Dr Theo Jones, then
Scoutmaster-General to the Army (and brother of General Michael
Jones, the victor at Rathmines), kept a diary covering the period from
13 March to July 1650. He records that on Wednesday 13 March,
Hewson's army set out from Dublin. He had a strong force of infantry,
including his own experienced regiment of foot, and a train of artillery.
Fourteen days' supplies of food were carried in knapsacks and commissary wagons.[14] Escort was provided by his own cavalry, strengthened by Colonel Shilbourn's troops of horse.

The army remustered at Naas, then approached the town and castle of

Carlow. The castle was held by some 200 of the enemy, but after a brief cannonade, sought terms for surrender. The way south was now open.

Hewson received direct orders from Cromwell's son-in-law, Henry Ireton, who had been appointed Cromwell's deputy following the death of Lieutenant General Michael Jones.

Messengers carrying dispatches between Colonel Hewson in Dublin and Cromwell at Army Headquarters in the south of the country, had to make their way through areas often scoured by Castlehaven's raiders and ran considerable risk of interception:

> "An Irishman, having been taken by Lord Castlehaven's guards at this time, desired to speak privately with his Lordship: and when he was brought in, he produced a yellow piece of wax, pretty round, which he was to swallow if he should be seized: within the ball there was an note to Cromwell from Colonel Hewson, to inform him that his forces were on the march to him from Dublin, but as Lord Castlehaven lay in his way desired orders what he should do. His Lordship copied the note; and the fellow having assured him of his return with Cromwell's answer, the note was rolled up as before, and the messenger sent away: within two or three days he returned with another such ball of wax inclosing Cromwell orders to Hewson, which Castlehaven kept: the Colonel however held on his march and passed the Barrow, eight or ten miles below his Lordship."[15]

Despite the loss of this particular message, Hewson did receive further orders to move south, following the eastern bank of the river Barrow and either secure a permanent river crossing, or bring Castlehaven to battle. Lord Castlehaven's mobile force still amounted to some 3,000 horse and foot, and though obviously this was not enough to take on Cromwell, it did amount to a continuing threat to the lines of communication between Cromwell and his main base in Dublin. In a letter dated 4 April 1650, published in *The Perfect Diurnal*, Hewson explained that he was unable to attack Castlehaven as he would not stand and fight, and he therefore decided to take the sturdy bridge at Leighlinbridge.

According to Cromwell's letter of 2 April 1650 to speaker Lenthall, Parliament's forces now controlled much of the west bank of the Barrow. Cromwell wrote:

> "In the end we had advertisement that Colonel Hewson was come to Loughlin (Leighlinbridge), where there was a very strong castle and pass over the Barrow: I sent him word that he should attempt it, which he did, and after some dispute reduced it: By which means we have a good pass over the Barrow, and entercourse between Munster and Leinster."

Cromwell was right to be pleased – the bridge was important because at that time it was the only bridge over the lower reaches of the river. And there was little "dispute" in taking it, as well as the protecting castle. Hewson obtained the surrender of the castle and garrison without losing a man. The document of surrender, dated 19 March, permitted the defenders to march out "with their arms, muskets laden, bandoleers filled, drums beating, and matches lighted, and with bag and baggage which is to them belonging, which they can carry away on their backs". Even so, they left behind a useful 800 bushels of corn, and some 200 weapons.[16]

By granting such generous terms to the trapped and helpless garrison, Hewson showed why he was regarded as an excellent soldier. Not only was he careful to avoid casualties to his own men (which raised their confidence in him), but he had secured this strong castle undamaged. Most importantly, he had not wasted time on a siege operation, understanding Cromwell's impatience for reinforcement. Indeed the speed of Hewson's advance was remarkable.

Cromwell's letter: "… I sent Colonel Hewson word, that he should march up to me, and we advancing likewise with our party met near by Goran (a populous town) where the enemy had a very strong castle, under the command of Colonel Hammond, a Kentishman, who was a principal actor in the Kentish insurrection …" (This referred to the Second Civil War two years earlier.)

HEWSON'S MARCH FROM DUBLIN TO GOWRAN IN MARCH 1650 TO JOIN CROMWELL

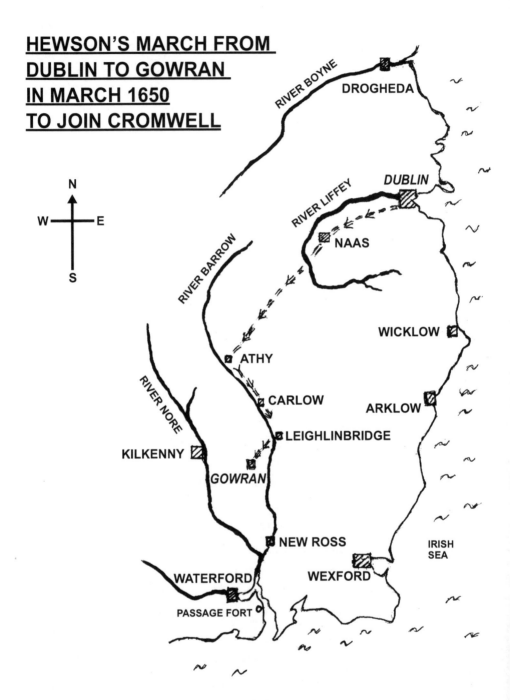

SCALE: 14 MILES TO 1 INCH

As ordered, Colonel Hewson's force immediately crossed to the west side of the Barrow, using the newly captured bridge, joined up with Parliamentary troops under Colonel Sankey, and surrounded the town and castle of Gowran (Goran). Professor Peter Gaunt describes the action:

> "The plague-ridden town of Gowran fell to Hewson's Parliamentarians without serious resistance ... The Royalists, however, retained control of the medieval castle, which stood outside the town walls and were still holding out when Cromwell arrived here on 19 March. The siege was stepped up and heavy cannon were placed before the castle on the 21st, the Royalist garrison lost heart and surrendered. The soldiers, members of Ormonde's own regiment, were allowed to march away, but their officers were shot and the castle burnt."[17]

Amongst the officers shot was the garrison commander, Colonel Hammond – perhaps because he had for a second time taken up arms against Parliament.

The stage was now set for Cromwell to move against Kilkenny.

By taking the towns surrounding the city he had effectively cut it off from assistance from the now disorganised Royalists. Their leader Ormonde was in the Limerick area, desperately seeking support from the Catholic Irish, while Lord Castlehaven's field force had no intention of confronting the combined strength of Cromwell and Hewson. Castlehaven's army was depleted by detachments he sent to the important town of Clonmel, and 1,200 men put in to augment Kilkenny's garrison. It should not be thought that Castlehaven lacked offensive spirit. While Hewson had been advancing down the east side of the River Barrow, Castlehaven on the west bank could operate with impunity. His force struck north, "surprising Athy and taking Hewson's garrison of 700 men, but he found the place untenable. 'Not knowing' ... he wrote ... 'what to do with my prisoners, I made a present of them to Cromwell, desiring him by letter to do the like for me'..."[18] This was one of the very few successes the Royalists managed against

Cromwell in the whole campaign.

On 22 March Cromwell's army marched to the outskirts of Kilkenny. Its governor, Sir Walter Butler, was in an unenviable position. Already short of supplies the fearful scourge of the plague had left less than 400 men alive out of his garrison of over 1,500 soldiers. However he bravely refused Cromwell's summons, though realising that he could expect no aid from Ormonde or Lord Castlehaven.

Kilkenny city stands on the western bank of the river Nore, which provides protection on one side. The main part is High Town, guarded on the landward side by strong walls. Towering over High Town is Kilkenny Castle. To the north of High Town was the poorer area known as Irish Town.

Operations commenced on the following morning, 23 March, with a failed cavalry attack on Irish Town. This may have been a feint, since in a simultaneous move Cromwell's men captured St Patrick's Church just outside the southern city wall, and unhindered, established a powerful battery. His cannon opened fire on the morning of 25 March, and by noon the pounding had opened a significant breach. To resist the inevitable assault, Butler ordered stout defences to be prepared behind the crumbling city wall, and placed his best troops in readiness.

Cromwell planned his assault on the breach carefully. As a diversion, Ewer's regiment attacked Irish Town, and successfully captured it. However, Ewer's attempts to break into High Town, the important area of the City, were beaten back. For the main assault Cromwell employed Hewson's, perhaps the most experienced, and certainly the most successful, foot regiment in his army.

The storming party was led by Hewson's Lieutenant Colonel Axtell: "Colonel Hewson led on the reserve very gallantly."[19] Hewson's men charged into withering musket fire from behind the defender's hastily thrown up barricades, and could advance no further:

"Twice the storming party at the breach strove to enter; each time they were repulsed; they lost Captain Higley and thirty or forty men. Hewson was slightly wounded; he received a shot in the back which … 'penetrated his buff coat, and a little bruised the flesh' … each time the breach was immediately repaired by the garrison. A third time the assailants were ordered to advance, but they would not obey."[20]

Scout-master Jones, in his diary, graphically mentions Hewson's wounding: "Col. Hewson Governor of Dublin was bruised in the shoulder with a bullet and then beshitt himself as Capt. Glegny affirmed." The almost indecent glee with which this embarrassing incident is recorded suggests that Hewson was not universally popular with his fellow officers.

One report says that some 600 Parliamentary troops fell at the breach, but this is undoubtedly an exaggeration. Hewson claimed that the order to advance had been given before his men were ready, and blamed his heavy losses on the extensive preparations the defenders had time to make. Cromwell blamed the regiment. In his letter to Parliament he wrote: "Our men upon the signal fell on upon the breach, which indeed was not performed with usual courage nor success." This criticism by Cromwell of soldiers who had clearly done their best seems unfair, and may have been the beginning of a cooling in the relationship between the two men.

Though the defenders had lost Irish Town, they still held High Town, and the formidable castle. Cromwell was very angry at his rebuff, but wished to avoid further fighting. He encouraged the townspeople to enter into negotiations to lead to surrender. Nevertheless he kept up the pressure by taking various outposts, and establishing a further battery to the east of the city. Butler, now down to fewer than 300 men, yielded. Certainly the mayor and older men were anxious to surrender before a final and bloody storming. On 27 March, terms were finally agreed, allowing Butler and his men to march out with honour, and protecting the persons and property of the townsmen.

Cromwell maintained the army's headquarters outside the city to avoid the plague. Lieutenant Colonel Axtell was named as governor of

SIEGE OF KILKENNY - 23 to 27 MARCH 1650

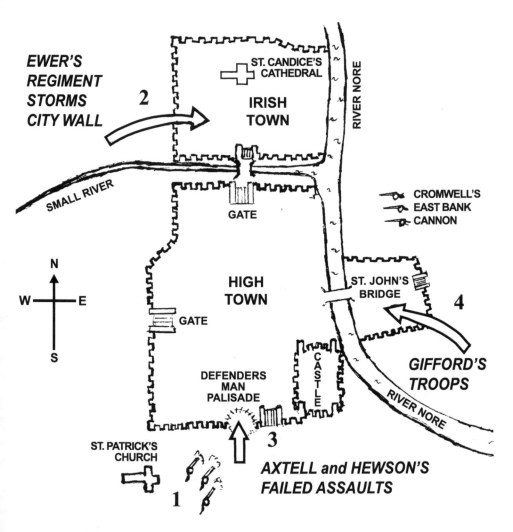

ACTIONS

1. CROMWELL'S GUNS BREACH CITY WALL.

2. EWER'S REGIMENT TAKES IRISH TOWN.

3. HEWSON'S REGIMENT TWICE THROWN BACK FROM BREACH.

4. GIFFORD FAILS TO CROSS ST JOHN'S BRIDGE.

the castle and city, which was quickly occupied. Why Hewson's efficient regiment was selected to form the garrison of this plague-infested town can only be a matter of speculation. Certainly this assignment was not popular with his radical troops, who vented their anger by profaning Kilkenny's churches, overthrowing altars, destroying crosses and showing contempt for anything sacred. St Canice's Cathedral, in the centre of Irish Town, became a particular target, with the stained glass windows shattered, and severe damage inflicted. The building was used as stabling for the troopers' horses for some considerable time. Hewson, himself, decided (or was ordered) to return to Dublin. It almost appears that Cromwell was determined to make an example of Hewson's regiment for its refusal to fight on at the breach.

Three days after Kilkenny's surrender Colonel Hewson's party quartered at Gowran on the road back to Dublin. He set off again, leaving behind the heavy culverin and mortar, perhaps because they prevented speedy progress. On the 1 April Hewson left Leighlin Bridge for Dublin, with an escort of two troops of horse. The reason for Colonel Hewson's urgency may well have been the need for specialised treatment for his left eye, which tradition avers, was injured in the Kilkenny fighting.

Back in that city, Hewson resumed his position as military governor. He organised supplies for the Parliamentary forces in the field, and on 30 April set out for Trim, almost due west of Dublin, with reinforcements of horse, foot and dragoons, as well as bringing cheese, biscuit and ammunition. On the 2 May Hewson returned to Dublin with a strong escort.

Down in Munster, Cromwell had embarked on his attempt to take Clonmel, an ancient walled town on the north bank of the river Suir, with a crossing bridge. Unlike previous towns which had largely English royalist garrisons, Clonmel was defended by a force of some 1500 hardy Ulster catholic fighting men, commanded by Black Hugh O'Neill, a veteran of continental wars. His weakness was a shortage of ammunition. Desperate pleas to the Royalist commander, Ormonde failed to produce any supplies, and by April 1650, Cromwell had drawn a noose around the town. On 27 April, Cromwell's guns were in position.

The sequence of events thereafter remains somewhat unclear. An initial assault, said to have been on 9 May, was bloodily repulsed. Continued battering by his cannon shattered part of the town's curtain wall, and Cromwell ordered an all out assault, possibly on the 17th. This was a total disaster, many hundreds of his best troops were slaughtered in a trap prepared by the ingenious O'Neill. Cromwell in person ordered his foot soldiers to make a second assault. They refused. Two regiments of horse then dismounted and gallantly advanced into the breach. Though fighting with the utmost bravery, they too were unable to enter the town, and suffered terrible losses. Cromwell accepted the inevitable and ordered retreat. He had lost some 2,000 of his finest men for nothing. His deputy, Ireton, considered the day's events as the heaviest defeat the Parliamentary army had ever experienced either in England or Ireland.

Cromwell's salvation came unexpectedly. "It is said that he had ordered the army to march away and abandon the place, when he espied something in the grass, which he took up and found to be a silver bullet. This incident suggested to him the straits to which the garrison was reduced."[21] Cromwell decided to bring up additional troops and try to starve out the defenders.

The story above is remarkably similar to the tradition found amongst a branch of the Hewsons in Ireland. It was claimed that during the siege of Kilkenny, Colonel Hewson made a practice of early morning strolls outside the city walls, seeking out weak spots that might be attacked in the day's operations. Of course he kept at a safe distance, but one morning a lucky musket shot struck him on the shoulder. At extreme range the ball failed to penetrate his tough leather buff coat. Idly Hewson picked up the ball, and recognising it as silver, realised that the defenders were virtually out of ammunition. Today it is impossible to say which is the true version of an event, which might indeed have happened.

Despite his success in inflicting grievous casualties on Cromwell's army, O'Neill recognised that it was impossible to hold out longer, so, with muffled hooves, his whole force quietly slipped out of Clonmel during the night. Meanwhile Cromwell had negotiated the town's surrender with the Mayor, and when he entered the following morning, found, to his wrath, that O'Neill and his soldiers had made their escape. With that success, the whole of southern Ireland was now cleared of effective Royalist opposition, and save only Limerick and Waterford, all the towns and cities were his.

That spring of 1650 had seen events taking an ominous turn for the Commonwealth government in London. It was unpopular at home – the execution of the King a year earlier had deeply angered many, whilst the continued high level of taxation to fund the Irish adventure was generally resented. The government further knew that the young Charles II was determined to win back his father's throne.

Though Cromwell's military success had eliminated any possibility of a Royalist invasion from Ireland, Charles' alternative strategy was alliance with the Scottish Presbyterians. This he pursued in meetings with representatives of the Kirk to establish on what terms Scottish forces would assist in a Royalist invasion of England. As early as 8 January 1650, Parliament had suggested Cromwell should return to London, though he claimed that the letter did not reach him until 22 March, just as his army was enveloping Kilkenny. Cromwell knew it was vital for him to break organised Royalist resistance in Ireland, and continued his campaign. A subsequent letter was more authoritative: "Affairs here are very urgent and we desire your presence and assistance."[22] Cromwell saw that his Deputy, Ireton, and the group of New Model veteran colonels supporting him, could complete the subjugation of Ireland. Cromwell sailed from Youghal for Bristol on 29 May 1650.

Perhaps his last known public act in Ireland was to send to Colonel Hewson in Dublin a letter requesting protection for the young Royalist, Lord Moore, Henry, Third Viscount of Drogheda, who had recently surrendered. The letter, dated 22 May, required Hewson to ensure that his soldiers offer no incivility to him "either by restraining his liberty or otherwise; it being a thing which I altogether disapprove and dislike that the soldiers should intermeddle in civil affairs farther than they are lawfully called upon".[23] The letter is signed, "Your loving friend, O. Cromwell". (It is not recorded whether Lord Moore's visit to Dublin was indeed free of incivility.)

CHAPTER 7

"Ireland - The Conquest"

Cromwell sailed from Ireland on 29 May 1650 (some sources give 26 May, others 27 May), and landed in England to a hero's welcome, and the heartfelt relief of the Commonwealth Government. The threat of invasion from Scotland was growing ever more ominous. In June the young Charles II landed in that country to claim his Scottish crown.

Meanwhile in Ireland, Henry Ireton, Cromwell's acting Lord Lieutenant and trusted son-in-law, continued Cromwell's military strategy of capturing the major towns still held by the Confederation of Irish and Royalist factions. By depriving the Confederation of a secure home territory, and thus denying it the funds that could be raised there, Ireton hoped to weaken and fragment his opponents. Unable to field an army sufficient to confront the powerful Parliamentary regiments, it was inevitable that Irish resistance would degenerate into a "hit and run" style of warfare. Repeatedly, the lightly armed Irish would strike vulnerable English supply columns and isolated garrisons, then retire to the protection of mountains and bogs before a punitive force could hunt them down. This was classic guerrilla warfare (though the term was unknown in the seventeenth century), and highly effective.

The war had taken on a changed ideological divide. Most of the English Royalists, and old Protestant landowners had surrendered to Cromwell. Now the main resistance came from the native Catholic Irish. Instead of the conflict being merely a political dispute between Parliament and Royalists, far deeper emotions were involved. The Irish had come to understand that Parliament intended to destroy the

Catholic Church once and for all, and fought the more desperately.

Colonel Hewson, back in Dublin as its Military Governor, had a key role in the Parliamentary strategy. His primary responsibility was to ensure the safety of the City. To this end he sought to extend the English controlled area westwards. His secondary responsibility was to ensure that supplies reached the forces in the field.

Scoutmaster-General Jones' diary records that Colonel Hewson left Dublin on 30 April 1650, with reinforcements for the regiments near Trim, operating under Colonel Reynolds. Trim was an important town to the south west of Dublin, defended by a substantial Norman castle still in reasonably good repair. Jones writes that on 1 May "Colonel Hewson ... brought provisions of bisquet cheese and amunition".[1] He goes on to explain that on the following day Hewson "sent for a guard to Dublin and had our foot left with him and six of our troopes". Hewson needed to commandeer an escort back to Dublin since his own regiment appears to have remained in Kilkenny under his second-in-command, Axtel.

Ireton intended to keep up the pressure on the Irish with a summer advance towards their heartland, the province of Connaught in the west of Ireland. Connaught was separated from the rest of Ireland by a natural defensive barrier, the long river Shannon, whose main crossing was at the strategic town of Athlone. The direct road running west from Dublin to Athlone was, however, barred by the Irish held fortress of Tecroghan, some seven miles from Trim. Both sides recognised the importance of Tecroghan. It was a strong position, a castle guarded by outworks, on a virtual island surrounded by water and treacherous bogs, with a numerous garrison. The efficient Colonel Reynolds first approached Tecroghan on 14 May 1650, but then made camp some miles distant to await the arrival of Colonel Moore with a considerable number of infantry, and the vital artillery train. At some stage Colonel Hewson rejoined Reynolds, and two days later the Parliamentary army laid formal siege. An Irish historian recorded, "Colonel Hewson and Colonel Reynolds, set down before Tecroghan, and, after summons, the Governor refusing to surrender, he drained away their water."[2] The

English cannon had the castle within range, but for once, it appears that they achieved little success.

While the Parliamentary army was involved in this operation, Irish irregular troops raided English held lands right up to the outskirts of Dublin, stealing cattle and burning crops. Though the Irish could not threaten the city itself, they planned to make it difficult for the Parliamentary forces to rely on local supplies. To protect his agricultural areas, Colonel Hewson ordered his own regiment back to Dublin. (When it had returned from the Kilkenny area is unknown.)

Meanwhile the Irish leaders Castlehaven and Clanricarde, had assembled a joint army of some 7,000 Connaught, Leinster, and Munster Catholics, a number far exceeding the Parliamentary strength of 1,400 foot and 1,200 horse. Even so, Castlehaven and Clanricarde were wary of engaging in a full-scale battle. Their move was to send an Irish force, manhandling supplies, to the beleaguered garrison in Tecroghan, attempting to get through the English blockade following secret paths through the woods and bogs. It was a failure. As Gilbert records, "Colonel Hewson has good successe against the Lord of Castlehaven, who attempted the relief of Tecroghan with 2000 foot through the bogs, one colonel and other officers were killed, and about a 100 foot souldiers, 300 got into the castle, all the rest were beaten back."[3]

What had happened was that the Irish on foot, weighted down with their weapons and bags of food and powder, had blundered into a waiting line of Parliamentary troops deployed in battle order. Further, the Parliamentary officers had chosen a position on firm ground, where their horse was able to operate to good effect. As Gilbert tells us, some few hundred Irish got through, the remainder were scattered. Clanricarde came to the conclusion that any further relief attempt was fruitless. He withdrew his own force to Connaught, and lacking funds to pay his men, largely disbanded. Alone, Castlehaven could do nothing, and returned with his soldiers to Munster. Though full of spirit, the abandoned garrison of Tecroghan accepted the inevitable, and surrendered on 25 June to honourable terms. The road to Athlone was now open.

The damage caused to the Irish cause was deeper than the loss of a strategic strong point. Clanricarde and Castlehaven could no longer work together, whilst mistrust developed between the Connaught Irish, and the Irish from the south. Events were playing into Ireton's hands.

In the south, Ireton himself had been successful. The major port of Waterford, which had stubbornly defied Cromwell the previous autumn, finally surrendered on 6 August.

Ireton's next move was against Athlone, but he took a circuitous route, marching his troops due north, parallel to the Wicklow Mountains. Perhaps he was stung by the Tories' raids up to the walls of Dublin, for he sent contingents to harry those Irish living in the mountains. Athlone did not surrender as he had been led to expect, so the disappointed Ireton decided to attack Limerick, his army encamping outside the city on 6 October, 1650. However conscious of the approach of winter, Ireton withdrew on 19 October, and dispersed his now exhausted soldiers to winter quarters in friendly towns.

It is worth noting that throughout 1650 the plague had been a factor in military operations – one remembers its crippling effect on the Irish defenders of Kilkenny. Equally badly affected were the Parliamentary troops. James Scott Wheeler writes, "In Dublin, a major garrison, as many as 1,300 people died per week as a result of the plague during the Summer of 1650. The disease killed the lieutenant-colonel, major, and many soldiers in Colonel Hewson's Dublin garrison in August and September 1650 alone, badly weakening the defences of that city."[4]

The activities of the Wicklow Tories remained a source of irritation to Hewson. Though ill disciplined and poorly armed, the Tories nevertheless represented a serious threat, for their numbers sometimes reached the thousands. Repeatedly, they raided the outskirts of Dublin, causing great alarm in the city. Hewson reacted by ordering the expulsion of all Catholics from Dublin, on the grounds that they might be providing information and assistance to the Tories.[5]

Colonel Hewson was provoked into making a successful punitive strike. An Irish historian writes, "Colonel Hewson's defeat of the Confederate horse in January 1651, and his reference to '200 Tories killed and taken' can be attributed to the parliamentary equation of Confederate cavalry and Tories."[6] If the Tories were destroying crops in English held areas, Hewson intended to repay the Irish. A letter to Speaker Lenthall from the Parliamentary Commissioners of Ireland, written in February, describes the operation. "The like attempt Colonel Hewson, Colonel Pretty and other parties have begun to make at Glanmellur the great fastness in Wickloe, and have there destroyed their corn and houses and all the provisions of the enemy they could meet with."[7]

Hewson's own regiment had returned to Dublin sometime in the spring of 1650, its lieutenant colonel, Axtel, remaining in Kilkenny as Military Governor. He was given another regiment, and took part in that year's campaign under Ireton. Who replaced Axtel as lieutenant colonel in Hewson's regiment is unclear, but his tenure was short, perishing, as previously noted, from the plague. William Arnop was appointed the regiment's major, i.e. third in command.

In the spring of 1651 the new Irish overall leader Clanricarde (who had replaced the Royalist Ormonde in August, 1650), formed a striking force of Ulster Catholics. It quickly occupied the counties of Westmeath, Longford and Cavan, to the northwest of Dublin. Colonels Hewson and Reynolds were ordered to repel the Irish advance.

This required a major military effort. The two colonels led separate columns. Reynolds advanced north into Westmeath, storming the castle of Dunore and seizing valuable food stocks. Meanwhile Hewson moved west from his advanced base at the stronghold of Trecroghan on 14 March, 1651, and joined forces with Reynolds near the castle of Ballymore. Whilst Reynolds was engaged in repairing and garrisoning in the castle, Hewson drove the Irish out of Ballinalack: "a considerable pass (over the Inny river) out of Westmeath into Longford".[8]

The next move was a combined operation. Hewson explained, "… the Commissary-General (Reynolds) and I agreed to march to Finea, where we heard was a great store of forces to entertain us". This castle, now know as Finagh, lies between Loughs Kinale and Sheelin, and was stoutly defended. The castle's defenders were supported by a strong contingent of Irish, under the command of one Phil O'Reilly, stationed in the nearby village of Togher. While Renolds skirmished with a separate force of Irish,

> "... Hewson advanced ... [and]... surprised O'Reilly one morning after his troops had engaged in a heavy drinking session the previous evening. O'Reilly was lucky to escape but over forty officers and 400 rank and file were captured; they were sent under strong guard to Dublin to await shipment as slaves to the sugar plantations in the West Indies."[9]

Next Hewson attacked a nearby castle. He set up cannon, but at the third shot the defenders panicked and fled. This availed them little, for Hewson's cavalry was then able to catch them in the open, and cut them down. Few escaped.

Finally Hewson advanced on Finagh castle itself. His initial assault was repelled, though with the loss of only two men. Reynolds force was also in the area. The garrison recognised its hopeless situation, and offered to surrender. The Irish were permitted to march away under safe conduct, though without their arms. There was now no organised Irish force in the counties of Longford and Cavan.

Following Cromwell's urgent departure from Ireland in the summer of 1650, the English Council of State had appointed two Commissioners charged with putting in place an effective civil administration, and re-establishing the virtually moribund English judicial system. These were Edmund Ludlow and Colonel John Jones. Two further Commissioners were deemed necessary, Miles Corbet and John Weaver. All four were then committed supporters of Cromwell. However they did not arrive in Ireland until January 1651. As the acting Lord Deputy, Henry Ireton, was in the field conducting the Parliamentary military campaign, it was inevitable much of the day to day administration of the country would fall to Colonel Hewson, as Governor of Dublin, the historic seat of English power. Backed by his own regiment he exercised considerable authority, even after the arrival of Parliamentary Commissioners.

To reflect his elevated status, and to provide a home for his family, who had joined him from England, Colonel Hewson had taken possession of Luttrellstown Castle, regarded as the second finest house in Ireland. Built by the Luttrells, one of the important families in the Pale in medieval times, the castle and township were situated in lovely countryside on the banks of the river Liffey, just an hour on horseback from Hewson's administrative centre in Dublin Castle.

Perhaps not without some sympathy for the displaced owner, Thomas Luttrell, Hewson kept him on as his head gardener. Hewson's occupation was regarded as a flagrant exercise of personal power. It particularly incensed the Adventurers, that body of English investors who in the early 1640s had advanced considerable sums to the Government towards the cost of the Irish wars, in return for the promise of a share in confiscated Irish lands. They saw Hewson's action as undermining the whole principle of this scheme.

Interestingly, good relations appear to have developed between the Hewson family, and the Luttrells. From a record of proceedings in Dublin:

> "Att a Court Martiall held at the Castell 19 Martii 1651, James Lutrill, Informant, Evan, Jones, Defendant, soldier under Captain Hewlett [of Hewson's regiment]:- 'This day the defendant being convicted for stealing the iron and sockett of a pump worth 5s of the Informant's goods, ordered that he shall ride the wooden horse at the Main-Garde, with two musketts att each heele, with the iron and sockett att his necke and an inscription on his breaste for one hower'."[10]

The "Main-Guarde" of the city was a strong post situated on the southern side of St Werburgh's Church, in Werburgh Street.

In May 1651, Henry Ireton called a council of senior officers to plan his military campaign to overrun Ireland west of the Shannon, and crush the Irish. It is not known whether Colonel Hewson was present, but he was allotted the task of moving his troops from Dublin to threaten Athlone from the river's east bank. Ireton's plan was to hem in that town from all sides – Sir Charles Coote with a strong force was to strike south from Ulster and approach from the west, whilst a mounted column under Colonel Reynolds crossed the river downstream, and then was to move north to join Coote.

On 9 June, 1651, at the direction of the new Parliamentary Commission in Ireland, Colonel Hewson wrote to the Speaker Lenthall, detailing recent military operations against the Irish holding out in Athlone and the west. His letter is somewhat rambling, and unfortunately lacking in dates. He describes receiving reports of the confusion amongst the Irish leaders, and their increasing despair at the successes of General Ireton and Sir Charles Coote, indeed on Father John, chaplain to the wounded Irish defender of Athlone, Lord Dillon, being "… Full of grief, the priest took to his beads".

On the 19 June Hewson wrote to the Irish Parliamentary Commissioners in Dublin reporting success: "I came this morning to Athlone, which is agreed to be delivered to your service." Lord Dillon surrendered to Coote, possibly on the 22nd, yielding valuable military provisions. These facilitated the Parliamentary operations deep into Connaught, whilst the capture of the Athlone bridge opened a direct supply route to Dublin. Hewson's letter continued, "I shall return with all possible speed to secure those parts about Dublin."[11] Clearly the harassing tactics of the Tories remained a problem.

Despite losses in battle, and still more from disease, a constant flow of reinforcements from England, as well as local recruitment of Protestants, had more than doubled Parliament's forces since Cromwell's landing in 1649. The costs of this army became an increasing burden on the English exchequer, so one of the first activities of the newly arrived Parliamentary Commissioners was to establish an effective tax raising system in Ireland. Early in 1651 the Commissioners divided the areas firmly under control into six "precincts", appointing Sub-Commissioners to work jointly with the local military commanders in collecting the excise, customs duty and property taxes. Hewson had control of the Dublin assessments, Axtel for the Kilkenny area, and

Hewson's son-in-law, Richard Lawrence, for Waterford. That spring an unusual task fell to Colonel Hewson: "Colonel Cooke was directed to provide fit preachers for Enniscorthy (at £30), and for Wexford (at £100); in May Colonel John Hewson was to appoint one for Naas ..."[12]

The Tanner collection of Irish documents, now held in the Bodleian Library, Oxford, contains an interesting letter dated 12 June, 1651, from Edmund Ludlow in Loughrea, Co. Galway, to the other Parliamentary Commissioners in Dublin. It informs them: "... my Lord Deputy (Ireton) who had ordered me to leave Com. Gen (Reynolds) his troope and Major Owens with my Lo: President and had commanded mee to write to yourselves and Col. Hewson to see them satisfied out of his treasury the last fortnight's pay, which is behind unto them."[13] This suggests that Hewson had retained personal control of the Dublin revenues.

It is unlikely that Hewson was able to respond to this request immediately, since before his return to Dublin, he went out of his way to garrison Raghereth (Raghra).

Once back in Dublin Colonel Hewson decided to punish the Irish irregulars hiding in the Wicklow Mountains who continued to harass the areas around the city. A letter dated the 1 July, 1651, to Parliament from its Commissioners in Ireland reported: "Last Monday, Colonel Hewson with a considerable body from hence marched into Wicklow. He doth now intend to make use of the scythes and sickles that were sent over in 1649, with which they intend to cut down the corn growing in those parts which the enemy is to live upon in winter time, and thereby, for want of bread and cattle the Tories may be left destitute of provisions, and so forced to submit and quit these places."[14]

As already mentioned, in the previous autumn, Hewson had ordered the expulsion of all Catholics from Dublin. This took time, but by the summer of 1651, most had gone. Hewson wrote to a London friend on the 19 June as follows:

"Mr Winter, a godly man, came with the Commissioners, and they (the remaining Catholics) flock to hear him with great desire; besides there is in Dublin, since January last, about 750 Papists forsaken their priests and the masse, and attends the public ordinance, I having appointed Mr Chambers, a minister, to instruct them at his own house once a week. They all repaire to him with much affection and desireth satisfaction. And though Dublin hath formerly swarmed with Papists, I know none (now) there but one, who is a Chirurgeon, and a peaceable man. It is much hoped the glad tidings of salvation will be acceptable in Ireland, and that this savage people may see the salvation of God; which that the Lord may accomplish shall be the desire of,

Your loving friend

John Hewson"[15]

The Mr Winter mentioned was Samuel Winter, a devoted and zealous minister, and appointed Provost of Trinity College, following the death from plague of the incumbent, Bishop Martin, in 1650. Winter's appointment was confirmed on 3 June, 1653, the formal document being signed by Oliver Cromwell.

The four Parliamentary Commissioners in Ireland wrote to Speaker Lenthall on the 25 June 1651 reporting the present military situation, and furnishing details of the surrender of Athlone. There is a note of complaint about Hewson's inadequate dispatches, "and though Colonel Hewson was there upon the place on this side of the Shannon, yet he cannot give us any particular account thereof".[16]

Military operations continued throughout July. Following Hewson's sweep through the Wicklow Mountains, he turned his attention to Irish held areas to the southwest of Dublin. In a letter written on the 1 August the Commissioners informed the English Council of State: "Col. Hewson hath done his work in Wicklow by destroying all the green corn there, and was a while in Queen's County upon the like business ..."

Demands were now being made on Hewson. He had earlier sent 300 foot to Sir Charles Coote in Connaught but the Lord Deputy

(Ireton) ordered that Colonel Hewson furnish him with 500 further foot. The Commissioners then wrote on the 2 August to the Council of State to express their view that "he is unable to comply and also conduct the Cavan operation, unless he is strengthened by the recruits newly arrived from England".[17] (The Cavan operation was a plan under which Hewson's and Venables' forces would join to occupy Co. Cavan.) According to the "Diary of Parliamentary Forces" for 3 August, "Collonel Hewson was ordered to draw downe with his forces towards Athlone and further into Connaught as occasion should be for assisting the Connaught army." It appears that Colonel Hewson decided to follow these orders rather than join Venables as required by the Commissioners. The "Diary of Parliamentary Forces" dated Wednesday 10 Aug records:

> "Clanricarde's party ... was about Ballilege ... Connaught side of the Shannon that ... the Commissary Generall and Coll. Hewson ... appointed to attend them marching towards them, Clanricarde's whole party dispersed not withstanding great advantages of places almost inaccessible ..."[18]

Hewson contemptuously remarked, "I found them unwilling to fight though their numbers be great."[19]

Following a resurgence in Irish military activity – they had successes near Dublin, and in Ulster (where they destroyed a supply of bread destined for Sir Charles Coote's regiments) – the Parliamentary Commissioners in Dublin appear to have become deeply alarmed. They wrote directly to Hewson on 3 September 1651, setting out the danger to Dublin and the garrisons in Leinster, posed by Irish incursions. They described an action near Baggotsrath in which a detached troop of Hewson's horse, commanded by Captain Howlett (or Hewlet), was worsted by Tories led by the notorious Scurlock from his hideout in the Wicklow Mountains. The Commissioners expressed fears that if Colonel Hewson pursued his operations in Connaught the enemy might seize Drogheda, Ross, or even Dublin, and requested the return of some horse and foot for their defence. Indeed the letter virtually recalls Hewson:

"… upon consideration of your weakness of body to attend field service as formerly, and indeed of the great want we have of you, both for counsel and action here, we are of the opinion it were very fitting you did come to this place, where there is now great want of you to these ends, and to that purpose have written to my Lord Deputy and do hearby signify the same to you."[20]

On the same day the Commissioners had written to the Lord Deputy (Ireton) setting out their fears. They suggested that Colonel Hewson be ordered back to Dublin, adding, "We understand that Col. Hewson is very infirm in health and unable to bear these marches which will be requisite in prosecuting the service in the field, and his presence and advice here would be very useful, which we humbly offer to your Lordship's consideration".[21] Clearly the nervous Commissioners felt that they would be a lot safer if Hewson was back commanding Dublin Castle. And possibly his state of health was not quite as incapacitating as implied!

Meanwhile, in England, on 3 September, 1651, Cromwell crushed, at the Battle of Worcester, the young Charles Stuart's invading Scottish army, finally ending any serious military threat from the Royalist cause.

Certainly Colonel Hewson was in no hurry to abandon active service. On 8 September, the Commissioners wrote again to Hewson, seeking his response. They claimed that, as all the Parliamentary forces in Ulster were absorbed into Colonel Venables' column, that Province was no longer vulnerable to Irish incursions.[22]

What happened is that a concerted effort was being made to hold off Clanricarde, the leader of the last significant Irish force. This is explained in a letter sent by the disappointed Commissioners on the 18 September to the Council of State in London, "Commissary-General Reynolds, Col. Hewson, Sir Theophilus Jones and Col. Venables have orders to conjoin and make a body about Athlone, to watch and follow Clanricarde and that body he was gathering to him about Jamestown (Co. Leitrim) out of Ulster and Leinster, to disturb the siege of Limerick or Galway…"[23] In the event, the siege of Limerick continued without intervention from Clanricarde, finally falling to the Parliamentary army on 28 October.

By this time Colonel Hewson was confident that the English occupation was secure. A record kept by the Commissioner John Jones of letters sent by post from Dublin included one dated the 9 October, 1651, to Thomas Scott in London, requesting him to move Parliament "for Colonel Hewson, that some Irish lands might be settled on him".[24] Whether Hewson had visions of retirement from the army, and settling down in a pacified (and Protestant) Ireland, or whether he planned to pre-empt his opponents, the Adventurers, in the anticipated redistribution of confiscated Irish land, can only be speculation.

With the Catholics driven out of Dublin (or underground), the City's churches were taken over by the various English Protestant sects. By 1651 the Independents had organised at least two separate congregations. The first, with John Rogers as preacher, was established in the medieval Christ Church Cathedral. Prominent members included Colonel Hewson, and other senior army officers. The second, using St Nicholas's Church, had Samuel Winter as pastor. He had come to Dublin early that year as Chaplain to the Parliamentary Commissioners, and as previously mentioned, Hewson had directed him to induct those Catholics prepared to convert to Protestantism as a means of remaining in Dublin. T. C. Barnard has identified Samuel Winters' congregation as mainly:

> "… civilians, and included the Cromwellian aldermen of Dublin. These differences (between the membership of the two groups) were not important in 1651. They became so in 1653 when Rogers, confronted with an offensive by the Baptists, returned to England. Many of his former congregation, including the important officers, embraced Baptism and became bitter opponents of the Independents led by Winter, who increasingly sided with civilian rule."[25]

The menace to the security of the Dublin area posed by the Wicklow Tories continued. These were led by the Lord of Westmeath and Sir Walter Duggan, and amounted to a serious force, according to the Commissioner's letter of the 28 October, 1651, to the Council of State, to total "between two or three thousand horse and foot".[26] During that month a joint operation against them was conducted by Colonels Hewson, Cooke (from Wexford to the south), and Sir Theophilus Jones, with 1,500 horse and foot, though the outcome was not recorded. However it seems that the threat was not eliminated since on the 30 October the Commissioners ordered "that Col. Hewson do raise 400 men for the public service".[27]

The Commissioners were seriously concerned about the financial difficulties facing the Dublin administration. A letter from them on the 25 November to the now mortally ill Ireton (he died the next day, and may never have seen it) details their problems and the steps taken to obtain supplies for the troops during the forthcoming winter "we have (upon advice with Col. Hewson, Sir Robert King and others) issued out orders for the furnishing of the stores at Trim, Mullingar, Carlow and Athy with 5000 barrels of corn, and all other garrisons within this precinct with three months' provision of corn …"[28] This corn was to be paid for out of the revenue assessments, and the Commissioners' concern was that the amounts remaining to be collected would be insufficient to meet the army's pay.

The capture of Limerick in October, 1651, ended organised Irish resistance in the south of the country, though bands of former soldiers and irregulars roamed the wilder parts, hindering English efforts to establish ordered rule. Henry Ireton's post as Commander-in-chief of the Army was filled by one of the Parliamentary Commissioners, Edmund Ludlow, a former Colonel. This effectively brought the Army under the control of the civil administration. In December a joint conference of the Commission and senior army officers to discuss policy was held at Kilkenny. Though some 30,000 Irish were still in arms, many of their leaders recognised the futility of further resistance and made overtures to be allowed to leave the country to take service under the Catholic Kings of France and Spain, and to bring their troops with them. A letter from the Commissioners and officers at the meeting, sent on 26 December, 1651 to the Council of State recommended that this be permitted. The signatories included Hewson, and his son-in-law, Richard Lawrence.[29] Colonel Richard Lawrence was then Military Governor of Waterford, Hewson's daughter Agnes being his second wife.

Colonel Hewson's private life was thrown into disarray early in January, 1652, with the death of his wife. According to valuable research by Professor Robert Temple, her name was Anne.[30] Whether Hewson had been able to return to Dublin before she died is unknown. As befitted the wife of the Military Governor, she was buried in Christ Church Cathedral on the 15 January, with "Heraldic Honours", the event being recorded in a "Funeral Entry" by the then Ulster King of Arms.[31] Unfortunately her grave was removed during restoration works at the Cathedral during the 1870s. During the same month the cathedral congregation, led by John Rogers, and of which Hewson was perhaps the most prominent member, received the Baptist message brought by Captain John Vernon and Adjutant – General William Allen.[32]

In early February 1652 yet another operation was mounted against the hostile Irish groups hiding out in the Wicklow mountains. This time a force led by Colonels Hewson and Pretty advanced into the fastness, and captured Glenmalure, the great fortress stronghold of the O'Byrnes, hidden in a beautiful valley to the south of Glendalough.[33] Certainly Colonel Hewson's forceful actions against the Tories were regarded as successful; the Venetian Ambassador in London reported to his masters in a letter sent on the 22 February: "It is stated that Colonel Hewson, the Governor, has chased them so effectually that they have not dared to approach for a long while".[34] However there was a dissenting opinion, "Colonel Cooke's report to the Commissioners of Parliament of March 1652 attested to the failure of Ludlow and Hewson's economic warfare and the extent to which Wicklow continued to serve as a bread basket for the torying confederates".[35]

Meanwhile, in England, the Commonwealth Government was struggling to meet the costs of its military occupations of Scotland and Ireland by sales of former Crown lands. Both individuals and organised bodies acquired property; it appears that regiments of the New

Model Army accounted for almost one half of the purchases. Possibly most of the land transferred to the regiments represents settlement of arrears of pay. Hewson's regiment was prominent, purchasing lands in Derbyshire, Lancashire, Suffolk, and Sussex to a total cost of £20,599. As an example, Captain Dan Henchman on behalf of the regiment, contracted on 26 February, 1652, for Derby Lot No. 5 (possibly High Peak), as shown in the Record of Sales endorsed on Parliamentary Surveys 1650-59.[36]

Colonel Hewson's formal participation in civil administration was further increased by an Order, issued on 24 March to him and others by the Commissioners of Parliament, to assist by sitting with them on Tuesday and Thursday afternoon to hear petitions.[37]

With the coming of spring in 1652 large-scale military operations recommenced; against Galway, the last remaining Irish held city, and against pockets of Irish resistance throughout the country. Success came in mid-April, when Galway surrendered.

During the latter part of April a series of meetings was held in Kilkenny between the Commissioners of Parliament in Ireland, and the senior Army Officers. They were deeply concerned about the repeated murders of the English settlers, and on 5 May a letter was sent to Lenthall, Speaker of the English Parliament, requesting guidance as to the extent of retribution to be visited on the Irish. Hewson was a signatory.[38]

A second letter was sent to Lenthall on 6 May from the Commissioners in Kilkenny, describing the process of surrenders now being made by scattered Irish forces around the country, their leaders having despaired following the fall of Galway. The Commissioners explained that the terms of surrender originally authorised to be offered by Colonel Venables to Irish contingents in Ulster, were not being offered generally. This course had been agreed unanimously by a Council of Officers. The letter went on to report that Commissary-General Reynolds, Colonel Hewson, Colonel Lawrence, Colonel Axtell, Adjutant-General Allen and others, had gone to negotiate a final treaty of surrender covering most of the remaining Irish groups.[39]

The treaty of Kilkenny was signed on 12 May, 1652, and marked the formal cessation of the war, though not of fighting, since recalcitrant bands of Irish continued to resist until well into the following year. In particular, the Irish forces in the far west, led by the Earl of Clanricarde, did not then capitulate. The principal signatory for the Irish was the Earl of Westmeath, who commanded the main Irish force in Leinster. For Parliament, the signatories were the senior officers sent by Ludlow, the Army Commander, to negotiate the surrender. However neither Colonel Hewson nor Colonel Lawrence signed the actual document. Lawrence's absence is not explained, but it is probable that whilst Hewson was at the Council of War held at Kilkenny on 9 May, when the terms required were decided, he then returned to Dublin.

Prolonged wars had brought misery to the Irish people, and devastation across the country. The economy was destroyed, disease and famine stalked the land. The Parliamentary surveyor, Sir William Petty, estimated that out of an Irish population of 1,500,000, some 600,000 disappeared.[40] As we will see in the following chapter, Irish suffering was to continue.

CHAPTER 8

"To Hell or Connaught"

Though the signing of the Treaty of Kilkenny on 12 May, 1652, may be said to mark an end to a formal state of war between the Parliamentary Government of England and the Irish Confederation, many Irish leaders, in various parts of the country, refused to lay down their arms. Defeated, nevertheless they determined to resist foreign invaders who made no secret of their intention to take away their freedom, their religion, and indeed their very soil.

And so military operations continued with, if anything, increased bitterness. In a letter sent from Cork on 5 June, the Commissioners Miles Corbett and John Jones, writing to Speaker Lenthall, referred to a gathering of the revived Irish forces at the castle of Donegale, which they had recently recaptured. The letter describes the movements of the English troops to counter this threat, and mentions "orders sent to Colonel Hewson to draw downe that way also: so it is hoped (through the helpe of Our Lord) they shall be inabled to finde out that enemy and ingage with him".[1]

Still in Cork, the two Commissioners wrote to Colonel Axtell on 19 June, advising him that Irish troops were assembling in County Cavan. To meet them, Sir Charles Coote was being reinforced with "part of the Leinster forces, besides four troops and 800 foot lately sent from Col. Hewson". Col Axtell was charged to keep a watchful eye on the Irish leader Colonel Grace, and also to strengthen existing garrisons along the River Shannon. However he was reminded that new garrisons may be established only where necessary, and then only "with advice with

Col Hewson or Col Sankey".[2] It is clear that the Commissioners had confidence in the military judgement of Colonel Hewson.

The operations were successful, and Colonels Hewson, Sankey and Axtell drove Grace's force out of both King's County (Leix) and Queen's County (Offaly), but the Irish managed to reach safety over the Shannon. On 24 June, 1652, the Army Commander, Ludlow, wrote to Speaker Lenthall from the "camp before Rosse" reporting that the General Council meeting in Kilkenny had resolved that the main part of the Parliamentary Army should now be sent against the enemy holding out in Kerry, and in the north. Forces were left with various commanders including Colonel Hewson, sufficient to meet any threat "in their several precincts".[3]

Sometime during the days of negotiation leading up to the signing of the Treaty of Kilkenny, Colonel Hewson had returned to Dublin. Whether he was called back to counter forays by recalcitrant Irish lurking in the Wicklow Mountains is speculation. Nevertheless the security situation was such that, on 12 May (the day the Treaty was finally signed), Hewson issued a Proclamation prohibiting the transport of victuals, or their sale, to any place on the south bank of the River Liffey.[4]

Barely had the Commonwealth Government in London triumphed in Ireland, when a fresh and more serious conflict broke out. This time the opponents were England's Protestant neighbours, the Dutch. Relations between the two countries had deteriorated, largely due to commercial rivalry, and English naval harassment of Dutch shipping. Matters came to a head with a trivial incident, when the Dutch admiral, Tromp, one morning in early May 1652, refused to dip his flag passing Dover Castle. An English fleet challenged him the following day, and Tromp opened fire. A fleet action developed; war followed. As part of the English government's wartime measures, the Commissioners in Cork wrote on 26 June to Colonel Hewson, in charge of the port of Dublin, requiring him to impound all Dutch ships (and to ensure the safety of their cargoes and fittings), until further orders.[5]

The military situation in Ireland was fast improving. A pincer movement, formed by the converging Parliamentary regiments of Colonels Coote and Venables (including "some part of the Leinster forces sent from Coll. Hewson"[6]) led to the surrender of the Earl of Clanricarde and the Irish groups holding out in Connaught. In reporting this success to Speaker Lenthall, in a letter sent on 22 July 1652, the Commissioners Miles Corbett and John Jones also referred to an earlier meeting of many of the army officers, apparently including Hewson, which had taken place in Clonmel. Certainly the conclusions of the meeting had been put into writing, and sent to the Commissioners by Colonel Hewson and Adjutant-General Allen.

At some date in July, Colonel Hewson was permitted to make a visit to England, his first since the fateful invasion of Ireland almost three years earlier. No doubt he crossed to Liverpool in a mail vessel, then his status and questionable health would doubtless require the onward journey to London to be made in the comfort of a private carriage. During that year, the purged Parliament (the Rump) had given some attention to the contentious issue of religion, setting up a committee for the propagation of the Gospel. A campaign to win over the Irish people to the Protestant faith was planned. Hewson was invited to a meeting at Oliver Cromwell's lodgings, close by the cockpit in Whitehall. As related,

> "Accordingly in July of that year (1652) it was directed that John Owen, Hugh Peters, and other devout ministers should meet at the Lieutenant-General's house at the cockpit in London, and there consult with Fleetwood, Colonel Hewson, and other officers of the Army on the advisability of sending godly persons into Ireland to preach there, the state engaging to provide fitting encouragement for them therein."[7]

It was important that Charles Fleetwood should attend, since Cromwell had decided to send Fleetwood, now his son-in-law, to Ireland as the new Lord Deputy. It is probable that Cromwell intended to strengthen his personal control over that country, since Ludlow and the other Commissioners clearly took their lead from those reactionary members in Parliament with whom Cromwell was fast losing patience. Fleetwood was by religious conviction inclined towards the more advanced sects. This, from the first, set him against those conservative congregations in Dublin drawing their membership from the City's Aldermen and prosperous merchants.

The fleet, which had brought Cromwell's invading army to Ireland in 1649, carried not only men and arms, but also substantial quantities of scythes and sickles, and a goodly supply of Bibles. The reaping instruments had been used to destroy the crops of the Irish to starve them into submission, whilst the Bibles were intended to provide sustenance for their souls. As part of the new enthusiasm to convert Ireland to Protestantism, the Council of State ordered, on 3 August, "the Governor of Dublin to give warrant to the commissary of the stores in Dublin, to issue the Bibles now in the stores, to the several companies of foot and troop of horse within the said precincts of Dublin".[8] Some two weeks later, the Council on 17 August, addressed a further instruction to the Governor of Dublin, "you are desired forthwith to deliver out of the stores under your charge one hundred Bibles unto Mr Robert Clarke to be by him disposed of, for the use of the forces and others, as may be for the propagation of the Gospel within the precinct of Galway".[9] It seems that Colonel Hewson stayed on in England, for a letter sent by the Irish Parliamentary Commissioner, Colonel John Jones, on 23 August, 1652, to one Mr Morgan Lloyd, refers to his brother Harry Jones (who was acting as Governor of Dublin) being busied with affairs of the world, "having the Government of Dublin cast upon him in Col. Hewson's absence".[10]

However, Hewson was back in Dublin by December. That month saw the visit to Dublin of two representatives of the Presbyterian Church in Ulster, Archibald Ferguson and Patrick Adair. The Dublin authorities regarded the Ulster Presbyterians as disloyal to the Commonwealth Government because they supported the idea of a Monarchy coupled with the Covenant; and at their assemblies prayed for Charles II, to the disgust of the Army. This was interpreted as opposition to the Government, and the Army in Ireland, now strongly influenced by

Anabaptists and Independents, tried to restrict their activities. Feeling against the Ulster Presbyterians had intensified following the coronation of Charles II at Scone in January 1651. By September 1652, the Antrim Ministers were regarded as disaffected, and indeed suspected of seeking to influence the people against the Commonwealth. These ministers refused to sign the Engagement (an undertaking to be faithful to the Commonwealth of England, as established without King, or Lords), so two delegates were invited to Dublin to explain their position. There, they "received much civility from Fleetwood and several of the officers, especially Colonels Sankey and Hewson, while others looked askance at them". Unfortunately the meeting ended on a sour note as Adair, stung by a slur on his honesty, protested at least they would not "kill Protestant Kings".

This remark went down badly, several present having been involved in the execution of Charles I. Fleetwood dismissed the deputation a day or two later.[11]

The Puritans, and the Army leaders, had little time for Christmas (one has only to recall the disorders in 1647 following the prohibition of the traditional Christmas Day football match of the Canterbury apprentices). They saw the festival as a Papist invention, and as an excuse for ungodly excess. So it is not surprising that a letter was sent on the 23 December (perhaps by the Parliamentary Commissioners) to Colonel Hewson, as commander of the Dublin precinct, recommending that 30 December be a day of fasting, humiliation, and prayer. The writers suggested that recent setbacks, particularly renewed outbreaks of the plague, indicated God's displeasure.[12]

The opening of 1653 brought an immediate answer to prayer. The Wicklow Tories, long a scourge of English settlers around Dublin, were dealt a devastating blow by the death of the leader of the O'Byrnes. It is recorded that Colonel Hewson paid £20 to Lieutenant Jacques on 6 February, as a bounty for the head of John Byrne. This removed the last serious threat to security around Dublin, and opened the way to the next development in the English conquest of Ireland.

After arranging for the religious conversion of Ireland, the

Government in London planned to confiscate its land. From the 12,000 or so troops that had landed with Cromwell in 1649, by July 1652 the English army in Ireland had expanded to 34,128 soldiers. Their arrears of pay then exceeded £1.5 million, well beyond the revenues of Ireland. The proposed solution was to satisfy the debt by grants of land to the soldiers. The expectation was that most would take up their entitlement on completion of their military service, thus ensuring that the most valuable parts of the country would be occupied by soldier-farmers of proven loyalty to the Government. Dispossessed Catholic Irish would be forced into the wilds of Connaught, or encouraged to emigrate.[13]

Parliament decided to pursue this course, and on 12 August 1652 passed an Act for the Settlement of Ireland. By an order dated 4 January 1653, Colonel Hewson, Colonel Sankey and others were to be appointed as a committee for the encouragement of tillage, and settling of land upon those who have served Parliament.[14] To enforce the Act, a Committee for Transplanting the Irish was established, with sweeping powers enforced by the military. Colonel Hewson and his son-in-law, Colonel Lawrence, were appointed to the Committee.

As a security measure, lands around garrison areas were to be cleared of Irish and Papists. Any found there were to be shot as spies and enemies, unless they had a pass or ticket of protection. Sometimes these were granted to allow the sowing or reaping of corn. For example, on 21 March 1653, the Committee for Transplanting the Irish allowed the inhabitants of Shanganah and Loughlinstown, five miles south of Dublin, six weeks to leave, and permitted them to have two persons to watch their growing crops and dwellings; "And Colonel Hewson was to grant them tickets of protection, to secure them from being shot by the English."[15] (Identification of Irish males was easy – they sported long drooping moustaches whilst true Englishmen were clean shaven!)

At the end of April, 1653, dramatic news arrived from London. As commander of the Army and head of the Council of State, Oliver Cromwell was the most powerful man in Britain. However he had not sought this position, and indeed tried to work with the Commons, or rather those Members of Parliament who had not been excluded from sitting by Colonel Pride's purge in late 1648, to establish a workable form of government for the new Commonwealth. This body of remaining Members, the so-called Rump, had consistently frustrated Cromwell's intentions of reforming the country's laws, and limiting the authority of the established church. He saw the Rump as acting only to protect its members' personal interests, and clinging to power by doing everything possible to avoid calling a fresh election. Furthermore he knew that the Rump hated and feared the Army. The bad relations between the Rump and the Army were exacerbated by Rump's support (largely from those Member's with commercial interests) for the ongoing conflict with the Dutch, with the consequent diversion of Government's funds to build up the Navy at the expense of the Army.

In August, 1652, a group of dissatisfied army officers had brought a petition to Cromwell calling for the dissolution of the Rump, and election of a new, more representative, Parliament. During the winter of 1652–53, Cromwell faced increasingly strident calls to replace the Rump.

The crisis came in April, 1653. On the morning of the 20th Cromwell attended the Commons. To his anger he found Members pushing through an Election Bill, which would have ensured them control of a successor Parliament, thus allowing the Rump's reactionary and delaying tactics to continue. After keeping silence for a while, Cromwell stood, and spoke. To Member's horror he listed their faults, and detailed how they had failed their country. He overrode their protests, declaring "you are no Parliament, I say you are no Parliament, I will put an end to your sitting". He then ordered his companion, Major General Harrison, to bring in a body of musketeers, and clear the chamber. Speaker Lenthall defiantly refused to leave his chair. A Captain Hewson, possibly the son of Colonel John Hewson, "enforced the unwilling Speaker to leave his beloved chair and mace".[16] After the shocked members had all left, Cromwell ordered the room to be locked. He put the key in his pocket and returned to his lodgings. Thus ended the Commonwealth, which had been established just four years earlier with high hopes for a godly England.

Following his expulsion of the Rump, Cromwell acted swiftly. Within ten days he signed a declaration that a replacement Parliament of "persons of approved fidelity and honesty" would be called. Meanwhile he appointed a less political Council of State, of seven Army officers and only three civilians, to act as an interim Government.

It is worth recalling the religious position in Ireland. Despite the conversion efforts of English preachers almost all the Irish remained staunchly Catholic. The Protestant English in 1653 were divided between those faithful to the traditional form of worship, and those congregations imbued with various biblical and radical beliefs. This has been touched on in the previous chapter. A belief in the necessity of physical Baptism for salvation had been held by many in the English army that landed in 1649, and was increasingly accepted, largely amongst the senior officers. Two ministers particularly, Thomas Patient and Christopher Blackwood, were influential. The former was preaching in Kilkenny by April 1650, where he converted the military governor, Colonel Axtell. His message spread to Waterford, where the military governor of that city, Colonel Lawrence, also joined the sect. In December, 1652, the Rev. Patient moved to Dublin, being replaced in Kilkenny by Blackwood. During 1653 the practice of Baptism became widely adopted amongst the English Protestants, with congregations being set up in the main garrison towns. All across Ireland this led to bitter divisions, the fault line being basically between the army officers, and the existing Protestant settlers. The newly arrived Lord Deputy, Charles Fleetwood, deplored the increasing acrimony but took no action. He personally favoured the Anabaptist position. Indeed in Dublin the chosen preacher to him and the general officers, was Patient. The senior officers who converted to Baptism used their authority to advance their belief, and many Baptist ministers were appointed all over Ireland. Peter Row, formerly a member of Patient's Waterford congregation, was installed at Naas as a result of Colonel Hewson's personal influence.[17]

The arrival of Baptist ministers may have been the reason for the move of the Rev. Thomas Huggins. He had been appointed as an Independent minister at St Thomas's Church, Dublin, in 1651. In June 1653 he was transferred to Wicklow. "He (Thomas Huggins) was in Wicklow acting as Chaplin to Colonel Hewson's regiment, but must have left Ireland for good shortly after as nothing further is recorded of him."[18] Perhaps he felt unable to accept the now prevailing Baptist ethos in the army.

Colonel John Hewson, sometime in 1653, acquired another responsibility. In addition to being the military Governor of Dublin he was also appointed as Sheriff of the County of Dublin. Presumably in recognition of his additional workload, a new post of Deputy Military Governor was created. This was given to the faithful Henry Jones, who had stood in for Hewson during his absence in London in the previous autumn. No doubt it was his duties on the Committee for Transplanting the Irish that had escalated Hewson's workload. The legal authority for the Committee to acquire land held by Irish landowners who had not supported Parliament, and to require them to re-settle in Connaught and Clare, had derived from the Act for the Settlement of Ireland passed in London in the previous August. Implementation was not so easy. The total debt owed by Government for arrears of military pay, other liabilities, and the claims of the original Adventurers, had to be established. Next the pool of available land had to be calculated, and finally an equitable arrangement for orderly distribution of the land in settlement of the debts needed to be prepared. The initial steps taken were an Order made on 2 July 1653 for the Irish landowners affected to move to designated areas in Connaught or Clare no later than 1 May, 1654; and an instruction to a surveyor to ascertain the available acreage for distribution in each county (it being appreciated that land in different parts of Ireland varied considerably in value).

The execution of the scheme was carried out with inhumanity. Thousands of men, women and children, the old and the sick, were driven out of their homes, and forced into the barren wastelands of the far west of Ireland, to survive as best they might. The scale of suffering was enormous.

The scheme produced two long-term outcomes. Firstly, the wholesale transfer of land ownership resulted in a Protestant English political ascendancy that endured for well over two centuries. Secondly, it fuelled a deeply rooted anti-English feeling that persists in some parts of Ireland even to this day.

CHAPTER 9

"Barebone's Parliament"
(The Nominated Parliament)

Following his impulsive dismissal of the Rump, Cromwell found himself faced with the problem of how to restore the machinery of government. As mentioned in the preceding chapter, his first action was to set up a small Council of State in place of the larger unwieldy Council. He appointed those he trusted, mainly military officers, and required them to conduct the state's day-to-day business.

With the support of these officers, Cromwell decided to establish a new body to be the country's "supreme authority". Its members were selected by Cromwell and Major General Harrison (the most fanatical of religious leaders in the army), with some being nominated by congregations around the country. A requirement was that the new members be persons "fearing God and of approved fidelity and honesty". Representatives were drawn from all parts, including Scotland and Ireland.

This nominated assembly first met on 4 July 1653, and on 6 July it resolved to call itself a Parliament, meeting in the old Commons Chamber. The new Parliament was much smaller than previous parliaments with some 144 members, 133 for England, 5 for Scotland and 6 for Ireland. The Irish members included Henry Cromwell, Colonel John Hewson, Vincent Gookin and Daniel Hutchinson, then Mayor of Dublin.

One of the first actions of Parliament was to elect a formal Council of State. John Hewson was elected to the Council to speak "for Ireland, or at least for Ireland's conquerors".[1] Politically, the new Parliament soon separated into a "Moderate" party (with around 84 adherents, including Hewson), and an "Advanced" party (of some 60 preachers and religious extremists).

The conduct of the religious fanatics quickly brought the whole Parliament into public contempt – earning the nickname "Barebone's Parliament", after one of its more outrageous members, "Praise God Barbon". Cromwell, and his Whitehall military staff, took no part in the new Parliament's proceedings, quickly recognising that its internal wranglings, and loss of public respect, rendered it incapable of developing into an effective organ of Government.

Sometime during that year, 1653, Cromwell was warned by Secretary Thurloe, who masterminded Cromwell's intelligence service, that Hewson was disaffected, and suspicious of Cromwell taking the throne. It appears that Hewson and Thomas Pride (who had conducted Pride's Purge in 1648, and a staunch revolutionary), had threatened to raise forces against Cromwell should he try to make himself King. Being aware that Hewson had no family money behind him, Cromwell then saw to it that he received no official funds even though he remained Governor of Dublin. This caused considerable financial difficulty for Hewson, who had suffered serious illnesses, incurring substantial medical expenses in Ireland which he could not now meet.[2]

During its first month, the new Parliament set up a group of members, the "Committee for the Affairs of Ireland", to exercise its authority over that country. Members included Henry Cromwell, Gookin, John Hewson and Daniel Hutchinson.

Unfortunately, no record of the proceedings of this committee appears in the surviving journals of the House. However it is known that its work included preparing reports for submission to the whole house, and planning legislation.[3] It was instructed "to meet at the Chair-Chamber in Whitehall".[4]

In November 1653 Parliament became embroiled in an acrimonious debate concerning Advowsons – the right to present one's own nominee to church positions. Frequently this right was owned by laypersons, being a marketable asset. Unfortunately this permitted the appointment of parish clergy for a variety of reasons, sometimes idiosyncratic, and often having little to do with spiritual qualities. The religious faction in the House sought to abolish the long established system of tithes, which traditionally funded a professional, university trained ministry. The moderate party professed to regard these attempts as heralding an attack, not merely on established custom, but on the very concept of private property itself. In a vote taken on the 17 November, the religious extremists prevailed by 60 to 43. Colonel Hewson acted as a teller on behalf of the retentionists.[5] It is clear that by now he was out of step with a significant number of members since he had not been re-elected to the Council of State in November.[6]

Back in Dublin, detailed arrangements for the seizure of Irish owned lands were progressing. On 21 November, the "Committee of Transplantation" was formed, headed by Hewson's son-in-law, Colonel Richard Lawrence, to ensure the transfer of the unfortunate land owners to Connaught. Though Hewson was then in London, almost certainly he became an active member the following year. The allocation of the resettlement land in Connaught to the dispossessed owners was to be the task of the so-called Loughrea Commissioners, who were appointed some six weeks later, on 6 January 1654.

Ignored by Cromwell, riven by feud, and derided by the people, Barebone's Parliament was put out of its misery in December 1653. The crisis started on the 10th, with a report from its Tithes Committee, with proposals for the removal of unfit ministers and appointment of suitable replacements. This split the House, and was used as a pretext by the conservative (and military) members to claim that the Parliament was heading in a direction harmful to the Commonwealth, and that it should be brought to an early end.

The 10 December had been a Saturday, so it must have been on the Sunday that the conservative members, with their military colleagues, planned a remarkable political coup. On Monday morning, the 12th, whilst the majority of religious members was attending a church service at Blackfriars, some forty conservative members arrived early in the Chamber. Claiming that they were unable to prevent what they termed "the confusion and despoliation of the nation", and led by Speaker Rous, they marched to Whitehall to inform a surprised and headshaking Cromwell that Parliament had dissolved, and that the government of the country was now returned to him. Meanwhile the religious members trickling back from Blackfriars found a deserted Commons chamber. Their unhappiness was completed when a contingent of musketeers, led by Colonels Goffe and White, civilly desired them to quit the building. Some were reluctant to go. The officers are reported to have enquired why they were waiting. One answered that they were seeking the Lord. To which one of the Colonels retorted, "come out of this place then, for to my knowledge, the Lord hath not been here this twelve years past".[7] The Nominated or Barebones's Parliament had lasted barely six months.

Though Cromwell may well have been genuinely unaware of the plot, it appears to have been contemplated for some time.

Contemporary sources suggest that the organisers of the coup included John Desborough, John Hewson, Sydenham, Sir Gilbert Pickering (whose younger brother John had been Hewson's commander in 1644), Montague and Philip Jones. The famous historian Samuel Gardiner was convinced that the mastermind was Major General John Lambert, and that he personally ordered the decisive intervention by Colonels Goffe and White.

General satisfaction followed the resignation of Barebone's Parliament – the extreme views of the religious zealots were particularly unpopular in the largely Presbyterian City. The plotters were exultant, and are said to have celebrated at a private party held in Sydenham's rooms. Doubtless John Hewson was one of the gathering.

It was no secret that a group of army officers had earlier drawn up an outline plan of government, sharing power between an elected Head of State (entitled the Lord Protector), a powerful Council of State, and a representative legislature.

Later on the day of the coup, 12 December, a delegation of officers called on Cromwell to accept their prepared constitution, the

"Instrument of Government". After some days' consideration, Cromwell agreed. On 16 December 1653, he was formally installed as Lord Protector.

As head of state, and also commander-in-chief of strong standing military forces, Cromwell was now in a position to establish an effective government. His Council of State was small, and dominated by serving or retired army officers.

Perhaps because of the tension between Cromwell and Hewson, it is not surprising that Hewson was omitted. Legislating by way of ordinances to be confirmed later by Parliament, the new administration quickly took control of government – its avowed aim to "heal and settle" the nation. The ruinously expensive war with the Dutch was ended by a treaty concluded in April 1654, whilst funds for the work of government were provided for under the Instrument, and did not therefore require the immediate calling of a Parliament.

Following the collapse of the Nominated parliament, Colonel Hewson was in no hurry to return to Dublin. Perhaps he was avoiding his creditors there, or found the fast moving London scene more to his taste.

During its brief existence, the Barebone's Parliament had, on 26 September, 1653, passed the Adventurers' Act. This established how the lands to be confiscated from the Irish were to be apportioned between the Adventurers (who had provided funds towards the successful military conquest), and other claims against the Government, principally arrears of soldiers' pay.

Under the Act, the Government reserved the towns of Ireland, church lands, and the counties of Dublin, Kildare, Carlow and Cork, for itself, to satisfy various debts and claims (including those made by some senior Army officers). As required by the Act, division of the remaining Irish land between the Adventurers and the regiments (in lieu of pay arrears) was carried out on 24 January, 1654, by a lottery held in Grocer's Hall in the City of London. Drawing for the Adventurers was Alderman Avery. Drawing for the regiments was Colonel Hewson (appointed personally by Cromwell).[8] Assisting Hewson was Major

Anthony Morgan, who, as we will see in a later chapter, was a correspondent of Henry Cromwell.

Hewson's pressing financial position finally forced him to petition the Lord Protector on 1 March for payment of the considerable pay arrears by now owing to him. Cromwell relented, and referred the petition to a Committee, which recommended, only fourteen days later, payment of a total of £2,134.16.3 [9] On 31 March a special ordinance was approved to authorise payment.[10]

In April 1654 the General Council of Officers in Ireland met in Dublin to consider the division of lands, and the satisfaction of pay arrears (no doubt on the basis of the results of the Grocer's Hall lottery). Detailed proposals were drawn up and sent to London. "These were 'offered' to the Lord Protector by '....the Lord Broghill, Col. Hewson, Col. Venables, Col. Ingolsby, Sir Robert King, and Master Hutchinson, Commissioners from Ireland,.......' together with a letter of congratulation expressing 'approbation of the present Government'. The matter was then referred to a Committee of the Council of State". [11]

Having rectified his financial affairs, Colonel Hewson prepared to return to his post in Dublin. His activities in London had not been limited to the political arena, for it is recorded that on the 8 June, "Colonel Hewson and his Lady, and many more men of quality and their families, sailed in the 'Truelove' from Liverpool for Dublin". Later Parliament made a special grant to him for the expenses incurred by taking up his residence in that city.[12] It thus appears that Hewson had also found time to court and marry a second wife.

Hewson resumed his duties as Military Governor of Dublin without delay. He had the authority to grant dispensation from transplantation. "Although it was supposed to be death for most Irish caught inside walled towns such as Dublin, dispensations were generally given to those whose trades or qualifications were needed. On June 5 Colonel Hewson allowed certain Irish to reside in the city."[13] This date cannot be reconciled with the previous paragraph, but possibly the document was backdated for administrative reasons.

What is certain is that Colonel Hewson and his bride took up residence in Luttrellstown Castle, his previous home in Ireland.

During the summer of 1654 Cromwell and his Council of State were making plans to set up the representative legislature envisaged in the "Instrument of Government". Inter alia, this provided that Ireland and Scotland each send 30 members to a new Parliament in Westminster.

In June, Cromwell, as Lord Protector, issued a writ to the Sheriff of County Dublin (Colonel Hewson), and to other county sheriffs, giving notice that a Parliament was to be convened in September, and commanding him to cause a fit person "to serve as Knight, with his sword girt, for said county, so that the said Knight may have full and sufficient power for himself and the people of that county".[14] It is perhaps no surprise that John Hewson of Luttrellstown was successful in the elections, though it is unclear where he had stood. The Dictionary of National Biography gives Dublin, other sources Co. Dublin, and David Esson reports that he was elected for the counties of Meath and Louth.[15] Be that as it may, Colonel Hewson returned to London. He was present in the Painted Chamber, Westminster, when the First Protectorate Parliament was opened by Cromwell on 3 September 1654, the day chosen by Cromwell as being his most auspicious day.

There was evidence of a plot for a Royalist rising in Ireland during that summer of 1654. According to ideas submitted to Charles II, "In Ireland, Carrickfergus, Galway, Londonderry, and probably Dublin and Athlone, might be gained without difficulty". The leaders were named as Colonel Stephens and another, identified only as "Fa", possibly one Fanshaw.[16] How far Colonel Hewson was aware of this plot is unknown.

The upturn in Hewson's fortunes continued. Barely had he made his home in Luttrellstown Castle than the Government in London issued an Order, dated 18 July 1654, granting the estate of Luttrellstown to him in lieu of pay arrears. Contemporaries alleged that this benefit represented rather more than a mere administrative set-off. Edmund Ludlow, a bitter opponent of Cromwell, alleged that the Lord Protector "began by bribes to corrupt others to his interest; and to this end ordered that arrears of Col. Hewetson for his English service to be paid in ready money, and his Irish arrears to be satisfied out of forfeited lands in the county of Dublin, at the rate of the adventurers, in such places as he should chose".[17] In addition to the Luttrellstown estate Hewson also acquired, in the county of Dublin, valuable lands at Kilmacud, near Booterstown, south of Dublin City.

The Luttrellstown estate was indeed of considerable value, being worth £2,500 a year in 1640. It had been held by the Luttrells, a staunchly Catholic but influential pro-English family, since Medieval times. In 1647, Thomas Luttrell made over the estate to Parliament for the use of Lord Broghill. He was succeeded as a tenant of the state by Colonel Hewson on the latter's appointment as Military Governor of Dublin. As earlier mentioned, in 1649, Thomas was allowed by Hewson to live in the stables, till the estate lands, and be the castle gardener. This arrangement worked well, and Hewson valued his assistance, for it is recorded that on 30 September 1654 Luttrell was dispensed from transplantation until 1 December as "his whole livelihood and his family's depended on improving the crop of corn that then in taking off the ground". Luttrell's wife, children and stock departed for Connaught on 1 June 1655.[18] It is to be assumed that Thomas had preceded them, taking up a replacement landholding allotted by the Loughrea Commissioners.

Though Colonel Hewson returned to Westminster as one of the Irish members in the 1654 Parliament, he remained Military Governor of Dublin, and retained Luttrellstown Castle as his Dublin home. Whether his new wife joined him in London is unknown.

CHAPTER 10

"The First Protectorate Parliament"
(The 1654 Parliament)

Cromwell formally opened this Parliament on 3 September, 1654, in the Painted Chamber, Westminster. His opening address urged members to support the terms of the Instrument of Government (a written constitution devised by a group of army officers when the demise of Barebone's Parliament appeared inevitable). He asked them to help him in his duty to heal and settle the divisions in the nation. In particular he desired members to ratify the numerous Ordinances that had been promulgated by the Council of State, thus giving legality to its decisions during the previous nine months. Equally pressing was the need for Parliament to authorise the levy of taxes to meet Government expenditure.

Meanwhile the arrangements for payment of the debts due to the Adventurers, and of arrears of soldiers' pay, out of confiscated Irish lands, had run into practical problems. On the 19 September, the Irish Council of State wrote to Cromwell saying that they were perplexed as to how to carry out the orders he had given for the prior satisfaction in full of the pay arrears of (inter alia) Colonel Hewson, bearing in mind that it now appeared that the available land in Ireland was not sufficient to satisfy more than two thirds of the debts charged thereon.[1] We may only surmise the terms of Cromwell's reply, for the next move of the perplexed Council was an Order dated 10 October 1654, "that Sir C. Coote, Sir H. Waller, Commissary-General Reynolds, Cols. Hewson and Lawrence, ... concerning the managing of the surveys of the forfeited lands in Ireland, and to propose some expedient unto us how the same may be carried on with most despatch and advantage to the Commonwealth".[2] In other words, the Irish Council simply passed the problem down to the officers!

To reinvigorate the transplantation scheme, the Council, on 26 October, issued a further instruction

> "... that Sir H. Waller, Col. Hewson and others, be appointed as a committee for ... the effectual and real prosecution of the work of transplanting the Irish into Connaught and Clare, and to make provision for them there according to their respective Qualifications, and to offer such further consideration therein as upon further debate they may judge fit."[3]

These orders from the Irish Council, specifically naming Colonel Hewson, suggest that he had absented himself from Westminster (as indeed had very many other members), and returned to Ireland by early October.

In fact there was plenty for Colonel Hewson to do in Ireland. A stricter Puritan outlook was influencing the Protectorate administration, and it is interesting to record that, on 28 November 1654, Captain Samuel Playford was recommended to Thomas Hooke (the new Mayor of Dublin) to inquire into recent disorders in the city. He was instructed to investigate offences such as keeping disorderly houses, the sale of drink by alehouses "at undue times ..., swearers, drunkards, blasphemers, Sabbath-breakers, adulterers, users of false weights and measurers ..." etc., etc.[4] Furthermore the Council was pressing for speedy implementation of the land clearance scheme – an Order was made on 30 November that all "transplantable persons" must have moved by 1 March, 1655.

The problem of the land survey remained. A first exercise had proved unsatisfactory – incomplete, and riddled with inaccuracies. However an intelligent mathematician, William Petty, then offered his services; and a relieved Council, on 11 December, formally instructed him to proceed. This technical land survey, the "Down survey", commenced without delay, much of the field work being carried out by teams of soldiers doubtless carrying arms for protection against the outraged landowners.

An annual irritation to the Puritan administration in Ireland was the popular attachment to the festivities of Christmas – viewed as a Popish invention, and an excuse for ungodly excess. It is not unsurprising therefore that, on 18 December, 1654, the Council issued an order to Colonel Hewson, Mayor Thomas Hooke, and two others, to consider ways of reforming the Christmas holiday.[5] There exists no known record of the outcome of their deliberations.

The arrival of 1655 coincided with Hewson's renewed involvement in military matters. On 3 January the Irish Council made an Order requiring him, and others, to establish a special hospital in Dublin "for the relief and accommodation of sick and wounded soldiers".[6]

In London Cromwell's hopes that the new Parliament would heal and settle the nation's divisions had been sadly disappointed. Its querulous proceedings led to public questioning of the legitimacy of his administration. Support for his government waned, Leveller pamphlets again appeared in the streets, and Presbyterian pulpits raged with denunciation of his efforts to advance tolerance towards other forms of worship. Early in that month, Cromwell, on guard against a Royalist uprising in England, ordered 3.000 foot and about 500 horse to be sent over from Ireland. Twenty-six companies of foot, drawn from various regiments, including four from Hewson's own, eventually arrived in England.

The troops to be sent to England were commanded by Colonel Sadler (foot), and Major Bolton (horse). But once on the quayside, some of the private soldiers refused to embark, and defied the orders of their senior officers. Fleetwood (the Lord Deputy in Ireland), and several field officers, called a court-martial on the spot. One of the ringleaders was sentenced to death, and one entire company was cashiered.

The sentences were immediately carried out, "hanging the man upon the mast of one of the ships: at this execution Col. Hewetson [Hewson], who had been lately obliged in matter of his arrears, as a mark of his gratitude gave orders that the poor man should be hanged higher than was at first designed".[7] This comment was from a contemporary, Edmund Ludlow, who repeatedly asserted that Cromwell had bought Hewson's support by personally ordering early settlement of his arrears of military pay. The remainder of the troops took ship without further trouble, and landed at Liverpool around 21 January 1655.

The political situation in England had further deteriorated. Cromwell and his Council of State needed Parliament to recognise the Instrument of Government, and to give support to his administration. This it failed to do, and indeed by the time winter had arrived, it had yet to pass a single piece of legislation. Cromwell saw that this undignified wrangling was undermining his authority, and unsettling the country. He acted decisively. On 22 January 1655 he dismissed Parliament. Sadly, he addressed members,… "It is not for the profit of these nations, nor fit for the common and public good for you to continue here any longer".[8]

Once again, supreme power rested, reluctantly, in Cromwell's hands. He tried to rule within the spirit of the Instrument, and took advice from the Council of State. This was his medium of government, and he relied on its members. He could count on George Monk, Blake, and the unfaltering loyalty of Edward Montague, "his [Cromwell's] kinsman, Disbrowe would give little trouble, nor would men like Whalley and Goffe and Sydenham and Hewson, though they might need humouring…".[9] Interestingly, Ludlow maintained that Hewson was far from being a thorough-going supporter of the Government.[10]

As a precaution, Cromwell put the Government of Ireland on a war footing. An Order made two days after the dismissal of Parliament appointed Colonel Hewson, and others, to be Commissioners, to carry out the Articles of War. This Order required them to settle disputes, and determine appeals, relating to the Articles, and enabled them to suspend proceedings in the Courts of Ireland or otherwise.[11]

Colonel Hewson continued to be involved in Irish administrative matters. On 12 February 1655, he was a member of a committee hearing the petition of a Mary Howard, requesting state provision for her support following the death of her husband on government service in Scotland.[12]

However the continuing preoccupation of the Government in Ireland was to make headway in the removal of the owners of the forfeited Irish lands. Under Orders dated 9 March, Colonel Hewson and others were required to draw up effective plans for the clearance and transplantation of owners from the counties of Dublin, Wicklow, Wexford, Carlow and Kildare; and to advance methods of encouraging English settlement.[13] By coincidence, the same day saw the publication in London of the pamphlet "The Interest of England in the Irish Transplantation". Written by Colonel Richard Lawrence, son-in-law of Colonel Hewson, and a brother of Henry Lawrence, the President of the Council in London, the pamphlet denied that the Irish Government contemplated a general transplantation. He claimed that transplantation was limited to land owners, and those who had been in arms against Parliament.[14]

The pressure to enforce transplantation continued. On 19 March 1655 Colonel Hewson and other senior officers were commissioned to use military force to carry out the plan. Persons required to transplant to Connaught or Clare, and without authority neglecting to do so, may be regarded as spies, and tried by Courts Martial.[15] Found guilty, they could be shot or hanged.

On 11 April, Sir H. Waller, Colonel Hewson and others, were instructed to attend a meeting at Cork House, Dublin, (the government's centre of the civil administration), to debate the business of the transplanting of the Irish inhabiting the five counties for which they were responsible.[16] In May an exemption to transplantation was introduced. A Declaration was made on 23 May that Irish Papists might claim exemption if they were able to demonstrate their "constant good affection to the Parliament of England".[17]

In England the long anticipated armed rebellion by Royalist supporters had erupted in March. Known as "Penrudduck's Rising", it was a futile attempt by a group of country gentlemen in Wiltshire. Apart from their servants and tenants they were unable to gather support. General Disbrowe's regular troops ignominiously crushed them. Perhaps the most significant aspect of the business was the harsh, indeed unlawful, treatment meted out to captured rebels by a Government that had previously studiously sought to follow conciliatory policies. None of the soldiers of Hewson's regiment, sent from Ireland two months earlier, was involved. Being politically reliable, Cromwell had retained them in London. There they featured in a bizarre incident.

Military discipline was increasingly influenced by Puritan morals. This was unfortunate for one Hugh Powell, a soldier in Captain Lieutenant Hoare's company of Hewson's regiment, then stationed at Whitehall. At a Court Martial held on the 15 June, he was found guilty of fornication and sentenced " to be whippt on the bare back with a whipcord lash, and have forty stripes while he is led through the four companies of the Irish forces before Whitehall ... and twenty stripes more after that at Putney".[18] The fate of the lady involved is not recorded.

Reviving prosperity in Britain led to an increasing demand for luxuries. Sugar particularly was in demand, and the new English plantations in Barbados were crying out for labour. Irish slaves fetched good prices there. The Irish Council had instructed that surrendered Tories be shipped to the Summer Islands (Barbados, etc.) as rogues and vagabonds. This led to a situation where many young persons, particularly girls, were being snatched in the streets of Irish towns, and smuggled overseas. The scandal provoked outrage, and on 6 July 1655, the Council recorded that some persons, both Irish and English, had been

> "... surreptitiously apprehended and forcibly put on board a ship in this harbour of Dublin, bound for that island, who are not comprehended as vagrants or idlers, it is ordered that the Governor and Mayor of Dublin do authorise persons to search the ship and such as they shall find there contrary thereunto, they are to secure and speedily to report and particulars thereof to the Council."[19]

(It was alleged that Colonel Coote had been involved in this trade, employing his soldiers to kidnap girls in daylight from the streets of Galway, regardless of their station in life.)

Cromwell was not convinced that the reports he was receiving from the Council in Ireland represented the true situation there. Perhaps it was a suggestion by Secretary Thurloe, who operated the Government's intelligence service, that persuaded Cromwell to raise his son, Henry Cromwell, to the rank of Major General, and appoint him commander of the Army in Ireland, with instructions to furnish his father with an independent assessment of the position in that country. Henry arrived in Ireland to assume his new duties on 9 July 1655.

Later in the same month, 24 July, Colonel Hewson in a surprising act of magnanimity, ordered that all Catholic priests held in the jails of Dublin (except those under suspicion of murder) "be delivered to Captain William Hazlewood's ship Globe to be transported to Cadiz or Malagar".[20]

The newly arrived Henry Cromwell took advantage of the rapidly improving security situation to order widespread reductions in the army in Ireland. Nineteen mounted troops, and forty-one companies of foot, were disbanded in August and September. Two companies of Hewson's regiment – those of Captains Turner (a brother of Colonel Hewsons's first wife, Anne), and Hincham (Daniel Hincksman, or Hinchman) – were paid off: they were allotted lands in Kilalea and Kericurrihie, in Co. Cork. Further disbandments took place the following year. In all the army was cut from 34,000 men to 19,000 "but it was sufficient to hold Ireland down".[21] On 20 August, 1655, Colonel Hewson and some other senior officers were appointed as a Committee to consider how to satisfy pay arrears due to maimed soldiers, aged widows, and orphans (who could not be expected to work grants of agricultural land), "and further consider how the State may most advantageously be enabled to buy the respective Debentures issued by the Commissioners of Accounts for such arrears".[22] In fact, the acquisition of Debentures of entitlement to land, issued in lieu of pay, by senior officers from common soldiers, using fraud or undue influence, became a notorious scandal. It is possible that the lands in Co. Leitrim, and at Roscrea in Co. Tipperary, held by the family of Colonel Hewson, and which escaped sequestration following the Restoration in 1660, were obtained in this way.

As the transplantation operation continued throughout 1655, the

Dublin authorities received increasing numbers of pleas for exemption. On 19 October, the officers responsible, including Sir H. Waller and Colonel Hewson, were instructed to clarify the conditions for the exemption of those Irish papists, who were the tenants and servants of Protestant landowners in the five counties under their jurisdiction.[23]

Needless to say, Irish hostility to transplantation was bitter. People, driven by invading foreigners into woods and bogs, homeless and starving, struck back at those who occupied their lands as and when possible.

A typical incident is mentioned by the Irish writer, the Rev. J.P. Prendergast,

> "... Denis Brennan and Murtagh Turner, persons lately in the army and pay of the State, troopers of Colonel Hewson, being engaged near the castle of Lackagh, in the same county of Kildare, repairing houses of some of the transplanted inhabitants, were barbarously murdered, to the great terror of the rest of the peaceable inhabitants of the county."

One wonders whether Murtagh Turner might have been related to Captain Turner, whose company was recently disbanded.

Retribution followed. According to a London newspaper, "Colonel Hewson is sent down to the Town where they were murdered and will secure them all to be sent to the West Indies: they will never change their bloody nature."[24] Hewson rounded up all the Irish of Lackagh, four ... "hanged for the benefit of the rest" ..., and the remaining thirty-seven were delivered to Captain Robert Colman, commander of the Wexford frigate, for shipment to Barbados. The area had been the scene of the activities of "Blind Donagh" O'Derrick, a notorious Tory, and Hewson was eager to claim the £30 reward for his head. However the Irish resistance leader avoided capture, though Hewson had the satisfaction of taking O'Derrick's wife. She was one of the unfortunates handed over to Captain Colman on the 27 November, 1655.[25]

Henry Cromwell, though he was only twenty-six years of age, quickly showed himself to be an able administrator. He followed his father's ideas of seeking to heal divisions, and bring together those of moderate views, be it in religion or politics. His attempts to establish a broad-minded Protestant church of Ireland antagonised the extreme sectarians, particularly the Anabaptist officers powerful in the army and in the Irish civil administration. The Lord Deputy, Fleetwood, was recalled to England in the autumn of 1655; Henry Cromwell took over his powers.

He found favour with many Independents in the army, and by November petitions for his formal appointment as Lord Deputy were circulating, though without Henry's approval.

> "The leaders of the Anabaptists, headed by Colonel Hewson, drew up a protest complaining that these petitions were a covert attack on Fleetwood, and asserting that the movement did not arise from affection to Henry Cromwell or the Protector, but from the desire of its promoters to weaken 'the godly interest' for their private ends."

The Protector's reply to this protest took the form of a letter to Hewson, which was circulated by the opposition as proof that Cromwell disapproved of any suggestion for Fleetwood's return.[26]

Apart from the Anabaptists' opposition to Henry Cromwell's tolerant approach in religious affairs, there was a more mercenary motive in the senior officers' attempts to retain Fleetwood: "Fleetwood believed thoroughly in the system by which the Irish were being ruthlessly driven from their lands, and the officers who were profiting by it, naturally did not care to have it interfered with" ... "This element of self-interest cannot be ignored in a consideration of the struggle to retain Fleetwood as a director of Irish affairs."[27] Fleetwood, himself an Anabaptist, though not a fanatic, did not support Hewson's plea to Cromwell for his return to Ireland.

Henry Cromwell, not unnaturally, was angered by Hewson's approach to his father behind his back. He wrote to Secretary Thurloe on the 19 December, 1655, complaining about allegations made against him: "If Colonel Hewson must be believed (with his three

Anabaptist sons) I must be made a liar, if not worse …"[28] And Henry Cromwell revenged himself on Hewson. He had Lieutenant Colonel Alexander Brayfield, who had served with Hewson, brought before a Court Martial, which condemned him to be cashiered. Despite his father's recommendation for clemency, Henry Cromwell allowed this severe punishment to stand because "Brayfield was a critic and intriguer belonging to the faction in the army led by Hewson which used to deride Henry as Absalom."[29]

January, 1656, saw the Dublin administration still struggling to enforce transplantation. Yet another committee, again including Colonel Hewson, was appointed on 1 February. Its task was to advise the Loughrea Commissioners how the transplanted Irish landowners were to be allocated lands in Connaught – "of like quality and quantity" – in proportion to the lands from which they had been expelled. Bearing in mind that Connaught and Clare were areas of largely uninhabitable wilderness, a satisfactory settlement was impossible. Astonishingly the committee took less than two weeks to do the work. By the 12 February, it had drawn up proposals, which were endorsed as formal instructions to the Loughrea Commissioners. This, at least, gave them some guideline, however inadequate, to make allocations.[30]

The Puritan administration in Ireland was concerned to punish use of the English Prayer Book, particularly by ministers with Episcopalian leanings.

> "On the 4 April 1656 it was ordered that Sir Hardress Waller, Sir R. King, Sir J. Temple, Colonels Hewson, Sankey and Lawrence; Winter, Harrison, Worth, Wooton, and Alderman Hooke should attend on Chief Justice Pepys and Chief Baron Corbet on the following Tuesday at 9 o'clock in the gallery chamber of the Castle for the purpose of perusing the Protector's order for approbation of ministers (dated 20 March 1654), and such further orders as had been subsequently passed by the Irish Council. This being done they were to frame a series of rules …"[31]

… for the trial of ministers.

The Committee, known as the Committee for the Approbation, or Trial, of Ministers, quickly produced draft rules; but these were unsatisfactory, for on 14 April the Irish Council referred them back, intimating that methods be found for discovering and ejecting ministers who were "weak, scandalous, popish, or ill-affected".[31] It might be noted that three members of the Committee were Anabaptists, Hewson, Lawrence and Sankey; and their appointment by Henry Cromwell suggests that he was still trying to work with them.[32]

Nevertheless it appears that Hewson no longer saw a future for himself in Ireland. He may well have made a visit to London in February, 1656, to re-establish his political contacts. This might explain why the February 1 Committee on Transplantation Rules worked with such uncharacteristic haste! There is a report in a London newsletter of the 26 February: "The beares in the beare garden were by order of Major Generall Barkestead Kill'd, and the heads of the game cocks in the severall pits wrung off by a company of foote soldiers."[33] This action, deeply resented by Londoners, was inspired by the ongoing Puritan suppression of gambling and unseemly assemblies. The historian, Macaulay, writing nearly two hundred years later, has offered a less praiseworthy motive: "the puritan hated bear baiting, not because it gave pain to the bear, but because it gave pleasure to the spectators".

This incident may well have been the occasion when Colonel Hewson was said to have dispatched bears with his own sword. Certainly Barkstead and Hewson had worked together in the past, particularly during the crisis in 1648, and Hewson may have renewed the acquaintanceship. It should be made clear that the suggestion that Hewson visited London in late February, 1656, is speculation – no documentary evidence either way has been found.

Sometime around mid 1656, Colonel Hewson, dissatisfied with serving under Henry Cromwell, left his post as Military Governor of Dublin, and returned to England. According to Robert Temple, he went back to Ireland briefly to settle his affairs, and transport his effects home to England, possibly settling in Surrey, but most probably in London. One wonders whether Hewson's new wife played any part in this decision.

It appears that thereafter Henry Cromwell had less trouble from the Anabaptists.

> "One factor in the continuation of peace was the withdrawal of some of the principal malcontents. Vernon and Carteret (a son-in-law of Hewson) crossed to England. Hewson went to London and proceeded to make trouble for Henry there, by disseminating the report that the Independents as well as the Baptists in Ireland were dissatisfied with him."[31]

Clearly, this was not the case.

In August Colonel Hewson was once more involved in an unsavoury affair. This concerned a Dr Harrison, who normally preached at Christ Church cathedral in Dublin, and was Henry Cromwell's chief chaplain. However at this time he was detained in London. Writing to Henry on 5 August, Dr Harrison complained that someone "had the malice to tell my Lord Deputy (Henry) that I was married to my maid and that not before there was neede ..." Clearly deeply upset, Harrison wrote again to Henry on the 12 August, mentioning his enemies' repeated calumnies. He wrote that he had been told that:

> "... even officers of the army are made to solicit H.H. [Oliver Cromwell] against my returne. Col. Hewson hath attempted to vilifie me to some of our church but hath not prevailed. I have dealt with him according to rule, he seemed satisfied and promised to make me so at his returne by bringing forth the authors of his most malicious groundlesse slanders."[32]

As we shall see, the ill-feeling between the Anabaptist faction and Henry Cromwell continued to fester.

CHAPTER 11

"The Second Protectorate Parliament"
(The 1656 Parliament)

The year 1656 saw Cromwell seeking, yet again, to establish an effective form of government, legitimated by an elected parliament. The spur was his administration's increasingly difficult financial situation. By the winter of 1655/6 annual income was falling short of annual expenditure by almost £250,000.[1] This could not go on.

Following Cromwell's dismissal of his first Protectorate Parliament in January 1655, he and his Council had tightened their grip on the country by imposing military rule. The country was divided into ten (later eleven) military districts, each controlled by a major-general. The generals were under detailed orders to preserve law and order, collect taxes, administer local government, and enforce Puritan standards of morality. All of which they did, with military efficiency. However such authoritarian direction from far-off London was far from welcome: "Provincial Englishmen had always tended to regard proclamations, regulations and commands from the centre as interesting suggestions rather than orders which must be precisely obeyed."[2] As might have been expected, the rule of the major generals, which rode roughshod over local sensibilities, and enforced with ruthless authority, aroused deep resentment throughout the land.

Cromwell and his Council also faced resentment from the influential merchant classes, who disputed taxation levied without Parliamentary approval. They recalled that the late King had attempted to do likewise. It became increasingly obvious that a new Parliament had to be installed, if only to disguise the reality that power was firmly in the hands of Cromwell and the Army. The major generals were confident that they could, with their local control, ensure that only members favourable to the current administration would be elected.

The election was called in the summer of 1656, and on 17 September the new Parliament assembled in Westminster.

Various difficulties needed to be resolved. One was that Major-general Thomas Kelsey was elected to represent Guildford in Surrey, but had also stood, and been successful, in Dover. "In 1656 Maj.-Gen. Kelsey was returned for Dover and for Guildford at the same General Election. He preferred to serve for Dover. At the consequent bye-election in Guildford the choice of the burgesses fell upon Col. John Newsome [This was a misspelling of Hewson]."[3] Presumably Hewson's election was less dramatic than that of one of his predecessors, Nicolas Picard, who, in the fourteenth century "commanded the respect and obedience of the burgesses by threatening to destroy the town by fire the next morning if his claims were not conceded forthwith";[4] he got his way. It is known that Colonel Hewson was appointed a Justice of the Peace.[5] This might have been in 1656, following his election as Member of Parliament for Guildford.

Hewson's election brought a further recognition. Of the 26 companies of foot temporarily brought over from Ireland in the previous year, to counter a feared Royalist uprising, only 13 had been returned. The remainder, including Hewson's four companies stationed in London, were retained permanently. In October 1656 the government resolved to form a regiment under the command of Colonel Hewson, consisting of the four companies in question, together with other companies that had been brought over at the same time. This new regiment, the 12th Regiment of Foot, was held on the English military establishment, and until 1660 bore Hewson's name.[6] No doubt the receipt of the pay and allowances for command of a second regiment (he still remained Colonel of his original regiment stationed in Dublin), helped meet the inevitable expenses of life in London as one of the Army grandees. And, "On 28 October, 1656, an Order in Council was made that Colonel

John Hewson be allowed a Chaplain for his regiment of Foot."[7]

Within days of the opening of the new Parliament it became clear that the major generals had miscalculated badly. Despite their efforts to secure the return of "friendly" members, a large number were deeply hostile to Cromwell's government, though it must be said that personally he commanded their respect. The Council of State took it upon itself to vet the new members, and shamelessly excluded more than a hundred potential trouble makers. Even so, the remaining members were not to be cowed. They strongly objected to the unlawful taxes levied since the First Protectorate Parliament was dissolved on 22 January 1655, and resolved that no further financial support would be given until military rule was lifted. In January 1657, Parliament rejected a tax bill required to fund the continuation of military rule, and with this defeat the hated administration of the major generals came to an end.

An equally emotional issue of dispute between the new Parliament and the government was Cromwell's personal policy of religious tolerance (except towards Papists and users of the Book of Common Prayer). The majority of members feared the increasing influence of the Society of Friends (The Quakers), and sought to make an example of a Quaker leader, James Naylor, who had committed public blasphemy. On 10 December, 1656, the Commons met to discuss his fate. The debate continued for several days, members suggesting exemplary punishments. Colonel Hewson took part repeatedly, calling for calm discussion. He refused his support for Naylor's death, and called for him to be invited to the Bar of the House to say why judgment ought not to be passed against him. Colonel Hewson: "I desire it may be asked him what he has to say."[8] Cromwell intervened, writing to the House pointing out that it was for the Courts and not Parliament to administer judicial process. However the House voted that Naylor should be branded, whipped and imprisoned.

On 16 December, the members considered the extreme language used by one James Noble, at the Committee for Drury House. It was resolved that the words he used were scandalous. The debate then was whether he should be punished, or treated as deranged. Colonel Hewson spoke: "He has been a soldier, and it is not proper to whip him."[9] In the end it was decided to send him to a lunatic asylum.

The "diary" of Thomas Burton, a contemporary, provides an insight into Colonel Hewson's willingness to speak in the House on a variety of matters. On 19 December, 1656, ten aldermen of London presented a petition from the City to debar those who do not contribute towards the support of the city's magistracy from being eligible to be free-men. Colonel Hewson asked the House to accept the petition: "The City has done you eminent service, never to be forgotten. This is the first petition that they ever troubled you with; it is no great matter. It is only to restore them to their ancient privileges and their order and government. I would have you give them thanks for their good serv-ice." After some discussion it was resolved that the petition be referred to a Committee, to meet tomorrow afternoon in the Court of Wards.[10]

The House made a point of sitting on Christmas Day – Papist celebrations would not be tolerated by the Godly. So it was on 25 December, 1656, that "An Act for Abolishing and Taking away Festivals commonly called Holy days" was read for the first time. An early speaker drew attention to the need to pass this measure, retailing with horror the extent to which Christmas was being observed: "One may pass from the Tower to Westminster and not a shop open, nor a creature stirring. It is a fit time now." Members agreed that Christmas should be banned, and Sir William Strickland proposed that the bill should be read the second time tomorrow, with Colonel Hewson sec-onding the motion.[11]

Immediately afterwards Major-General Desborough proposed a Bill "for continuance of a tax upon some people, for the maintenance of the militia" – in effect making decimation tax already levied on the richer Royalists, permanent. He argued that, as they threatened public peace, they should pay for its maintenance. The difficulty was that his proposal was against the Act of Indemnity, which Parliament had passed on 24 February 1651–52. Many Army officers supported the proposal. Colonel Hewson argued:

"You are not laying a tax upon the people, but upon your enemies, whose estates are at the devotion of your enemies. They
are active people, whom they well employ to your destruction. I
grant the Act of Oblivion is a sacred thing, and your public faith
ought to be kept; but I hope you only pardon offences, not what
is to come. If they have digged pits or laid snares since, against
the honest party, that you will not be asleep, but look about you.
You are disobliged from the Act of Oblivion. I desire that a Bill
may be brought in, to lay an assessment upon the Cavaliers."[12]

Hewson had his way, and Desborough was given leave to bring in his
Bill. In the end though, it was rejected on 29 January, 1657.

The next day, 26 December, once more saw the House sitting.
Colonel Hewson spoke during the second reading of a Bill for the provision of maintenance of a minister at Newport, in the Isle of Wight.[13]

He was again on his feet in a discussion of Cromwell's letter to
Members, read out by Mr Speaker (Rouse). Cromwell desired to be
informed of the grounds on which they had punished James Naylor without his consent. What reply could they make? Members had differing
views as to the jurisdiction of the House. And different accounts were
given as to how severely the sentence had been carried out. Colonel
Hewson brought Members back to the main issue. He proposed that
a Committee might be appointed "to find out a way how to give his
Highness an account in this business. If the person was favoured in the
punishment, it was the lenity of the executioner, not of the sentence. I
was against it in my opinion".[14] A long debate followed but no resolution.

A notable part of the work of the Second Protectorate Parliament
was to consider, and (if agreed), confirm the various ordinances,
proclamations, taxes, instructions to major generals, etc., issued by
Cromwell's administration since he dismissed the First Parliament
nearly two years earlier. Many were of doubtful legality and required
the authority of Parliament. Members decided to embody all ordinances to be confirmed into one bill, mentioning each specifically.
Each was nominated, and required to be individually approved for
inclusion. Sometimes there was lively debate, sometimes general

assent. "Colonel Hewson was heard to give his yea to his own ordinance – for arrears of pay – which caused a laughter."[15]

There was quite a human touch during the sitting of the House on 2 January, 1657. Mr Speaker Rouse started to give a second reading to a Bill touching the Exportation of Fish, but on seeing that it was incomplete, lacking title, and with blanks for rates of customs duty, in a temper threw it from him. Colonel Hewson stood up to calm matters, and suggested that the House adjourn until the following Monday morning. He addressed the Speaker: "In regard our preservation depends much on your health, I desire you would put that question." This was done, and the adjournment approved. The offending Bill was committed to the Committee of Trade.[16]

On 16 January, 1657, Hewson wrote to Cromwell, perhaps petitioning for the return of Fleetwood to Ireland to replace Henry Cromwell, Hewson's enemy.[17]

In February emerged the defining political issue of the year. This was a proposal in Parliament to make Cromwell king, under a new constitution. The idea was far from new, but had effectively surfaced the previous October, when an Irish member, Colonel William Jephson, proposed that the office of Protector should become hereditary. His suggestion was not accepted by the House, but the issue of succession following Cromwell's death continued to exercise Member's minds.

On 23 February, 1657, Sir Christopher Packe, a former Lord Mayor of London, introduced kingship proposals to the House. Their authorship remains obscure, but it is unlikely to have been Packe, since the prominent lawyer Bulstrode Whitelock had earlier been approached to do so and had declined.[18]

The basic proposal was that Cromwell should become king, with the power to nominate his successor. The army leaders flatly opposed the idea, but a majority of the civilian members looked forward to a return to some form of the ancient monarchal constitution. Most Irish members supported the proposal, but one, Major Anthony Morgan, wrote on the next day to Henry Cromwell that they were "all for it but Cooper, Huson and Sankey".[19]

The senior army officers reacted swiftly. Four days after Packe's proposals, a deputation of over 100 officers presented themselves to Cromwell. He addressed them forcibly, claiming that he neither sought nor desired the crown, but tried to conform to the goodwill of Parliament. He refused to discuss the matter further, but said that he would talk with a small delegation of six or seven. This confrontation kept the lid on the military unrest, though "Lambert, Sydenham, Hewson and Disbrowe were as sullen as ever".[20]

Parliament, nevertheless, commenced discussions on the new constitution, to be entitled "the Humble Petition and Advice". The objections of the army members were simply outvoted by civilian members, who sought to reduce the power of the Council of State (which mainly comprised senior officers), and increase that of Parliament. In March the House decided to restore the Upper Chamber, and on the 25th of that month, voted through a motion formally inviting Cromwell to accept the office and title of king.

Most senior officers remained bitterly opposed to the offer of kingship to Cromwell. In a letter dated 31 March 1657, Colonel Thomas Cooper writing to Henry Cromwell in Dublin comments, "Lambert, Sydenham and Desborough still stand out upon the sullen posture. Fleetwood does not mutiny but lament". Hewson is "as obstinate as could be imagined".[21] Another report to Henry Cromwell, written on the same day by Colonel Jephson, seems almost identical, "but Hewson as obstinate as could bee imagin'd or wisht". The original letter is Lansdowne MSS. 822, and should show whether the author was Thos. Cooper or Jephson.[22] However, bearing in mind the uncertainties of the post in those troubled times, it is more than possible that there were indeed two similar accounts sent on the same day.

On Saturday 4 April, Bulstrode Whitelock reported to Parliament that Cromwell had refused the Crown. The news elated the Army members. Though this was "no small discouragement" to the supporters of the Petition and Advice they did not give up, and proposed that Parliament should adhere to its former vote and renew the offer. The debate was short and sharp. Hewson and Desborough (Disbrowe) opposed the motion, but it was carried by a small majority. Once again the civilian members had defeated the military officers.

Two days later, on Monday 6 April, the debate was resumed. This time the supporters of the proposal turned out in force. They decided to set out the reasons why Parliament should continue its support for the Humble Petition and Advice,

> "... but some violent things were said against the proposal. 'Mr Speaker' ... Colonel Hewson was reported to have declared,... 'this Parliament in which we are is worse than the Devil; for he offered the Kingdoms of the World to Christ but once, and we must offer it twice; and for it give reasons to destroy not only ourselves but all the three nations with us'."[23]

On the 8 April 1657 Parliament again requested Cromwell to heed the Petition and Advice. His reply was ambiguous, leaving Parliament in suspense.

Some two weeks after this debate, the House granted Hewson leave of absence for two months to return to Ireland to wind up his affairs in that country, and arrange the management of his Luttrellstown estate.[24] It appears that Hewson let the estate to Sir William Berry (or Bury) Kt., who was shown as occupant in a 1659 Census.[25]

The Lord Deputy of Ireland, Henry Cromwell, anticipated that the movement in England to crown his father might provoke unrest when the news reached Dublin. In particular, he was concerned about its effect on the Anabaptist faction, still strong in the army and civil administration. Henry wrote to trusted army commanders,

> "... to look out for any signs of disturbance, and to check any attempts at petitions. Fearing especially the influence of Richard Lawrence and John Jones, encouraged by Hewson, who had returned to Ireland on private business, he made such changes in the disposition of the forces at Dublin as should so far as possible nullify that influence. Allen and Vernon, too, were holding meetings, and Axtell's behaviour caused him some uneasiness."[26]

Back in Westminster, all awaited Cromwell's decision as to whether he would accept the kingship. He had yet to make up his mind, and on 1 May, sent a message to the Commons promising a speedy reply. He admitted that he was sorely tempted: his biographer Antonia Fraser writes, "In fact it was perfectly possible at this point to sympathise with the hostile comment of Colonel Hewson: this Parliament is worse than the Devil, for he had only offered Christ the Kingdom of the World once, where as they were doing it twice."[27] However a week later, on 8 May 1657, Cromwell finally refused the title of King though not the office, and indeed subsequently maintained a kingly style as Head of State. He, reluctantly, had to accept that he could not afford to antagonise the leaders of the army that kept his administration in power.

Henry Cromwell's concern that Hewson's reappearance in Ireland would ferment trouble was only too well founded. It came to light in June that they (Hewson and his son-in-law, Colonel Richard Lawrence) had been promoting a letter from the officers to Fleetwod, rejoicing in Cromwell's refusal of the Crown. They had secured its fifteen signatures, according to Henry, by dubious methods. On the grounds of this action he forbade Hewson and Lawrence to leave for England, and in spite of Thurloe's attempts to make light of the affair, and Fleetwood's defence of Hewson, declared publicly against the letter. His objections to what might seem a harmless expression of opinion were based upon the fact that indirect methods had been used, and that the matter did not come up immediately after the refusal of the crown, but much later when the settlement of the government was well under way.[28]

An unusual, and unbiased, source of political information of the time is found in the series of reports by Venetian ambassadors in London to their Government. The letter sent 22 June 1657 relates ... "A report has been current here for some days that sixteen officers of the Army and two Members of Parliament, one of whom is Colonel Hewson, Governor of Dublin, fell in with an Ostend ship on their passage from England to Ireland, by which they were captured and carried to Flanders". This report was apparently based on unfounded rumour and might well reflect wishful thinking in some London political circles![29] Subsequent reports by the ambassadors make no further reference to this tale.

It is not known when Henry Cromwell allowed Hewson to leave Ireland. Possibly he was advised to do so by Thurloe, who was in regular correspondence with him. Henry's antipathy to Hewson may also have been the motive for his cashiering of Lt. Col. Brayfield, who commanded Hewson's regiment in Ireland. This action was defended in Henry's letter to Thurloe sent on 9 September, on the grounds that Brayfield was "... a supporter of Colonel Hewson".[30]

However Henry Cromwell retained the confidence of his father, and as part of his restructuring of the Government, was on the 17th November 1657 re-appointed Lord Deputy in Ireland, thus dashing the hopes of the Anabaptist faction who wanted the return of Fleetwood. The new constitution also required a second chamber, a revival of the House of Lords which the Commonwealth had abolished in 1649. The members of this Upper House were selected by Cromwell, largely drawn from his supporters in the Commons. As Head of State – de facto King-Cromwell claimed the right to award honours, and "knighted" his appointees to the new House of Lords, Hewson being created a peer on 5 December. These honours were not universally accepted. The Royalist, Lucy Hutchinson, was scornful; he (Cromwell) "... wanted not many fools, both of the army and the gentry, to accept of, and strut in, his mock titles.[31]

On 10 December, 1657, formal writs were issued for Cromwell's new House of Lords. The idea was that it should be able to reject unpalatable legislation emanating from a potentially hostile Commons. Cromwell gave seats to those he thought would support him. These included many senior army officers, including Fleetwood, Desborough, Hewson, Goffe, Pride, Barkstead, Tomlinson and Berry. Notably excluded was General Lambert, who allegedly saw himself as Cromwell's successor. There was argument whether the new chamber should be called "House of Lords" or "The Other Place". Resolved by adopting the term "Upper House".

The first meeting of the Upper House was called on 20 January 1658, but many "Lords" failed to attend, only about forty-two of the sixty-three summoned took their seats. Some absentees may have feared repercussions if the Stuart monarchy was to return, hereditary nobles may have preferred not to mix with members of the lower classes. Antonia Fraser writes "... Afterwards the reluctance of the hereditary peers was ascribed by men like Ludlow to mere social snobbery – Warwick, he said, would not condescend to sit between Colonels Hewson and Pride, one of whom had been a shoemaker and the other a drayman in civilian life."[32] However, a member of the Commons defended their right to sit ... "the command of a regiment of foot gave as much influence as the possession of an estate."[33]

The next day one of the absentees made his appearance "this day, James Lord Berry, having taken the Oath in the room within the painted Chamber, ... came into the house and tooke his place next to John Lord Hewson on the bench in the second Rowe on the Left hand."[34]

January 20th, 1658, was the day the new House of Lords convened. On the same day the Commons, which had been in recess, re-assembled. Its membership had altered. Many of the elected members hostile to Cromwell, who had been excluded by the Council of State when Parliament first met in September 1656, had been able to take their places. The Protector's party in the house was also fatally weakened by the elevation of so many of Cromwell's supporters to the Upper House. The groups opposed to Cromwell's (and military) administration now dominated the Commons, blocking his policies. The business of government stalled. Cromwell reacted with anger, and on 4 February 1658, called both Houses together. In a sharp speech he rebuked them for sowing disaffection in the country, and concluded by declaring Parliament dissolved. Once again, responsibility for government rested on Cromwell alone.

CHAPTER 12

"The Death of Oliver Cromwell"

When Oliver Cromwell sent the members of Parliament back to their homes on February 4 1658, he was accepting an unpalatable reality. He had recognised that there could be no accommodation with a republican majority which sought to pull down his regime, and bring the army under its control. The concluding words of his address dismissing Parliament were, "Let God be judge between you and me."

Cromwell's failure, over the years, to enlist the support of successive Parliaments for his plans to build a united and tolerant Britain, deeply distressed him. He believed that he was doing the Lord's work yet was increasingly conscious that time was not on his side. Each passing month saw his Government falling ever deeper into debt, his health was failing, and military rule was losing support both in City and Shire. Some historians claim that his will to continue as Lord Protector faltered. To add to his unhappiness, he suffered bereavement – first a son-in-law in February, then the crushing loss of his beloved daughter, Elizabeth. After enduring a protracted and agonising illness she died in August. During that summer he aged visibly. Shortly after Elizabeth's funeral, Cromwell went down with a fever. Though he rallied briefly, his condition rapidly worsened, the end coming on 3 September 1658. Sometime before death he nominated his son Richard to succeed him as Lord Protector.

There is a paucity of information concerning Colonel Hewson's activities during this period. The so-called Upper House had been closed along with the Commons when Parliament had been dismissed, so it may be assumed that Hewson spent his time involved in military matters, or at home. There is some possibility that he was in poor health.

The proclamation of Richard Cromwell as Lord Protector was generally accepted. General Lambert, who earlier appeared to be the natural successor to Oliver Cromwell, kept a low profile. Richard was a very different sort of man from his forceful father, having been living quietly as a country squire. Surprisingly, in view of his lack of military experience, the army made no open objection to his taking command, though without his father's strong personality it was perhaps inevitable that various factions developed amongst the more politically active officers.

Secretary Thurloe wrote four days after Cromwell's death to Henry Cromwell, still in charge in Ireland, informing him that Richard had assumed the Protectorship without dissent, but "there are some secret murmurings in the army as if His Highness were not generall of the army as his father was; and would looke upon him and the army as divided and as if the conduct of the army should be elsewhere and in other hands; but I am not able to say what this will come to. I think conceit of any such thinge is dangerous".[1] On 14 September Fauconburg wrote also to Henry on much the same lines: "Certainly somewhat is brewing underhand. A caball there is of persons and great ones held very closely, resolve, it's feared, to rule themselves or set all on fire."[2]

Nevertheless the murmurers were not prepared to speak out openly. A large group of army officers, stated by Fauconburg to include Fleetwood, Sydenham, Berry and Huson, met at Whitehall on 20 September, "and heard Fleetwood explain that they had come together to consider and address to His Highness. It was then read and signed, all present striving who should be first".[3] Fleetwood, accompanied by the signatories, presented the address to Richard the following morning. Fauconburg remained suspicious of the activities of this group of sectarian army officers. Writing again to Henry Cromwell on 28 September: "matters are drawing towards ruine ... the cabal gets ground [grows] apace ..." and reports that the group was now demanding the power of granting commissions, and vetoing appointments to the Council.[4]

Henry Cromwell was anxious to receive information from Fauconburg and Secretary Thurloe about the activities of the sectarian army leaders in London since he still regarded the Anabaptist faction in Ireland (which he suspected drew its lead from Colonel Hewson) as a threat to political stability. However Henry remained firmly in control of that country, with an army that mustered at 14,000 or 15,000, excluding garrison troops. His position was further strengthened on 6 October, when Richard formally confirmed him as Lord Lieutenant of Ireland. Although Hewson was now resident in England he owned considerable estates in Ireland (including Luttrellstown), and drew rents therefrom. A document of the time listing the Irish regiments, shows regiments of foot held by both John Hewson, and his son-in-law, Richard Lawrence. Hewson's companies in Ireland were under the day to day command of his Lieutenant-Colonel, William Arnop.[5]

During October and November regular meetings were being held at St James on Fridays, attended by "two or three hundred officers". Their discontent focussed on a variety of grievances – dislike of hereditary rulers with a House of Lords (the "good old cause"), arrears of pay, allegations of alleged victimisation, e.g. Lambert's case, and a feeling that officers dismissed by Oliver Cromwell should have their commissions restored. The officers, led by Fleetwood, submitted a petition to Richard Cromwell in early October, but their main requests were refused. The unrest continued, some army leaders were said to be holding daily conferences with the heads of the civilian Republican Party. Whilst these rumours were doubtless exaggerated, they may have been caused by a sort of coalition between the group of officers known as the Commonwealthsmen, and some of the more extreme Wallingford House group of officers. Clearly these factions in the army leadership would not be cut and dried, but the Commonwealthsmen included Colonels Ashfield, Lilburne and Fitch, Lieutenant Colonels Mason, Moss and Farley, and appeared to have the general support of the junior army officers. The Wallingford House group, who took their name from their usual meeting place (Fleetwood's residence), included Fleetwood, Berry, Disbrowe, Clerk, Kelsey, and other leaders, including Hewson. It was Berry, Hewson and perhaps Disbrowe, who were alleged to have been working with the Commonwealthsmen. The faction continuing to support the Lord Protector included Major-Generals Whalley, Goffe and Howard, Goodrick, Colonel Ingoldsby and many senior officers in the Irish and Scottish armies. Needless to say the divided leadership of the army offered encouragement to those wishing to bring down Richard Cromwell's Protectorate government.

The officers' agitation was interrupted by the State Funeral of Oliver Cromwell, on 23 November. As befitted one of the outstanding Englishmen of all time, "This great funeral was performed with very great majesty". So wrote a contemporary. The formal procession was from the lying-in-state at Somerset House in the Strand, to the Abbey Church of Westminster. Immediately following the coffin, preceding even the mourners, pride of place was given to the Banner of England. Lords Tomlinson and Hewson had the honour of carrying the Banner.

Through the winter, the Friday meetings of the Wallingford House clique of senior officers continued, nominally for devotions. Usually they met now at Disbrowe's residence. Hewson, Cooper and Robert Lilburne regularly attended. They aimed to wrest command of the army "out of the feeble hands of Richard".[6] Disbrowe was sent to request that the new Protector put command of the army into the hands of someone who would have their confidence – and immediately named Fleetwood. Richard flatly refused this demand.

But perhaps Richard's most pressing problem was his administration's desperate need for revenue. Only a lawfully elected Parliament could authorise raising increased taxes. His Government called fresh elections, and on 27 January 1659, the third Protectorate Parliament assembled.

CHAPTER 13

"Fall of the Protectorate"

Richard Cromwell, the new Protector, was a very different man from his forceful father. Contemporaries spoke of his personal charm and undoubted intelligence. But being plucked from the rural life of his modest Hampshire estate, he found London politics a trying business. Lacking military experience, he had little other than his father's name to command the army's allegiance; this was not enough. And without public backing from the army leaders, his influence over a new Parliament was weakened from the start.

The third Protectorate Parliament met on 27 January 1659. It had been summoned by Richard primarily to find a way to solve his Government's revenue shortfall.

In composition the new Parliament was largely a continuation of the 1656 Parliament, which Oliver Cromwell had angrily dismissed less than a year earlier. Most members were country gentlemen, largely Presbyterian, opposed to personal rule, distrustful of the army, and devoted to a reduction, rather than an increase, in taxation. The experienced republican politicians, Sir Arthur Hesilrige and Thomas Scot, were quickly able to form an opposition majority in the Commons. The government persuaded the Commons to accept the restored Upper House, and this, at least, it controlled.

Colonel John Hewson resumed his place in the Upper House. Not long after, he received special recognition of his military achievements. On 7 March 1659, he was admitted to the Honourable Artillery Company, which must have been particularly pleasing to one brought up in the city of London. Hewson's signature may be found in *The Ancient Vellum Book of the Honourable Artillery Company: Being the Roll of Members from 1611 to 1682.*[1]

At first Richard's new Parliament co-operated with his administration. The problem of finance was recognised, and members sought to establish the extent of government debt, and the extent of the revenue shortfall. However, within weeks, things began to go wrong. Richard's republican opponents stirred up unrest in the lower ranks of the army. Richard attempted to placate the republican majority over the army. Events came to a head in April. After confrontation with the Council of Officers, he told the officers that their Council was abolished, and that they must leave London. Fleetwood, who spoke for the senior officers, and Disbrowe, known for his personal dislike of the new Protector, counter-demanded on the 21 April that Richard dissolve Parliament. The officers called on their troops to rendezvous, leaving Richard without any military support. Now powerless, Richard had to yield to the army leaders, and on 22 April, dissolved Parliament.

This left the Council of Officers in control of the country, yet without a legal mandate – a situation that had to be remedied as soon as possible. Their discussions are recalled in a letter written on 2 May by Gilbert Mabbott to Henry Cromwell in Ireland,

> "The last weeke a counsell of officers sat at Wallingford house consisting of these lords, viz: Fleetwood, Disbrowe, Sidenham, Cowper, Hewson and Berry...... and others lately added. They have spent much time in considering of a government and incline to ye calling of ye Long Parliament and nominating a counsell whoe are said shall have a checke or negative upon them ..."[2]

And it appears that on the same day several officers consulted with eminent members of the Long Parliament concerning its recall.[3] The junior officers, and radical rank and file, were pressing for re-establishment of the purged Long Parliament (the Rump). On 5 May the Council of Officers agreed, and on 7 May the Rump was recalled. This ended the Protectorate.

Richard Cromwell, however, was unwilling to be sidelined so easily. He secretly sought military aid from General Monck in Scotland, and his brother Henry ruling Ireland, but without success. Monck's troops supported the re-established Rump Parliament, whilst Henry, appalled at the turn of events, also found the army in Ireland unwilling to intervene. Henry did not last long; on 7 June he was recalled, and replaced by Commissioners appointed by the English Parliament. Richard finally accepted the situation, and resentfully returned to private life.

The re-established Rump Parliament actually consisted of only some sixty-five active members, and was small enough to act effectively. The recent unashamed exercise of military muscle convinced them that Parliament, not the army, had to rule the country. Accordingly the Speaker of the Commons, and not the army leader, Fleetwood, was charged with granting commissions to all officers. This allowed Parliament to dismiss Richard's remaining supporters from the military.

Both Colonel Hewson's regiments were regarded by the new regime as reliable, and the list of officers of his English regiment approved by Parliament on 13 June 1659, showed few changes. Lieutenant Colonel John Duckenfield (from Cooper's regiment) was appointed as its lieutenant–colonel, and Edward Hoare confirmed as its major. Many of the regiment's officers were long serving; three if not more of the captains had fought under Hewson with the old regiment in his Irish campaigns.[4]

Parliament was concerned about the level of support Henry Cromwell had built up in Ireland during his years as Lord Lieutenant. Henry had established good relations with the long established Protestant Old English land owners, as well as the largely Presbyterian merchants in the main cities. His policy had been to curtail the influence of the radical and Anabaptist groups in army and civil administration. These, he suspected, were led by Hewson and his faction. In place of Henry Cromwell, Parliament promptly appointed a team of Commissioners to run the country. These were radical in outlook, and the Baptist element quickly recovered its political dominance. In the new climate, Colonel Hewson saw his opportunity and returned to Ireland, rightly expecting to exercise considerable influence.

The new Commission's first act was to pre-empt any military action by Henry's supporters. On 22 June, "The halberdiers in the castle [Dublin Castle] were sent back to their dragoon regiment and the absentee Hewson's major (of his Irish regiment), Henry Jones, was ordered to move his company into their place".[5] The Commissioner's orders to the Major General of the foot in Ireland, Sir Hardress Waller, were comprehensive "that he do forthwith draw into the castle of Dublin Col. Hewson's company of foot and such other forces as he shall judge fit for the security of the said place, the magazine and the stores there, and for as doing this shall be his warrant".[6] In July the castle defences were strengthened, the gates repaired, and arrangements to block access commenced.

The Parliamentary Commissioners then remodelled the entire army in Ireland. On 8 July 1659, Edward Ludlow received a Commission as Commander-in-Chief of the army in Ireland. Colonel Hewson, back in Ireland, secured appointment as Commander-in-Chief of the Foot during his stay in Ireland. He now controlled the eleven foot regiments which formed the army backbone. But with this appointment, command of his Irish regiment was transferred on 13 July to Henry Markham. However Markham does not appear to have taken up command of his new regiment, preferring to remain in England. The lieutenant-colonel who had commanded the regiment during Hewson's prolonged absences in London, William Arnop, was removed and replaced by the regiment's major, Henry Jones. Whether Jones' promotion was in any fashion connected with his marriage to one of Hewson's daughters can only be speculation! The regiment was also brought up to strength by incorporating companies from disbanded regiments, or what were termed "loose companies" – that is, unregimented companies.

Meanwhile, back in London, the initial good relations between the Rump, and the army Grandees, who had brought members back from the political wilderness, had soured. Parliament had decided that the army had to be brought to heel, yet failed to raise taxation so that the government's debts could be reduced; or, more urgently, arrears of military pay satisfied! This Parliament was almost as unpopular as rule by the swordsmen, not least because the general populace feared its radical and sectarian members would attack conservative property and traditional church values.

Such popular disquiet encouraged Royalist plots. Most came to nothing, but in Cheshire a prominent landowner, Sir George Booth, raised a substantial military force. Initially he was successful, seizing the city of Chester and large areas of North Wales and southern Lancashire. The army leader, Fleetwood, ordered General Lambert north with a small but experienced brigade, the infantry element being Colonel Hewson's reliable English regiment. Since Hewson was in Ireland, it was led by his lieutenant colonel, John Duckenfield.

Lambert's troops caught up with the Royalists near Nantwich on 19 August 1659.

> "A skirmish, rather than a battle, ensued. The ground was too broken up by hedges to use the horse at first but the foot, mainly Hewson's, drove their opponents over Winnington Bridge and secured it so that the horse could pass over. Then ensued a brief fight performed by the horse ... on both sides like Englishmen! Lambert's men prevailed, and soon Booth's army was scattered in all directions, most escaping in the enclosures where horse could not follow."[7]

Lambert's letter to the Speaker, sent on 20 August, commended Duckenfield: "He showed himself a worthy servant this day to you and his country..."[8]

Emboldened by their success in crushing Booth's rebellion, the officers in Lambert's force resolved to petition Parliament to address their concerns. John Duckenfield took a leading part in drawing up this document, which was signed by some fifty officers at Derby, on the 16 September 1659. Requesting punitive measures against the Royalists, various political reforms and, unsurprisingly, settlement of pay arrears, the Derby Petition in no way represented an attack on Parliament. However members so regarded it, and, wrongly, assumed that the Grandees were behind the soldiers' action. A second petition followed, and feeling that Parliament's position was being threatened, members voted to cashier Lambert and eight leading colonels. This was unfair, as it appears that the original petition was prepared without Lambert's approval.[9]

The army's Council of Officers reconvened. Parliament, fearing action by the disaffected troops, summoned supposedly loyal regiments to protect them. As Richard Cromwell had found earlier, the junior officers, and rank and file, had views of their own, and these did not include supporting a Parliament that had let them down. The next day, 13 October, the army leaders acted against Parliament.

In this open military coup, Hewson's regiment, under John Duckenfield's command, played a leading part. It was Duckenfield who stopped the Speaker's coach at the gate of Palace Yard. Duckenfield's men told Speaker Lenthall, when he claimed to be their commander, that "they knew no such thing; that if he had marched before them over Warrington [Winnington] Bridge, they should have known him".[10] This time the army leaders had had enough of Parliament, and dispersed the members. The responsibility of government now rested solely with the Council of Officers. It appears that Colonel Hewson played no part in this conflict between a Parliament determined to discipline its troops, and an army that felt it had to defend its rightful claims. Presumably Hewson had remained at his post in Dublin.

Though Fleetwood resumed his position as army Commander-in-Chief, it was the energetic General Lambert who took charge. The army leaders, on the 26 October 1659, named a Committee of Safety to carry on government on a temporary basis. Efforts were made to make it as broad-based as possible. The twenty-three members included civilians prominent in public life, Sir Henry Vane, and the lawyer Bulstrode Whitlock. In an attempt to win the support (and the financial backing) of the City, two London Aldermen were recruited. Also included was Henry Lawrence, one-time President of the Council, who was the elder brother of Colonel Richard Lawrence, Hewson's son-in-law. Military members selected included Colonel John Hewson, though now described as Major General, doubtless in recognition of his commanding role in the army in Ireland.[11] The first meeting of the new Committee was held two days later.

The stopgap role of the Committee was acknowledged, and on 1 November 1659, it nominated a subcommittee of fourteen, "To consider of and prepare a form of government to be settled over the three nations in the way of a free state and commonwealth, and to present it [to] the Committee of Safety for their further considerations".[12] This learned group included Fleetwood, Whitlock, Vane, Lambert, Desborow and Colonel Hewson, as well as the Scottish lawyer Warristoun.

The repeated use of military force against an elected Parliament, clearly only to protect the careers of a handful of army leaders, was deeply unpopular, particularly in Presbyterian London. A poor harvest (leading to rising food prices), and unchecked privateering by Spanish vessels, damaging English trade, all combined to fuel a rising tide of popular discontent.

CHAPTER 14

"The Slide into Chaos"

Through the political dramas of the summer and autumn of 1659, no part had been played by the army in Scotland. This was about to change.

The commander of the army in Scotland was General George Monck, an able professional soldier. In many respects he was the de facto Lord Protector of that country, his disciplined troops maintaining order, whilst he left civil administration largely in the hands of the Scots. Government revenues were collected efficiently; hence his soldiers were paid better, and more importantly, regularly, than the army in England. Monck was first and foremost a soldier's soldier, barely a day passed when he was not visiting his regiments. He handpicked his officers, weeding out radicals, and those whose loyalty was suspect. He had forged a united and effective army, physically hardened by years of campaigning through Highland bogs and mountains.

Unlike the military leaders in London, who schemed to share political power with Parliament, Monck believed that his duty lay in obeying the orders of the lawful civil authority. Writers have described his political outlook as "conservative", and certainly he viewed the radical elements in both Parliament, and the Council of Officers, with distrust.

During that autumn of 1659, Parliament and the Council of Officers both sought his support. It became apparent that he intended to intervene in English affairs – his army was making obvious preparations to march south. No one, however, could fathom his intentions.

On 13 October the army Grandees expelled the Rump, (those members of the Commons who had not been excluded in Pride's Purge in 1648), an action without a shred of legal justification. The news reached George Monck later that month. As mentioned in the previous chapter, the men of Hewson's regiment played a leading part in the army coup, though Hewson himself was undoubtedly still in Dublin. The army seizure of power must have disturbed Monck, arousing his fears that the now unchecked radical element in the Council of Officers would push through extreme measures, further destabilising the country. Monck publicly declared that he opposed the Grandees' action, and maintained the primacy of legally constituted authority.

The Council of Officers determined to resist any move into England by Monck. Lambert assembled a substantial army, the core being his own regiments and troops drawn from the regiments quartered around London. Playing for time, Lambert opened negotiations with Monck, whilst his own army, now some 12,000 strong, advanced north, first occupying York, then Newcastle. Monck, too, was anxious to defer a clash. His preparations were far from complete, and he knew that his men hardly relished the prospect of bloody battle against former comrades. Monck counted upon the approaching winter weather, and the increasingly poor morale of Lambert's underpaid soldiers, to redress his numerical inferiority. Monck wrote, assuring London's Lord Mayor that he merely intended to restore the authority of Parliament, and sent envoys to negotiate for recall of the Purged Parliament as it existed in 1648.

By the end of November 1659, the country was restless, London itself becoming ungovernable. On 3 December, the officers of the Portsmouth garrison mutinied, took control of the town, and openly declared their support for Parliament. In an attempt to suppress this mutiny the Council of Officers sent a contingent of Hewson's regiment to quieten the situation. However the Portsmouth garrison was supported by ships of the navy which blockaded the Thames (cutting off London's vital winter coal supply). This added to the pressure on the military leaders, whose manifestly unlawful rule was being increasingly challenged. There were noisy demands for the recall of Parliament, and even for the free election of a new Parliament. Many hoped that a new Parliament might invite Charles to reclaim his throne.

It was the City of London which saw popular defiance of military rule. Elections for the City's Common Council had brought in young members bitterly opposed to army tyranny. The City's inhabitants turned increasingly against the troops, with repeated attacks on soldiers unwise enough to venture into its narrow streets. Led by the politically volatile apprentices, calling for a "free Parliament", rioting broke out in early December. On 5 December the mob drove out any soldiers it found, and barred the city's gates.

The army leaders determined to quell this uprising. That day, Colonel Hewson (returned from Ireland) ordered his regiment to break down the Temple Gate. He led his men into the City. Inflamed by this assault on their ancient privileges, the City's furious inhabitants hurled abuse, roof tiles, turnip tops and any noxious matter available, down onto the heads of the marching soldiers. One account explains:

> "All shops were shut, Hewson was hailed by cries of 'A cobbler, a cobbler', and any soldiers that straggled were disarmed and kicked by apprentices. Growing bolder, the lads kicked a football among the soldiers, and stoned them as the proclamation was read aloud. At last the soldiers' patience gave way and, apparently at Hewson's orders, they fired into the angry mob that confronted them. Some apprentices were killed, and more wounded by bullets or swords. At length the crowd dispersed. The soldiers stood on guard all night at the gates but were withdrawn the next day, perhaps after a deputation of aldermen and common councillors to the Committee of Safety had excused the riot and denied any share in it."[1]

The London Trained Bands (the City's own military force) had not attempted to quell the disorder, "but had been content, according to Pepys, to exchange sour looks with Hewson's men".[2]

As might be expected, Hewson was highly unpopular in London following the riot, and "Satires in verse and prose were heaped upon him: 'A Hymn to the Gentle Craft, or Hewson's Lamentation': 'The Outcry of the London Prentices for Justice upon Lord John Hewson,' and so on."[3] More seriously, a Coroner's Jury held that the army officers, particularly Hewson, were guilty of murder. The diary of Samuel Pepys records, in his entry for 8 December 1659,

> "The Coroner's inquest upon the death of those that were slain on Monday have given it as Murder and place it upon Colonel Huson, who gave his Soldiers order to fire. The Grand Jury at the Sessions this week in The Old Bailey desired of my Lord Mayor that the Soldiers might be moved out of the town, who answering that he knew not well with the Safety of the City how to do it, they offered in open Court to indict their officers and undertake to bring them before his Lordship ..."

Pepys was himself in Cornhill on 5 December, and had witnessed an apprentice killed – shot through the head.

The army leaders were now in an impossible situation. Serious military action against a recalcitrant City would make collection of taxes impossible, and without pay, the soldiers on whom they depended would simply melt away. In their desperation to restore order around London, the Grandees ordered General Lambert, still in Newcastle, to bring back his army. What they had not appreciated was that Lambert's regiments had voted with their boots, deserting in hundreds and thousands, mainly to join General Monck's army. Lambert returned to Whitehall with difficulty, not bringing an army, but almost as a fugitive.

Meanwhile Dublin had seen a dramatic coup. As recorded in the previous chapter, the radical Anabaptist faction, headed by Colonel Hewson and his three sons-in-law, now dominated the Army in Ireland, having dismissed those officers who had supported Henry Cromwell. However a group of Dublin politicians who supported the ousted Parliament, and a number of self-seeking Army officers, appreciated the opportunity presented by the paralysis of the Council of Officers in London, and the near certainty of General Monck moving his troops south to take control of the Kingdom.

At this time Colonel Hewson was in London, unable to influence events in Ireland. His Irish regiment was commanded by his lieuten-ant-colonel, Henry Jones, and Major John Bennett. The key to British rule in Ireland, Dublin Castle, was apparently secure in the hands of its garrison of Hewson's men.

At 5 pm on 13 December 1659, military power in Ireland was snatched from Colonel Hewson. In a surprise attack by foot soldiers led by a Captain Bond, the castle was seized in the name of Parliament. The coup was headed by Sir Theophilus Jones, supported by officers who backed Parliament against the military regime in London. The plotters successfully arrested Hewson's commanders, Henry Jones and Major Bennett. Simultaneously, Colonel Charles Coote, who had been appointed the military governor of Galway by Cromwell, cap-tured that town. Many of the leaders of the Army in Ireland, mostly supporters of Hewson, were in London; and it was not difficult for the Parliamentary party, largely old English Irish, to take control of the whole country.

The power of the Army leaders in London, the Grandees, was ebb-ing fast. All realised that, were Monck to march on London, he could not be resisted. On 23 December, the Council of Officers met, but quickly dispersed, intending to take individual actions to calm the situ-ation. They never reassembled.

We need now to return to the matter of Hewson's regiment in Ireland. Some time earlier, one Colonel Henry Markham had been appointed as its colonel. However he never crossed to Dublin to take up his command, which explains why Hewson remained in effective control. Henry Markham, in fact, was unable to come to Ireland, since in November he had been put in prison for delivering the letter from Monck to the Lord Mayor of London, which Lambert had denounced as a forgery. Released in December, a vengeful Markham, doubtless with the support of the junior officers, then helped to organise the fateful demonstration of the soldiery in Lincoln's Inn Fields on 24 December 1659, at which the regiments declared their return to obedi-ence to Parliament.

"On 24 December Hewson's regiment and the rest of the troops in

London submitted. Assembling in Lincoln's Inn Fields, they marched to Chancery Lane, and at the gate of the Roll's House the officers made their apologies to the Speaker...... 'owning him in words also ...... as their general and the father of their country'." (4) On that day Mr Speaker received back the key to Parliament House. Without their regiments the Grandees were nothing. Most returned to their homes, or left London.

Hastily reassembling, the first action of the Rump Parliament was to secure its own power by continuing the exclusion of those members purged in 1648. The Rump largely represented Presbyterian and individual interests and had no taste for sweeping reforms. Needless to say this selfish manoeuvre was badly received by the country, and the popular agitation for a new "free" Parliament intensified. The now triumphant members sought vengeance against their old enemies, the army leaders. Sir Arthur Hesilrige, the most powerful member, sought to protect the Grandees, but Parliament ordered those who had remained in London to leave, and threatened their arrest.

A wholesale purge of officers who had supported the Grandees followed. In the north, Monck dismissed those he found in the regiments that had marched to Newcastle under Lambert (and which now were under his command), whilst Parliament itself dealt with the southern regiments. In all, half of the more senior officers were forced out of the army, and a widespread reshuffle of commands destroyed any remaining cohesion in the demoralised English army.

Colonel Hewson's personal position was now serious. Were he to attempt to flee to Ireland, his enemies there would doubtless arrest him as soon as he set foot in that country. Furthermore this would inflame Parliament against him. In event Parliament treated him with leniency. As punishment for his support of the army's action against the Rump, and the charge of murder levied against him for the shootings during the Apprentice's Riot of 5 December, he was relieved of command of his regiment. However the Commons proceeded no further against him. A humbled Hewson wrote on 6 January, 1660, to thank the House "for their grace and favour in granting him his pardon".[5]

Command of his regiment in England was given to John Streeter, formerly Quarter-master General of the Foot in Ireland up to September, 1653. Hewson's lieutenant-colonel, John Dukenfield, was less fortunate, being cashiered. No doubt the Speaker remembered the incivility heaped upon him by Dukenfield's men during the army's coup just two months earlier!

The calculated emasculation of the army by Hesilrige and his Commons supporters proved a serious mistake. Emboldened, General Monck finally advanced south on New Year's Day, 1660. Though only a little over 5000 in number, his soldiers were veterans, sternly disciplined, backed by ample supplies, and marching on London.

In Ireland, the pro-Parliament officers, who in December had wrested control of Dublin from Hewson's radical Anabaptists, arrested the Government of the Grandees. They secured the support of officers drawn from the conservative minded "Old Protestants". These were the pre-civil war English settlers, headed by Lord Broghill. Once established in power, the coup leaders preferred to await on events in England.

This chapter has charted the ebb and flow of power between the army leaders and a self-seeking group of politicians, the Rump. It records the final acceptance by the soldiers of the supremacy of Parliament, and Parliament's actions rendering its own army virtually useless. England was open to Monck's advance.

This chapter closes as it started – with widespread speculation about the real intentions of General George Monck. As one Royalist commented in frustration, "He is the black Monk and I cannot see through him."

CHAPTER 15

"The Restoration"

The Speaker received the key to Parliament on 24 December 1659 from a despairing Fleetwood, though members did not re-assemble until two days later. The Commons promptly took public revenge against the now powerless army leaders. Most of the Grandees were summarily dismissed, including Lambert, Hewson, Disbrowe and Fairfax.

Claiming the necessity to restore law and order in London (and perhaps with an eye to their own protection), members voted to invite General Monck to accept appointment as the new Commander-in-Chief, and to move his army south. Monck had not needed this invitation – his regiments were marching by New Year's Day. To ensure the goodwill of the virtually leaderless troops around London (at least until the arrival of General Monck's disciplined army), the House promised early payment of one month's arrears, and voted through the necessary increased tax assessment.

Pursuing its own agenda, the Rump also voted to replace absent members, and declared its intention to establish a national church. Unfortunately members were totally inward looking, seemingly oblivious to the growing contempt of ordinary people, and the ever-insistent demand for a "free" Parliament. They failed to understand that they were as unpopular as the fallen swordsmen.

Towards mid-January 1660, Monck marched south from York; the winter snows testing the discipline and fortitude of his men. On the way, he sent word to the Parliamentary leaders that they should give orders for the existing London regiments to be dispersed around the country, freeing quarters for his men.

His army arrived in the capital on 2 February. Watching largely in silence, London's populace was surely awed by the formidable authority of Monck's marching columns. He himself rode in style, at the head of escorting lifeguards, making clear to all that he was his own man. Sir Arthur Hesilrige, and his fellow members, must have secretly questioned their own futures whilst watching this overt display of military force!

However, quelling any private apprehensions, members calmly instructed Monck to use his troops to suppress the continued agitation in the City for a "free" Parliament. He politely accepted their order, but held back from taking action. For some days he walked a tightrope, giving offence neither to the City nor Parliament, yet ensuring that his officers continued to support him. To demonstrate loyalty to the House, on 8 February, Monck instructed his soldiers to dismantle part of the City's Temple Gate. When he saw the degree of outrage this aroused, he reported back to the Speaker that he had done enough; and, significantly, called for the House to admit those members who had been excluded since Pride's purge in 1648. This was a critical move because the excluded members were drawn largely from the propertied and landowning classes, and opposed to radical constitutional or religious changes. Their number would take voting control of the House out of the hands of Hesilrige and his cronies. Since Monck's proposal was one of the demands of the City Fathers, this made clear to all his political direction.

Monck carefully allowed his officers to develop a conviction that the existing Commons was a self-serving tyranny and must go, whilst the sympathy of his rank and file went out to the people of London in their clamour for a "free" Parliament.

Seeing which way the wind was now blowing, Hesilrige declared London's Common Council dissolved, and attempted to rush through Parliament a bill sacking Monck as Commander-in-Chief.

On 11 February Monck made his decisive move. He and his senior commanders sent a joint letter to the Speaker protesting at Parliament's use of force against the citizens of London, and giving members six days to issue writs calling for a free national election. He made clear that the Rump must terminate its long existence.

Hesilrige was livid but impotent. London's population rejoiced that the end of the hated Rump was in sight. Monck and his troops were feted. Church bells rang, and that night the City's skyline was lit by bonfires. Pepys noted in his diary that he had counted thirty-one from his vantage point on a bridge over the Thames.

Though Monck had enforced his will on the Rump, allowing at least the appearance of seeking their co-operation, he had less sympathy for the now scattered Grandees. He had not forgotten that, only months earlier, they had sent Lambert with 12,000 men against him. Lambert was now in hiding, his immediate arrest was ordered.

Ten days later, Monck allowed the long excluded members to enter Parliament. Though only some seventy of the two hundred excluded by Hewson and Pride in 1648 took their seats, this was enough to out vote Hesilrige and his supporters. It will not be forgotten that the members originally excluded were those suspected of, or who had, sympathy with the late King Charles. With their return a whole new political climate was developing.

Under pressure from Monck, the restored Long Parliament issued writs for a new election, and finally dissolved itself on 16 March, 1660.

Everything hinged on Monck being able to keep the army united and supporting his political moves. He started breaking up regiments that might have favoured a return to republican ideas, and forbade his officers from meeting in military councils "to interpose in civil things".[1]

Although Monck had publicly pointed out earlier the divisiveness of an attempt to restore the Monarchy, it was evident now that this would find backing in all levels of society. By early March, Monck had entered into secret negotiations with Charles II and his advisors in the Spanish Netherlands, to establish the terms under which the King might return.

The long awaited election of a new Parliament stirred intense public interest. Though Royalists were officially barred from standing, it is remarkable that some sixty were successfully elected. Some of the old republican notables stood, like Lambert from his cell in the Tower of London, but fared disastrously. In general there was widespread rejection of candidates with Independent or Commonwealth opinions. When the new Parliament, the so-called Convention Parliament, met on 25 April 1660, there was no doubt that members enthusiastically supported the popular demand for the return of the King.

Die-hard Republicans, and old soldiers clinging to dreams of the "good old cause", made a final effort to stem the tide. Attempts were made to undermine the loyalty of the army by the dissemination of pamphlets written to fill the soldiers with fears of a return to Kingship. The flashpoint came on 10 April when the extremist Lambert escaped from the Tower, and called to arms all true republicans. His old comrades, Fleetwood, Disbrowe, and most of the former army grandees were cautious not to become involved. Nevertheless his appeal found an answer. Troops from at least six regiments of horse joined him, and risings in support were reported in over nine counties.

It was not enough. Without the backing of the ordinary people, there was no way Lambert could be successful. On 22 April his scratch rebel army was confronted near Daventry by Government troops from London. This force was made up of 500 foot soldiers from Hewson's former regiment (which had been given to John Streeter), with some ancillary horse. Lambert's men refused to fight old comrades, and scattered. He was recaptured attempting to escape when his mount became mired in a sodden field. His second-in-command, Colonel Daniel Axtell, was also taken. Mopping up of the remaining bands of republicans followed; the rebellion was effectively put down within days.

Hewson was suspected of complicity with Lambert, perhaps because of his long association with Axtell. In a proclamation issued by the Council of State on 21 April, Hewson (and other leading republican officers), were required to surrender themselves to the Council at Whitehall. Hewson protested to Monck that he now lived privately, and held converse with none, so as to avoid all jealousy, and also that he was very lame of the gout.[2]

In affairs of state, events were moving fast. Charles, anxious to take advantage of the popular call for his return, willingly accepted the terms proposed by Monck. The formal acceptance document, now known as the Declaration of Breda, was presented to the Commons and the recalled Lords, on 1 May, 1660. With enthusiasm, both Houses voted on the following day to bring back the Monarchy. The army had, eleven years before, executed the King; now it had enabled his son's return to the throne. The nation celebrated, church bells rang, bonfires lit the night skies, and the people drank to the health of their King.

Charles II was proclaimed King on 8 May 1660. Hewson anticipated that Parliament would attempt to ingratiate itself with the monarch and, like several of those responsible for the execution of the new King's father, deemed it wise to leave England. On the 14 May, the Commons resolved "that all those persons who sat in judgment upon the late King's Majesty when the sentence was pronounced for his condemnation be forthwith secured".[3] On the 17th the House voted for the seizure of the estates of those regicides who had fled instead of allowing themselves to be arrested. On the same day, a vote for closing all the ports to prevent their escape was also passed.

By then, however, Hewson was probably already in Amsterdam.[4] Certainly on the 21st the Commons was informed of Hewson's escape from the country.

The authorities in Ireland followed suit. A report from Dublin in the *Mercurius Publicus*, May 31–June 7, advised: "the commissioners for the Government have ordered the estates of ... Colonel Axtell, ...Colonel Hewson, and Colonel John Jones, to be sequestered".[5]

His Majesty landed at Dover on 25 May 1660 to claim his kingdom. It was a bright sunny morning – the clouds of intolerant puritan rule had lifted for ever.

CHAPTER 16

"The various deaths of Colonel Hewson"

Having made his escape from England early in May, 1660, to the temporary safety of Amsterdam, Colonel John Hewson must have reflected on the events of the past half-year with something akin to horror.

It was only in the previous October that Hewson had been a member of the Kingdom's ruling body, the military led Committee of Safety. In Ireland, as Commander-in-Chief of the Foot, with eleven regiments under his orders, he was the most powerful army leader. The centre of British domination of Ireland, Dublin Castle, was his. Financially he was well provided for – he drew pay as Colonel of his English regiment, the pay of his Irish rank (roughly equivalent to Major-General), plus pay as Colonel of his Irish Regiment (since Henry Markham had not assumed command). In addition he received rents from the valuable Luttrellstown estate, from lands to the south of Dublin, and doubtless other properties. We do not have information concerning his residence in England, nor the extent of the dowry brought in by his second wife.

Seven months later Hewson was a fugitive in a foreign land. Concealment was not easy. Even if he could speak Dutch, his English accent would be immediately apparent. Walking abroad, his heavy build, and patch over his lost left eye, made him a distinctive figure. In his haste to leave, Hewson would not have had the time to realise his investments, and must have been beset by financial problems from the outset. Compounding this, evidence suggests that his health was poor, which would necessitate unwelcome physicians' bills. Even if he could contact his wife, or friends in England, the transfer of funds might be traced by Government agents. And who could he trust? His capture would indeed be well rewarded.

In the months following the restoration of Charles II, his government sought to inflict retribution on his father's executioners. Three colonels of the New Model Army suffered death on the scaffold, and a gibbet was erected in London's Cheapside with Hewson's name on it. This may have misled both Pepys and Evelyn to assume that he too had been taken. In fact, Colonel Hewson remained in hiding in Amsterdam.[1]

Sir George Downing, envoy extraordinary for the King in Holland, was hunting down the regicides. He reported to the government in England, by letter dated 15 July 1661, "I hear that Okey and some others of them are in Strasbourg, and have purchased their freedom there publicly; and that Hewson is sick, but intends thither also with one or two more by the first occasion."[2]

Possibly Colonel Hewson never did recover – Wood asserts that he died in Amsterdam the following year.[3] Noble agrees, whilst Granger refers to his death "in obscurity" in Amsterdam.[4]

It is interesting that in "The King's Revenge", based on recent research, the authors, Don Jordan and Michael Walsh, assert that Hewson had died in early September 1661 and in Rotterdam, rather than Amsterdam.

Downing was working with a Scot, Sir William Davidson, a committed Royalist merchant trading in Amsterdam. Davidson tried to serve writs on "Dendy and two more of them", but without success, as the fugitives continually kept on the move. An article about Downing explains his difficulties:

> "Davidson seemed to despair of success, and since they could not take any of the living, he suggested that they might avenge themselves on the dead. Hewson had died recently at Amsterdam, and the Scot thought it would be some satisfaction to tear his body out of its grave and dispatch it for England. Downing thought this ghoulish suggestion worthy to be transmitted to Clarendon

(a leading member of the government in London), and asked for his "Lordship's mind" as to it. Clarendon could hardly have had any objection to the desecration of Hewson's grave and the mutilation of his remains, but to secure these objects would have been expensive and might have caused trouble with Holland. Apparently he had nothing to say in answer to the suggestion, or if he made any response it must have been unfavourable."[5]

It is possible that had Davison proceeded with his suggestion, he would have opened an empty coffin. Hewson may well have fabricated his own death in a desperate attempt to throw the king's agents off his trail.

The subsequent references to Colonel Hewson centre on Rouen, in Normandy. On the face of it, it seems so unlikely that he would seek refuge there that his pursuers probably did not even consider this possibility. The dangers of Rouen were obvious. It was on the popular route to Paris via Southampton and carried the risk of recognition by English travellers. Worse, France did not offer the security of a Protestant regime. As C. H. Firth has noted, "The danger which republican exiles incurred in France was very considerable. In January 1663, Johnston of Warriston was seized at Rouen, and lodged at Dieppe Castle, whence he was transported to England for trial. In May 1663 he was shipped to Scotland, where he was tried and condemned to death."[6]

The apprehension of Archibald Johnston must have been an unpleasant shock for Colonel Hewson. It is not inconceivable that he had made his way to Rouen, rather than to Strasbourg, at Johnston's invitation. They were known to each other, both had sat in Cromwell's Upper House, and Hewson had been a member of the Committee of Safety, of which Johnston appears to have been permanent president. Perhaps the men were friends. Both were fiercely opposed to the idea of kingship, and both shared a vision of life rooted in Old Testament values. At all events, Hewson seems to have remained, since there was a report that he "died of starvation at Rouen in 1664".[7]

It is evident that the English authorities had not accepted the story of Hewson's death in Amsterdam in 1662 and were still looking for him. In March 1666 a wandering tobacco-seller, who had been arrested in England in the belief that he was Hewson, claimed that he was in Rouen when Hewson died there.[8] One can only wonder what suspicions prompted the tobacco-seller's arrest, and why his odd explanation was accepted.

There remains an area for speculation. A set of playing cards issued about 1675 showed "C. Hewson" on the Knave of Clubs.[9] This might have been the name of the card maker (following French practice), or a jibe against "Cobbler Hewson", derived from the satirical pamphlet *Walk, Knaves, Walk*. Evidence suggests that the cards were not produced in England. Rouen was one of the two places of card manufacture in France at the time. Clearly the full story of Hewson's death remains to be told.

CHAPTER 17

"The man himself"

And what of the man himself?

We have a good idea of how he looked. A contemporary painting, now lost, was reproduced in engravings made in the 1740s, one
of which is held in the National Portrait Gallery in London. Others
remain in private hands.

The painting was a formal study of Colonel Hewson, clearly
intended to celebrate his successful martial career. It depicts a heavily built man, indeed with impressive girth. His face is not unattrac-
tive, eyes set well apart, and with a leader's aquiline nose. His face is
turned so that the left, blinded, eye is partly hidden. The mouth is tight,
almost bitter. Delicately trimmed stubble, and a pencil thin moustache,
add an appearance of some authority. He has a high, unfurrowed brow
suggesting character and intelligence. His hair is long and fashionably curled. The pose is that of a man confidently the master of all he
surveys.

In contrast, an unflattering cartoon drawing, perhaps expressing
the popular fury at the shooting down of the London apprentices in
December 1659, shows a furtive weaselly figure, with eyepatch and
flamboyant moustache. His left hand holds a heavy sword of more
heraldic than effective design, presumably to make the point that crude
military force, rather than personal distinction, had given Hewson his
position. Both illustrations show his blinded eye. The circumstances
of its loss during military operations in Ireland are unknown, though it
has been suggested that the injury was sustained in early 1650, during

the seige of Kilkenny. No direct evidence has been brought forward, but Hewson's urgent return to Dublin following the city's surrender might be explained by a need for specialist medical attention.

The portrait correctly conveys Hewson's aggressive self confidence. He was always ready to speak his mind, even when unwelcome. An example was his championing of the claims of the common soldiers against the wishes of the senior officers during the 1647 army unrest. Perhaps more risky personally was his blunt advice to Cromwell, then the Lord Protector, to reject Parliament's pressing offer of the Crown.

He could look after himself. One recalls his famous encounter with the notorious highwayman, John Cottingham (who was better known as Mulsack). The tale is that Cottingham and his accomplice, Tom Cheyney, set on Colonel Hewson as he was riding through Hounslow Heath, apparently alone. They were not to know that his regiment was following close behind. Hewson defied them. He defended himself until some of the leading troopers, seeing what was going on, came galloping to his support. Cottingham, having a good horse, escaped; but after a stiff fight, the surrounded Cheyney was captured.

Indeed Hewson's bravery cannot be questioned. Time and time again he led his men to success in the face of the hottest enemy fire. His conduct in leading the forlorn hope against the walls of Bridgwater Town, his part in the halting of the fleering parliamentary ranks at Naseby, leading them back into the fray, and his unstoppable onrush in the savage hand to hand fighting at Maidstone in 1648, are but better known examples.

Perhaps, like Cromwell, he was fired by the conviction that he was fighting the battles of the Lord; and he would prevail. Certainly his sermons and letters reveal an Old Testament certainty that those who opposed him represented the powers of Evil. Naturally this applied to Irish Papists, who deserved to be put to the sword.

When first we hear of John Hewson, in the late 1630s, he was known in the City as a fiery preacher. He held a religious and political outlook which rejected state regulation of worship. In particular he denounced Presbyterianism. Such Independents claimed the right to hold autonomous meetings, and advocated freedom of choice and individual belief. Politically they wished to abolish Kingship, a notion understandably unpopular with the authorities.

Hewson endeavoured to impose his violent and extreme opinions on all he could: in Chapter 3 the incidents at Steeple Aston are mentioned, including the Sunday when his troops took over the village church, and Hewson "occupied the pulpit both morning and afternoon, proving in his sermon the lawful minister of the parish to be Antichrist by thirteen marks of a false prophet".[1] In Drogheda, in 1649, he is reputed to have preached for hours on end.

Appointed the Military Governor of Dublin in September 1649, Hewson attended services at Christ Church, the cathedral church of the Holy Trinity. It appears that these were often led by the Independent pastor, Samuel Winter. However around 1651 Winter was displaced by John Rogers, who quickly gained influence over Hewson and his wife, Anne. John Rogers has been described as "a man of considerable learning, but of violent prejudices". It is reported that Rogers accompanied Hewson on military expeditions, perhaps as Chaplin to the troops.[2] Following the military conquest of Ireland there was a great need for Protestant clergy to convert the Catholic native population. Representatives of many sects followed the army from England. Particularly influential in Ireland was Thomas Patient, a "Particular" Baptist. These believed that Christ died only to save the elect. Patient had originally belonged to the Church of England but had become a Baptist while in New England, "... He arrived in Ireland in 1650 and after preaching in both Kilkenny and Waterford managed to win over to his side the governors of both cities, Daniel Axtell and Richard Lawrence respectively."[3] "Though few in number, Baptist ministers entered in controversy with the other Protestant sects, especially the Independents. For instance Patient's congregation in Waterford challenged the open communion practised in Dublin by John Roger's flock, finding them 'guilty of their sin of disobedience.' As a result of the ensuing argument Roger's congregation was dissolved, while Patient became one of the preachers at Christ Church..."[4]

This doctrinal dispute resulted in a political division in the English administration in Dublin. The ousted Rogers, and his supporters, formed a new congregation in St Nicholas' church, drawing in most of the civil officials, and English traders. Colonel Hewson stayed at Christ Church and became closely associated with the Baptists, but was never called an Anabaptist by those who used the term correctly.[5] However his three sons-in-law were so described.

It may be that the passing years dimmed the fire of his religious extremism, or political considerations supervened, but by the time of the Barebone's Parliament (1653), Hewson was firmly in the moderate camp. Professor Woolwrych writes, "...but his religious stance in Barebone's Parliament is interesting. He belonged to the congregation in Dublin which from 1650 to 1652 had for its pastor John Rogers, who became notorious during 1653 as a Fifth Monarchy man. Hewson, though not a Baptist himself, was later strongly identified with the 'Anabaptist' faction in Ireland which was to be such a thorn in the side of Henry Cromwell, while Lord Lieutenant of Ireland."

It is incontestable that there was a deeply repulsive side to Colonel Hewson. His almost gleeful order to hang a mutinous soldier far higher than was required attracted comment even from his hardly squeamish fellow officers, while his part in the burning to death of dozens of helpless Irish soldiers in the conflagration at St Peter's church in Drogheda, suggests a positive streak of cruelty. He played a major part (perhaps the leading role) in forcing thousands of Irish men, women and children, from their homes, to perish of cold and starvation in the stony wastelands of Connaught. The deliberate infliction of such suffering has left an indelible stain on the English reputation in Ireland. The "Cromwellian transplantation" has never been forgotten.

Furthermore it does appear that Colonel Hewson was unashamedly ambitious. Examination of the events of 1647 shows that he was a leader in the agitation for soldier's rights. Yet within six months he was repressing military unrest, and was firmly on the side of the senior officers – which, of course, advanced his career.

In money matters he seems to have been tight fisted. During a period (October 1648) of acute delay in payment of the troops, many regimental officers paid the men from their own pockets. Hewson did not and his desperate soldiers were forced almost into brigandage for survival. It is possible, of course, that Hewson himself was in financial difficulty. Certainly he petitioned Cromwell for settlement of his personal arrears of military pay, claiming that he urgently needed money to settle his medical bills. Once he received a generous settlement his financial affairs turned the corner and he became well off. It seems probable that, during the late 1650s, Hewson (like other senior officers in Ireland) was engaged in buying, at well below their true value, the entitlements to land which his men received in lieu of actual pay. By taking advantage of their need for ready money he was able to acquire legal rights to large tracts of Irish land. These he was able to transfer into the nominal ownership of members of his family, or into the names of trustees. Such lands were not forfeited to the Crown following the Restoration in the 1660s and, certainly in Co Leitrim, remained in the hands of his descendants until the early 20th century. An American family of Hewson's claims that lands near Roscrea in Co Tipperary were also originally owned by Colonel Hewson.

Though Hewson's family probably came originally from Kentish land owners, his father was a London shoemaker. Hewson carried on the business and apparently owned a shop in Tothill Street, in Westminster. Perhaps members of the Royal Court, and politicians, were clients. The business, far from being that of a poor cobbler, as depicted by his detractors, was a fairly large scale manufacturing concern – it is recorded that he won a contract to supply shoes to the Parliamentary army.

Hewson lacked a university or legal education, nor could he claim the social advantage of being landed gentry. Some aristocrats looked down on him; when Cromwell's "House of Lords" first met in January 1658, the Earl of Warwick... "would not be persuaded to sit with Colonel Hewson and Colonel Pride"[6]

Hewson's manner was at times extraordinarily rude. In his participation in the religious discussion at Oxford on 12 November 1646 he was described as "a most categorical disputant, yet so rude. We wondered [at] so much true logic and false English..."[7] It appears that so offensive was Hewson that the Oxford divines refused to continue the debate!

Hewson took a particular dislike to Henry Cromwell (son of the Protector); perhaps he resented a youngster being placed over the heads of experienced officers who had secured Ireland for Parliament. In 1655 Hewson went behind Henry's back and wrote directly to Oliver Cromwell, belittling him... "His Lordship [Henry] is young and to be pitied". In the spring of 1656 Hewson returned to London and there continued his spiteful campaign against Henry "by disseminating the report that the Independents as well as the Baptists in Ireland were dissatisfied with him"[8] This damaging accusation was untrue, and Hewson knew this.

Hewson attempted to hurt Henry later in the year by spreading slanderous accusations against one Dr Harrison, who was Henry Cromwell's chaplain in Dublin, preaching at Christ Church. Dr Harrison, visiting London, wrote to his patron on 5 August 1656 that someone... "had the malice to tell my Lord Deputy that I was married to my maid and that not before there was neede". On 12 August, Dr Harrison wrote again to Henry Cromwell complaining of his enemies' calumnies... "Even officers of the army are made to solicit H H against my returne. Col Hewson hath attempted to vilify me to some of our church but hath not prevailed". It seems that Hewson mollified Harrison, blaming others for the malicious rumours.[9]

The foregoing paragraphs present an unfavourable picture of Colonel Hewson. It is difficult indeed to find any unselfish or generous actions. One possible example that comes to mind might be his order in 1654 or 1655, as Governor of Dublin, that all Catholic priests in the city's prisons "...as are not under suspicion of murder..." should be released for transportation to Spain.[10] Another might be his considerate offer, following Pride's Purge of the Commons in December 1648, to release sick or elderly Members under arrest, to find more comfortable overnight accommodation, on their promise to surrender themselves at his lodgings in Whitehall by 9 o'clock the following morning.

Perhaps Colonel Hewson had the best insight of all, when he described himself as a "… child of wrath".

CHAPTER 18

"Family, Friends and Enemies"

We do not know for certain when John Hewson was born, but 1599 might not be too wide of the mark. This statement is based on the recently published, "The King's Revenge", by Jordan and Walsh, which mentions that Hewson was sixty years old when he ordered his soldiers to fire on the rioting London apprentices in December, 1659. Interestingly, the Record of Members held in the archives of Parliament shows John Hewson to have been born in 1620, and dying in 1668. The first date is certainly incorrect and the second highly unlikely. According to research by Robert Temple, his father was also called John, his mother Margery.[1] The family seems originally to have been connected with the Husons of Tenterden, in the county of Kent.[2] And, certainly, Hewson regarded himself as being of gentle stock.

The Tenterden connection has recently been confirmed by the discovery that the coat of arms engraved on his first wife's memorial stone in Christchurch Cathdral, Dublin, is virtually identical to the Huson arms on an 18th Century gravestone in Tenterden parish churchyard (343 in Section D).

Whether John Hewson was the only son is not known. The records of the Cordwainers [leather workers] Company in the City of London, in the 1640s, in addition to John Hewson, show also a Symon Hewson, both of Bell Yard. Symon may have been a brother, or an uncle.

John Hewson's social standing was recognised by his immediate commission as captain in the Earl of Essex's Regiment of Foot, when it was raised in 1642. And also by his marriage to Anne Turner, daughter of an ancient Kentish family. Her brother, Captain Edward Turner, in later years served under his brother-in-law, commanding a company in Hewsons's Regiment.

John Hewson married Anne, presumably in Kent, in the 1620s or early 1630s, though no record of his marriage licence has been found. This may well be due to the family's opposition to the official church. The marriage was blessed with three daughters and at least one son. Agnes became the second wife of Colonel Richard Lawrence, an active and intelligent officer in the Parliamentary army, and one who played a leading role in the Cromwellian settlement in Ireland. The other two daughters also married well, one to Dr Philip Carteret, Advocate-General to the Army in Ireland, and the other to Colonel John Jones, who was prominent in Irish affairs in the 1650s. All three of Colonel John Hewson's sons-in-law were aggressive Anabaptists. With him, they headed a radical religious and political faction in Dublin.

Hewson's wife, Anne, died not long after joining him in Dublin, where he was Military Governor. Following an official funeral service at the city's Christchurch Cathedral on 15 January 1652, she was buried in the cathedral crypt. He was not long a widower. While attending Parliament in London during the winter of the 1653–4, Colonel Hewson remarried. In June 1654 he brought his new bride to live in magnificent Luttrelstown Castle, which he had accepted in lieu of part of his arrears of army pay.

When Colonel Hewson sailed for Ireland in 1649 with Cromwell's invading army, he left his family in England. Some six months later, his regiment included a Captain Hewson. On 1 March 1650 Colonel Hewson wrote to the Governor of the Irish held fortress of Ballysonan, which he was besieging, offering to send Captain Hewson to negotiate terms for surrender.[3] What is not clear is whether this Captain Hewson is Captain Geoffrey Hughson, "who was commissioned into the Middlesex Militia" on 20 November 1650. Robert Temple suggests that Geoffrey might be Hewson's eldest son[4] (which implies that there were others).

A Captain Hewson, most likely the same, played a part in Cromwell's dramatic expulsion of the Rump on 20 April 1653. As a contemporary Royalist newsletter describes the event, "Cromwell called the Members a company of oppressive perfidious fellows; ... and Captain Hewson enforced the unwilling Speaker to leave his beloved chair and mace."[5] Another account mentions Captain Hewson as actually taking the Speaker by the arm, and forcefully leading him down from his seat.[6] At the same time, Cromwell famously commanded one of the other soldiers to "take away that bauble", indicating the mace.

As described in Chapter 16, in 1660 Colonel Hewson went into hiding on the Continent, leaving his wife and children in England and Ireland. In his book, *Lives of the English Regicides*, published in 1798, the Reverend Mark Noble concludes his chapter on Hewson, "what became of his family is unknown; the posterity of these men so highly guilty having ever been ashamed of owning from whom they descend."[7] Until the nineteenth century, the Regicides had been condemned as despicable traitors, only since then did the Parliamentary challenge to Royal absolutism become respectable. No wonder that Hewson's descendants remained in obscurity.

Today at least five families claim him as their ancestor, two with the tradition that their farming lands in Ireland were originally owned by him. One family had a farm in Co. Leitrim, at least until the 1920s, when it was burnt out during the "troubles". The other had lands near Roscrea, Co. Tipperary. Neither family has succeeded in establishing a conclusive genealogical link.

According to details posted on the internet, a Norfolk family of Husons claims descent from Colonel Hewson, though details are not given. In support, the family possessed a silver tankard inscribed with his name spelled Hewson.

Again the line of descent has not been established, but it may well be that a revolutionary hero of the American War of Independence, John Hewson, was also descended from Colonel Hewson. He was born in 1744, son of Peter Hewson, a London woollen draper. Peter claimed Colonel Hewson was his ancestor. Also related to this family was Dr William Hewson, a famous London surgeon in the 1770s.

Colonel Hewson had numerous acquaintances, but as far as can be ascertained, few real friends. One can only assume that this was his choice. Perhaps his longest relationship was with his fellow radical London preacher in the 1630s, Hugh Peters. Their paths crossed repeatedly.

Peters was born in Cornwall in 1598. He took an MA at Trinity College, Cambridge, which enabled him to obtain a ministry in London. Here he became a leading Puritan preacher, well known to the Winthrop family, and undoubtedly to the fiery young John Hewson, who also knew the Winthrops. Peters has been described as plump, red faced, excitable and coarse – earning the nickname "Jack Pudding". His invectives against the established church incurred the wrath of the Bishop of London. Peters avoided trouble by leaving for Holland, where in 1629 he was appointed preacher to the English community in Rotterdam. Even here his outspoken comments created bad feeling; in 1635 he sought freedom in New England. He renewed his acquaintance with John Winthrop, and was elected as the minister for Salem. Peters soon rose to be a leading member of the Colony's elite. In 1641 he was sent to England by the Boston authorities as one of their representatives in London. He quickly became involved in public affairs, playing a leading part in bringing down Archbishop Laud.

Peters was a passionate and earthy speaker, who became the outstanding military chaplain in the New Model Army. His pre-battle addresses to the massed ranks of Cromwell's soldiers must have contributed mightily to the victories at Naseby, Bridgewater, and the storming of Basing House, Hewson fought in these engagements, and Peter's exhortations "to smite the enemies of the Lord" surely resonated with his own deeply held Old Testament sentiments.

Hewson and Peters took part In the 1647 Putney debates, both taking the side of the Grandees. Unfortunately for Peters, he (like Hewson) was prominent in the trial of King Charles, apparently leading the outcry "Execution! Execution!" This outrageous behaviour rendered him intensely unpopular with moderate opinion, as well as with Royalists. One way and another he made numerous enemies.

Hewson and Peters were thrown together again during the 1649 invasion of Ireland, when both worked closely with Cromwell.

Peters soon returned to England, and in 1650 was appointed preacher at Whitehall. He became influential in Government, won the confidence of Cromwell, and was made a member of the Commons' law reform committee. For some years he was at the heart of events, but increasing ill health limited his activities.

Following General Monck's arrival in London in 1660, Peters fell from favour. After the Restoration in May of that year, Peters was hunted down as a regicide, and arrested. Though he managed to prove that he was not present at Charles' beheading, his conduct at the trial deemed him to be a traitor. Peters was executed at Charing Cross on 16 October 1660.

Another acquaintance of Hewson's youth was Thomas Hewson, presumably a relative, possibly an uncle. Thomas was a Puritan, an established clothier, and, not uncommon in those days, often browbeat and insulted his employees. One of his apprentices was Lilburne, who deeply resented this treatment. He took the very unusual course of bringing an action against his master in the Court of the Lord High Chamberlain. Thomas Hewson could respect a young man who stood up for his rights: the dispute was settled amicably. Within a few years Lilburne was acting as Thomas Hewson's ally in the Puritan agitation against the overweening power of the Bishops of the established church. Both were present when, in 1637, the ears of John Bastwick and William Prynne were cut off by order of the Court of Star Chamber. Whether John Hewson was also in the angry crowd gathered around the pillory, is not recorded.

Colonel Hewson certainly had a close relationship, in his last few years, with the Scottish lawyer, Archibald Johnston, Lord Warriston. Johnston was born in Edinburgh in 1611, and called to the Edinburgh Bar in 1633. He was active in the resistance of 1637 to the introduction to Scotland of the Book of Common Prayer. Subsequently he took part in the Berwick negotiations of 1639. Apparently he addressed King Charles I with "outspoken bluntness", and refused to hold his tongue. However Charles found it necessary to attempt to placate the Covenanters, and created Johnston a Judge of the Scottish Court of Session, with the title Lord Warriston. Warriston led the negotiations in 1647, which resulted in the Scots army handing over the King to the English Parliament in return for money. Warriston joined Charles II at Perth after the Dunbar defeat of 3 September 1650, and loudly blamed the young King's immorality for the disaster. Charles was greatly offended, and developed a personal hatred of Warriston.

Sometime in the 1650s, Warriston moved to London, and took his seat in Cromwell's House of Lords. Possibly it was here that he first met Colonel John Hewson. Following the dispersal of the Rump Parliament at the end of 1659, Lambert set up the Committee of Safety, of which Warriston became Permanent President. As Hewson was also a member, the two men worked together. They seemed kindred spirits, both hated Kingship, and both took their inspiration from the Old Testament.

Following the Restoration in 1660, Charles II ordered the apprehension of Warriston. The King had not forgotten nor forgiven his humiliation at Perth. Warriston escaped to Holland. But this was too dangerous, and he moved to Hamburg. For some reason he left there in the spring of 1661, and took refuge in Bolbeck, near Le Havre. Riddle suggests that someone had recognised him in Hamburg. Warriston lived at Bolbeck in complete secrecy for nearly two years. "But in the Spring of 1663, his wife joined him at Rouen. She was followed by an English government agent, who seized Warriston while he was at his prayers, and took him to the French authorities and demanded his extradition to England."[8] "The magistrates in Rouen imprisoned Warriston and referred the matter to the King's Council in Paris."[8] The Council decided to refuse the request for extradition, but was overruled by Louis XIV, who ordered Warriston to be handed over. Warriston was shipped to England. Subsequently he was transferred to Edinburgh, where he was put to death. It is quite possible that Colonel Hewson had been with Warriston in Rouen; if so, Warriston's arrest must have been an unpleasant reminder of how precarious was his own situation. Though he might have considered seeking refuge in a safe Protestant country, the probability is that ill health, or lack of funds, prevented his so doing.

Hewson's political career owed much to his friendship with Henry Walker – scathingly known as "Pious Harvey" for his biblical utterances. Walker was the publisher of the successful London broadsheet *Perfect Occurrences*, and while Hewson was serving in Ireland, the two kept up a regular correspondence. First-hand accounts of Cromwell's campaign sent by Hewson appeared in *Perfect Occurrences*, and would have been eagerly read and discussed in London's taverns and coffee houses. Besides boosting sales of the newspaper, the letters brought Colonel Hewson's name to public notice. Most important was Hewson's letter, giving his version of the storming of Drogheda, published in *Perfect Occurrences* on Friday, 5 October 1649.

At the time of the beheading of Charles I, at the end of January 1649, wild rumours swirled around London that one of the two disguised executioners was Henry Walker. Almost certainly this was untrue.

It is said that a man may be known by the company he keeps – the reader may draw his own conclusions from Hewson's friends. Equally revealing are his enemies.

Best known was Henry Cromwell, born in 1628, and the fourth son of Oliver Cromwell. Henry served under his father in the Irish Campaign of 1649 and 1650, and there may well have encountered Colonel Hewson. He became a member of Cromwell's "Barebone's" Parliament of 1653. Following the dissolution of this Parliament at the end of the year, his father sent him to Dublin to discover the attitude of the officers of the Army in Ireland, and to counteract the influence of the Anabaptist faction. This was in March 1654, and presumably resulted from Secretary Thurloe's warnings to Oliver Cromwell that Hewson was disaffected, and suspicious of Cromwell taking the throne. Thurloe reported that Colonel Thomas Pride and Hewson had threatened to raise forces against Cromwell should he try to make himself King. Hewson would have quickly guessed the reason for Henry

Cromwell's arrival in Ireland, and resentment was understandable. Henry reported to London that the Lord Deputy of Ireland, Fleetwood, was deeply involved with Hewson and the Anabaptists, and recommended Fleetwood's recall to England.

In September 1655 Fleetwood left Ireland, though he retained his formal title of Lord Deputy. Authority passed to Henry Cromwell, who was appointed Commander-in-Chief of the Army in Ireland. Henry supported Colonel Hewson in the work of exiling Irish land owners to Connaught, and seizing their properties for the use of the Government, but strengthened his own position by establishing good relations with the substantial body of Protestant land owners loyal to Parliament, and with the mercantile class. The Anabaptist faction felt their grip on Government threatened by Henry's policies, and tried to undermine his position, sending unfavourable reports about Henry to London.

The differences between Henry Cromwell, and the Anabaptist faction headed by Hewson, came to a head in November and December, 1655.

> "While some of the English officers in Ireland had welcomed the change in the actual command, others, particularly Fleetwood's friends, the Anabaptists had taken offence at the stronger hand of the new young Commander-in-Chief, whom they insultingly nicknamed Absalom, and regretted the easy-going times under Fleetwood – easy-going for them, not for the Irish! One of these Anabaptist Officers, Colonel John Hewson, organised a petition to the Protector begging for the return of Fleetwood and his 'sweet healing peaceable spirit'."[9]

As might be expected, Oliver Cromwell rejected this suggestion, and publicly endorsed his son in November, 1657, giving him Fleetwood's formal position of Lord Deputy.

That this rebuff only fuelled Hewson's resentment against Henry Cromwell perhaps explains the shameful accusation he made against Dr Harrison, Henry's chaplain. This is mentioned in the previous chapter.

Following Oliver Cromwell's death on 3 September 1658, Henry continued governing Ireland until his recall to England by Parliament in 1659. He played no further part in public affairs: retiring to his home in Cambridgeshire.

An enemy of Colonel Hewson, far more dangerous, was George Downing. He was a member of the influential Winthrop clan, and a nephew of John Winthrop, who was well regarded in London's Puritan community, and who later became Governor of the Mayflower Colony of Massachusetts. At his uncle's invitation, young Downing joined the Salem settlers (whose preacher was Hugh Peters). He entered the newly established Harvard College, and was its second graduate. Downing returned to England in 1645, as the First Civil War was coming to an end.

George Downing entered politics, and became a Member of Parliament. He supported Oliver Cromwell, and was a signatory to the Death Warrant of Charles I, executed in 1649. Cromwell rewarded Downing in 1650 by commissioning him as Scoutmaster-General of his Scottish Army. Nevertheless Downing favoured the traditional form of government, and headed a movement in the Commons to offer the crown to Cromwell. Cromwell trusted Downing; recognising his ability, he employed him as his personal emissary in foreign affairs.

In 1657 Cromwell appointed him as his representative in the Hague. In April 1660, aware of the inevitability of Charles II taking the throne, Downing sought to make his peace with the new King. He secured his own safety by agreeing to track down and betray fellow regicides, personally planning the entrapment and arrest of Colonels Okey and Barkstead, and Miles Corbett, at Delft. The three were transported to England and executed.

George Downing was despised by his contemporaries – accused of servility, avarice and treachery. He was particularly anxious to secure Colonel Hewson, whom he knew had made his escape to Holland. He failed to do so, and believed that Hewson had evaded him by death. Hewson's reported funeral in Amsterdam in 1662 might well have been a charade designed to convince Downing. Even so, he remained a threat, and this might explain Hewson's seeking refuge in Rouen.

Hewson and Downing would, of course, have known each other, not only through the John Winthrop connection, but also for their parts in the trial of Charles I.

Whilst Henry Cromwell and Sir George Downing were the most prominent of Hewson's enemies, it must be said that many more, particularly in the City of London, and in Ireland, would have cursed his name.

CHAPTER 19

"Arms and the Man"

In the seventeenth century, anyone with social aspirations sought his own arms. Actually this was a practical status symbol. Legal documents, particularly property deeds, in addition to signature, normally needed authentication by wax seals impressed with the deponent's arms, or monogram.

In the case of Colonel John Hewson, we have knowledge of the arms he used from his seal, since this appears on the 1649 Death Warrant of King Charles I. These are described by Temple as being horses/chevrons.[1] Apparently the same seal was used in an original document of 1647 held in the British Library. Temple is supported by Noble, writing in 1798.

The problem is that these arms differ from those of the Husons of Tenterden, Kent. According to Burke, the Huson arms are "Quarterly, gu and erm., an eagle displayed or.". Their crest was "a ram's head erased ar. Horned or".[2]

However, by 1652, Hewson was claiming the Huson arms. The memorial arms of his wife, buried on the 15 January that year in Christ Church Cathedral in Dublin, have been recorded as "Quarterly, gu. and erm. an eagle displ. or, in the dexter chief quarter a lion pass. ar". To explain – "displ." means displayed, i.e. wings spread; the "dexter chief quarter" is also known as the first quarter, and "pass." is walking. The full record is in John Hewetson's *Memoirs of the House of Hewetson or Hewson of Ireland*.[3] It is no longer possible to confirm these details since Hewson's wife's memorial was destroyed during cathedral renovations in the late 19th century. This is the strongest evidence that Hewson was connected with the Husons of Tenterden.

The Reverend Mark Noble, writing in the 1798, questioned how Colonel Hewson acquired the right to bear arms. His remarks might well reflect the prejudice of the time against the regicides ... "Colonel Hewson, also ... sprung from the dregs of the people, first a cobler, then a shoemaker", ... a natural and easy ascent, unquestionably... "bore for his arms, (as appears by his seal) two horses counter salient, a sword erect in base, and four annulets." The Reverend Noble therefore suggests... "Query, did they receive arms from the heralds, or did they assume them without?" [4].

It is unlikely that Colonel Hewson falsely assumed these arms. The College of Heralds would have destroyed his reputation. A possible mode of legal (if hardly honourable) acquisition of arms has been described:

> "Sir Thomas Smith (see vol. ii. p. 456, ad fin.) has set such a question at rest, by showing how, at least in 1565, one of the novi homines, of any rank, could procure the herald's 'slender help to fame'; now, by the progress of plebeian education, becoming every day more slender. If he would only, by an allowed and well-understood palmistry, conciliate 'a King of Heralds', that prime officer in the court of honour, 'his visual nerve being thus invigorated, would presently discover among "old registers" arms, if not supporters, belonging to the applicant's remote 'ancestors'."[5]

However the Hewson arms survived the political and social obliteration of Colonel John Hewson and his family following the Restoration. A well known family of Hewsons, resident in Hunter Street, Brunswick Square, London, in the late eighteenth and early nineteenth centuries, used arms described, "Quarterly, gu. and erm. an eagle displ. or. in the first quarter a lion pass. guard. ar.".[6] This family claimed descent from Colonel Hewson, though the link has not been traced. No doubt the College of Heralds accepted the claim.

This family claimed as its crest "a bull's head, or in the mouth a torch emitting flames".[7] Presumably this crest would have been that of Colonel Hewson, and possibly derived from the Husons of Tenterden. The tradition amongst the family of Hewsons in Co. Leitrim in the early twentieth century, who also appear to have been descended from Colonel John Hewson, that its crest was "the rising sun" appears to result from confusion with the crest of the Hewsons of Castle Hewson in Co. Limerick, which is a "radiant sun". The Castle Hewson family has no connection with the Husons of Tenterden, or with Colonel Hewson's family in London, having originally settled in Ireland as early as the thirteenth century from Yorkshire or Lincolnshire.

CHAPTER 20

"Man of Property"

Down the centuries, ownership of land conferred social status. Particularly in country areas, landowners exercised great influence over the lives of tenants and local people. In the absence of properly regulated financial institutions, or of a trustworthy banking system, land was the only secure investment. Ownership carried the right to vote, and, a not unimportant consideration in coastal towns, exemption from arbitrary impressment into the King's navy.

We do not know whether John Hewson owned property in Bell Yard in the City of London, or in Tothill Street in Westminster, places where it appears he carried on his shoe making business. Or if he did, when or how he disposed of them.

Colonel Hewson was in serious financial difficulties in early 1654. On 1 March he was driven to petition Cromwell for early payment of his arrears of military pay. We cannot know what passed between the two men but Cromwell referred the petition to a Commons Committee, which on the 14 March recommended that a total of £2,134.16s.3d be paid.[1] A mere two weeks later, on 31 March, the Commons passed an ordinance for payment.[2] The hand of Cromwell may well have been behind this expeditious treatment, bearing in mind that other officers of similar rank were having to wait years before settlement of their arrears. Tradition has it that loud hilarity broke out in the House when members observed that amongst voices raised in support of the payment, was that of one Colonel Hewson!

The matter of Colonel Hewson's arrears came before the House again on 18 July, when the Irish estate known as Luttrellstown was granted to him in part settlement of his arrears for his service in Ireland. As the estate had, in 1640, a rental value of £2,500 a year,[3] it is clear that its true value was many times this figure, and suggests that Hewson was being unduly favoured. Certainly this was the view of some contemporaries. Ludlow did not mince words. Cromwell "began by bribes to corrupt others to his interest; and to this end ordered the arrears of Col. Hewetson for his English service to be paid in ready money, and his Irish arrears to be satisfied out of forfeited lands in the county of Dublin, at the rate of the adventurers, in such places as he should chose".[4]

Colonel Hewson was already familiar with Luttrellstown Castle since he had occupied it as his personal residence in 1649, when appointed military governor of Dublin. Most likely he persuaded Cromwell to allow him to become its owner.

The Luttrellstown estate has always been prized. Situated some miles to the west of Dublin, in Castleknock Barony, it overlooks the River Liffey, and adjoins the main road to the city. In the nineteenth century, Prince Pückler Muskau described it in rapturous terms, as having an approach "indeed the most delightful in its kind that can be imagined. Scenery, by nature most beautiful, is improved by art to the highest degree of its capability... Gay shrubs and wild flowers, the softest turf and giant trees ... fill the narrow glen through which the path winds" to the Castle itself. In Hewson's day the castle was regarded as a most desirable residence – second only in Ireland to Malahide Castle, which had been taken by Cromwell for his official residence.

Rebuilt during the fifteenth century, Luttrelstown Castle was again rebuilt in the early eighteenth century, with further substantial renovations carried out in the nineteenth and early twentieth centuries. Little can be seen today of the original structure.

Since the early Middle Ages the area around Dublin, known as the Pale, had been the base of English power in Ireland. It was essential that its military fortifications should remain in trustworthy hands.

Early in the thirteenth century, King John granted Luttrellstown Castle and surrounding lands to the English knight, Sir Geoffrey Luttrell. The estate continued in the possession of this loyal Anglo-Norman family, with only one interruption, until the eighteenth century. In the nineteenth century the estate was purchased by the wealthy Guinness family (whose world renowned brewery was just a few miles down the adjoining river Liffey), and quickly became a rendezvous for the cream of Anglo-Irish society. Guests included Queen Victoria; and, much later, Grace Kelly. These days the castle, often called Woodlands, is an exclusive hotel and was in the headlines as being the scene of the lavish wedding of the footballer David Beckham, to Victoria Adams, perhaps better known as "Posh Spice".

The one interruption in the Luttrell family's 500 years' ownership of the estate took place in 1647, when Thomas Luttrell made it over to Parliament, "for Lord Broghill, who was afterwards succeeded as tenant to the state by Colonel Hewson, Governor of Dublin".[5] The precise circumstances in which Thomas was forced to surrender his family inheritance are not known, but since he was a leading Catholic, and his father had been a vehement supporter of the defeated King Charles, he would have had little choice.

As stated earlier, in 1649, after Cromwell's successful invasion of Ireland, Luttrellstown Castle became the official residence of Colonel Hewson. Thomas Luttrell, however, remained on the scene as Hewson's head gardener, being allowed to live in the stables with his family, and to cultivate part of the land for his own benefit. Relations between the deposed owner and the new occupant were surprisingly good. Although under the draconian Transplantation orders Thomas Luttrell was required to quit his home and move to the wilds of Connaught, on 30 September, 1654, Colonel Hewson gave special permission for him to remain on the estate until his private crops could be safely harvested.[6] Exactly when in 1655 Thomas went to Connaught is unknown, but his wife, children and farm stock were forced to travel by June of that year.

Though Hewson returned to England in 1656 to advance his political career, he continued as owner of the Luttrellstown estate. In his absence he granted tenancy to Sir William Berry (or Bury). In *A Census of Ireland, c.1659*, the House at Luttrellstowne, and Luttrellstowne Mill, are shown as held by Sir William as Tituladoe.[7] Interestingly, this Census also indicates that by then Thomas Luttrell had managed to come back from exile in Connaught, since he is entered as being the Tituladoe for Poocestowne, which is close by Luttrellstown.[8] Colonel Hewson's own title to Luttrellstown was confirmed in 1659, when the castle was granted to him in free (fee) farm, together with extensive lands in Co. Dublin estimated at nearly 7,000 acres. Sir William Berry is mentioned as being the tenant in occupation.

Following the Restoration of Charles II in 1660, the regicides were attainted by Parliament, their property being forfeited to the Crown.[9] Hewson's lands were granted to others. Sir Allan Broderick (Viscount Middleton) acquired half.[10] However, Thomas Luttrell had by then resumed occupation of Luttrellstown. He was protected by a personal letter from Charles II to the Duke of Ormonde, Lord Lieutenant of Ireland, dated the 17 June 1661, and issued under Sign Manual and the Privy Seal… "Thomas Lutterell, not to be disturbed in the possession of Luttrellstown by reason of our Grant to others of Hewson's estate."[11]

By the Act for the Settlement of Ireland, passed in 1662, properties in Ireland of the regicides were awarded to the Duke of York, afterwards James II.[12] This meant that Sir Allan Broderick lost his half share of Hewson's estates, though an order for compensation was made. Tenacious Thomas Luttrell still continued in occupation, and in later years, his family recovered full legal ownership of the Luttrellstown estate.

Colonel Hewson's second Irish estate was at Kilmacud, lands situated to the south of Dublin, near the present Booterstown. This estate was also considerable. During the 15th century it contained only two substantial houses, but by the 1660s there were four. The 1659 census recorded thirteen inhabitants, eleven of whom were English.

In the early 17th century the lands at Kilmacud had been owned by the Archbolds, a Catholic family long established in the Pale. Doubtless, like the Luttrells, they had supported the King, and were similarly punished. Parliament took over the family land, and transferred it to Colonel Hewson, probably in 1654, as part of the settlement of his arrears of military pay.

At the Restoration, the Kilmacud lands were forfeited to the Crown. Charles II awarded one half to his brother, the Duke of York, but the other half returned to the family, being granted to Richard Archbold, a Protestant descendant of the original owners.

As the fighting in Ireland gradually petered out during the mid-1650s, large parts of the Cromwellian army of occupation were disbanded. Not only had these troops to receive their outstanding pay, most soldiers serving in Ireland were owed considerable arrears. The Government's total liability far exceeded its cash resources, and due to poor harvests and the slow recovery of the Irish economy after the war, there was little prospect of raising adequate tax revenue to meet the shortfall. Initially soldiers were given an option to accept confiscated land in lieu of their outstanding pay, but as the Government's financial difficulties escalated, this was made compulsory.

Instead of cash, soldiers received paper debentures to the value of their arrears, entitling them to farming land confiscated from the defeated Irish, or Royalist supporters. The debentures were transferable. Soldiers, desperate for real money, sold them to land speculators, usually their own regimental officers. It has been stated that "two thirds of the soldiers sold their arrears to their officers".[13] A contemporary land expert, Petty, records that in 1653 debentures were freely sold for 4 or 5 shillings per £1 nominal value.[14] In many instances soldiers who had taken the option to receive plots of land, decided against farming, and sold the land, often to return to a more familiar life back home in England.

This unprecedented availability of farming land tended to force property values even lower, so that those with ready money might easily build up large holdings of prime agricultural land. Colonel Hewson was in a most advantageous position. Not only had he received a substantial capital sum in the 1654 settlement of his arrears of pay, but he was also in receipt of the income from his Luttrellstown and Kilmacud estates, as well as (until 1656) his salary as Governor of Dublin.

Most of the confiscated arable land in co. Leitrim, and also areas in the south of Ireland, in Co. Cork, and possibly in Co. Tipperary, was designated for distribution to soldiers in Hewson's regiment. There is no doubt that much of this land found its way into Colonel Hewson's hands. The regicides were fully aware of their likely fate should the young King Charles, now in exile, recover his Crown. It may be assumed that Hewson attempted to frustrate possible sequestration by vesting the legal title in the names of relatives or trustees. Certainly two families of Hewson, in Co. Leitrim (near Drumahaire), and in Co. Tipperary (at Roscrea), which claim direct descent from Colonel Hewson, assert that their lands were originally his.[15]

There is also evidence that Colonel Hewson had taken possession of an Irish estate belonging to Richard Belling, Esquire. On 25 January 1661, King Charles II wrote to the Lords Justices of Ireland ordering that the lands be restored. The original letter is held on the Bodleian Library.[16]

Colonel Hewson's enemies must have smiled when a man of such wealth and power ended his days in sickness and poverty.

CHAPTER 21

References Chapter 1

(1) Noble, Revd. M., *Lives of the Regicides*. Vol. 1. 1798, London, p.352

(2) Taft, B., *The Council of Officers' Agreement of the People. The Historical Journal*. Vol. XXVII. 1985, pp.170–171

(3) Manning, B. *The Crisis of the English Revolution*. 1992, London

(4) Temple, R K. G. Unpublished M. Phil. *Thesis The English Regicides*. February 1988

(5) *Dictionary of National Biography*. 1921 Edition, pp.702–703

(6) Hewetson, J. *Memoirs of the House of Hewetson or Hewson of Ireland*. 1901, London, pp.204–6

*(7) Manuscript record of the Cordwainer's Company, held in the London Guildhall Museum

(8) Tolmie, M. *The Triumph of the Saints*. 1977, Cambridge University Press, pp.36 & 44

(9) Woolrych, A. *Commonwealth to Protectorate*. 1982, pp.182–183

(10) Parry, R. H. (Ed.) 1970 *The English Civil War and After, 1642–1658*, p.46

References Chapter 2

(1) Tolmie, M., *The Triumph of the Saints*. 1977, Cambridge University Press, p.156

(2) Davies, G., *The Parliamentary Army under the Earl of Essex*. English Historical Review. Vol. 49, p.35

(3) Wharton, Nehemiah. *Archaeologia, XXXV*, 326

(4) Public Record Office. S.P. 28/4/376

(5) Harris, quoting an unnamed source

(6) Bradley, K., *English Civil War*. Issue No. 6, Partizan Press

(7) Frazier, A., *Cromwell, Our Chief of Men*. 1973, p.125

(8) Ashe's account of the battle in Vicars, Vol. 3, pp.269–282

(9)   *Parliament Scout.* 4–11 July 1644

(10) Foard, G., *Colonel John Pickering's Regiment of Foot, 1644 – 1645.* ISBN 0-946014-25-6, p.65

(11) Holmes, C., *The Eastern Association.* 1974, p.168

(12) Ashley, M., *The English Civil War.* 1992, p.124

(13) Foard, G., *"Naseby: The Decisive Campaign.* 1995, p.64

(14) Public Records Office. SP 28/35. fol. 633

(15) P.R.O. SP 28/140, part 2, fol. 6

(16) Young, P., *"Naseby, 1645.* p.318

(17) Sprigge

(18) Sprigge, p.95

(19) Gentles, I., *The New Model Army in England, Ireland & Scotland.* 1994, pp.69–70

(20) Kingdom's Weekly, No.110

(21) Sprigge, p.114

(22) Bradley, K. Article in English Civil War Notes and Queries, Issue No. 6. Partizan Press

(23) Mercurius Civicus, 22 October 1645

(24) Young, P. and Emberton, W., *Sieges of the Great Civil War, 1642– 1646.* 1978, pp.96 & 97

(25) At the Council of War during the Oxford siege, Hewson was still recorded as a Lieutenant Colonel. Sprigge, p.277

References Chapter 3

(1)   Firth, C. H., *Cromwell's Army.* ISBN 1-85367-120-7, p.332

(2)   Gentles, I., *The New Model Army in England, Ireland and Scotland.* 1992, p.102

(3)   Moderate Intelligencer, 17–27 Sept. 1646, E355/8, p.655m Mercurius Civicus, 16–23 July 1646, E 345/17, p.231

(4)   Kishlansky, M. A. *The Rise of the New Model Army.* ISBN 0-521-22751-8, 1979

(5) Gentles, I., *The New Model Army in England, Ireland and Scotland.*" 1994, p.102 "A Publike Conference betwixt Six Presbyterian Ministers and Some Independent Commanders, November, 12ᵗʰ, 1646." E. 363/4, pp. 2-5, 11-14. also E.363/6

(6) Clarke Papers. Vol.1, p.16. ISBN 0-86193-133-5

(7) Firth C. H., *The Regimental History of Cromwell's Army.* Oxford, 1940, p.405

(8) Gentles, I., *The New Model Army in England, Ireland and Scotland.* 1994, p.159

(9) Clarke Papers. Vol.1, ISBN 0-86193-133-5

(10) Denton, B., *The Crisis in the Army, 1647.* Partizan Press, 1984

(11) Gentles, I., *The New Model Army in England, Ireland and Scotland.* 1994, p.161

(12) Clarke Papers. Vol.1, p.22 ISBN 0-86193-133-5

(13) Clarke Papers. Vol.1, p.43

(14) Clarke Papers. Vol.1, p.51

(15) Kingston. A. *Hertfordshire during the Great Civil War.*" London, 1894, p.65

(16) Fraser, A., *Cromwell, Our Chief of Men.* London, 1973, p.196

(17) Gentles, I., *The New Model Army in England, Ireland and Scotland.*" 1994, p.96

(18) Clarke Papers. Vol.1, p.141

(19) Berry & Lee., *A Cromwellian Major General.* Clarendon Press., 1983, p.47

(20) Williamson, H. R., *Four Stuart Portraits.* 1949, p.124

(21) Wilson, J., *"Fairfax.* 1985. ISBN 0-7195-4207-3 p.122

(22) Woodhouse, A. S. P., *Puritanism and Liberty.* 1992, ISBN 0-460-87206-0, p.112

(23) Woolrych, A., *Soldiers and Statesmen.* Clarendon Press, 1987, p.278

(24) Gentles, I. *The New Model Army in England, Ireland and Scotland.* 1994, p.218

(25) – ibid – p.219

(26) Firth C. H., *The Regimental History of Cromwell's Army*. Oxford University Press, 1940, p.406

(27) Woolrych, A., *Soldiers and Statesmen*. Clarendon Press, 1987, p.310

(28) Gentles, I., *The New Model Army in England, Ireland and Scotland*. 1994, p.227

(29) Woolrych, A., *Soldiers and Statesmen*. Clarendon Press, 1987, p.312, 313

(30) Fraser, A., *Cromwell, Our Chief of Men*. 1973, p.228

(31) Rushworth, vii, 943.

References Chapter 4

(1) Abell, H. F., "*Kent and the Great Civil War*. 1901, p.173

(2) Gentles, I., *The New Model Army in England, Ireland and Scotland*. 1994, p.237

(3) Carlyle, T., *Cromwell's Letters and Speeches*. Quoting Clarke Papers, ii, et seq.

(4) Everitt, A. M., *The Community of Kent and the Great Rebellion 1640 – 60*. 1966, p.241

(5) Everitt, A. M., *The Community of Kent and the Great Rebellion 1640 – 60*. 1966, p.235

(6) Clarke Papers. Vol. II., p.11, ISBN 0-86193-133-5

(7) Firth C. H., *The Regimental History of Cromwell's Army*." 1940 Oxford University Press, p.326

(8) Clarke Papers. Vol. II. p.19

(9) Rushworth, vii, p.974

(10) Ludlow, E., *Memoirs*. Ed. Firth. Clarendon Press, 1894, Vol. I, pp.193–4

(11) Fairfax Correspondence, vol.4, p.32–3.

(12) Everitt, A. M., *The Community of Kent and the Great Rebellion 1640–60*. 1966, p.267

(13) Firth, C. H., *The Regimental History of Cromwell's Army*. Oxford University Press, 1940, p.407

(14) Rushworth, vii, 1149, 1229

(15) Information taken from English Heritage Guides to Deal Castle and Walmer Castle, and Laker's *History of Deal*

References Chapter 5

(1) British Library E.527 (23), quoted at p.19 of *The Crisis of the English Revolution*, by Brian Manning. 1992, ISBN 0-906224-73X

(2) Gentles, I., *The New Model Army in England, Ireland and Scotland*. 1994, P.270

(3) – ibid – p.272

(4) Underdown, D., *"Pride's Purge*. 1971, p.135

(5) Underdown, D., *Pride's Purge*. 1971, p.135

(6) Ludlow, E. 1, 211-12

(7) Firth, C. H., *The Regimental History of Cromwell's Army*. Oxford University Press, 1940, p.366

(8) Underdown, D., *"Pride's Purge*. 1971, p.151

(9) Underdown, D., *Pride's Purge*. 1971, p.162

(10) Gentles, I., *The New Model Army in England, Ireland and Scotland*. 1994, pp.290–1

(11) Woodhouse, A. S. P., *Puritanism and Liberty*. 1992, ISBN 0-460-87206-0, p.128

(12) Clarke Papers. Vol. II. ISBN 0-86193-133-5, p.77

(13) Taft, B., *Voting lists of the Council of Officers, December, 1648*. Bulletin of the Institute of Historical Research. L ii, 1979, pp.138–154

(14) Clarke Papers. Vol. II., ISBN 0-86193-133-5, p.134

(15) Taft, B. –ibid–

(16) Taft, B. –ibid–

(17) Clarke Papers. Vol. II. p.LVii

(18) Carlyle, *Cromwell's Letters and Speeches*. Letter dated 22 December 1648, addressed to Colonel Whitchott (Whitcote), then the Governor of Windsor Castle.

(19) Temple, R. K. G., *The English Regicides*, 1988. Unpublished thesis.

(20) Wedgwood, C. V., *The Trial of Charles I*. 1964, ISBN 85456-616-3. p.423

(21) Muddiman, J.G., *Trial of King Charles the First*. William Hodge

& Co. Ltd., 1928, p.94

(22) Muddiman, J.G., *Trial of King Charles the First*. William Hodge & Co. Ltd., 1928, p.148

(23) Shaw, H., *The Levellers*. Seminar Studies in History, Longmans, 1968

(24) Foard, G., *Colonel John Pickering's Regiment of Foot*. 1994. p.117

(25) Clarke Papers, Vol. II p.192 ISBN 0-86193-133-5.

(26) Clarke Papers, Vol. II p.190 ISBN 0-86193-133-5.

(27) Gentles, I., *The New Model Army in England, Scotland & Ireland*. 1994, p.319

(28) Gregg, P., *Freeborn John*. 1961, p.268

(29) Gardiner, S. R., *History of the Commonwealth and Protectorate 1649–1660*, Vol. I, London, 1897, pp.49–50.

(30) Gentles, I., *The New Model Army in England, Scotland & Ireland*. 1994, p.352

(31) Firth, C. H., *The Regimental History of Cromwell's Army*. Oxford University Press, 1940, pp.408, 409.

(32) Gentles, I., *The New Model Army in England, Scotland & Ireland*. 1994, p.328

(33) Gentles, I. *"The New Model Army in England, Scotland & Ireland."* 1994. p.335

(34) Gentles, I., *The New Model Army in England, Scotland & Ireland*. 1994, p.335

(35) Gardiner, S. R., *History of the Commonwealth and Protectorate 1649–1660*, Vol. I, London, 1897, p.61

(36) Prendergast, J. P., *The Cromwellian Settlement of Ireland."* London, 1870, p.187

(37) Fraser, A., *Cromwell, Our Chief of Men*. London, 1973, p.319

(38) Firth, C. H., *The Regimental History of Cromwell's Army*. Oxford University Press, 1940, p.408

(39) Gilbert, J. T. (Ed.), *A Contemporary History of Affairs in Ireland from 1641–1652*. Dublin, 1880. The primary source is XVI, Carte Papers, XXV, p.25

References Chapter 6

(1) Coonan, T. L., *The Irish Catholic Confederacy and the Puritan Revolution*. London, 1954, p.295

(2) Wheeler, J. S., *Cromwell in Ireland*. Dublin, 1999, 0-7171-2884-9, p.86

(3) Reilly, T., *Cromwell, an Honourable Enemy*. 1999, p.67

(4) Gentles, I., *The New Model Army in England, Ireland and Scotland*. 1994, p.360

(5) Ludlow, E., *Memoirs*, Vol. I, pp.302–3.

(6) Ludlow, E., *Memoirs*, Vol. I, pp.302–3.

(7) Hewetson, J., *Memoirs of the House of Hewetson or Hewson, etc.* 1901, London, p.205

(8) Murphy, *Cromwell in Ireland*. Dublin, 1883. pp.141–142

(9) Borlase, E., *The History of the Execrable Irish Rebellion*. London, 1680

(10) Prendergast, J. F., *The Cromwellian Settlement*. London, 1870, p.334

(11) Wheeler, J. S., *Cromwell in Ireland*. 1999, ISBN 0-7171-2884-9. p.132

(12) Cromwell's letter of 2 April, 1650, to Speaker Lenthal.

(13) Seymour, Revd. St. J. D.*The Puritans in Ireland 1647-1661*. Oxford University Press, 1921, p.20

(14) Wheeler, J. F., *Cromwell in Ireland*. 1999, p.132

(15) Warner, Fernando, *The History of the Rebellion and Civil-War in Ireland*. London, 1767 and Dublin, 1768, p.495

(16) Murphy, *Cromwell in Ireland*. Dublin, 1883, pp.289–90

(17) Gaunt, P., *The Cromwellian Gazetteer*. 1987, ISBN 0-75090-063-6. p.216

(18) Bagwell, R., *Ireland under the Stuarts*. 1909, Vol. II, p.217

(19) Murphy. *Cromwell in Ireland*. Dublin, 1883, p.298

(20) Murphy. *Cromwell in Ireland*. Dublin, 1883, p.299

(21) Murphy. *Cromwell in Ireland*. Dublin, 1883, p.337

(22) Calendar of State Papers (1650) p.62

(23) Bagwell, R., *Ireland under the Stuarts*." Vol. II, 1642–60, Longman Green & Co., 1909, pp.223–24

References Chapter 7

(1) O'Meagher, C., *Diary of Dr. Jones, Scoutmaster-General to the Army of the Commonwealth.* Journal of Royal Society of Antiquaries of Ireland, 1893, Vol.3, pp.44–54

(2) Gilbert, J. T., *A Contemporary History of Affairs in Ireland.* Dublin, 1880, Vol. III, Part 1, p.166

(3) Gilbert, J. T., *A Contemporary History of Affairs in Ireland.* Dublin, 1880, Vol. III, Part 1, p.166

(4) Wheeler, J. S., *Cromwell in Ireland.* 1999, ISBN 0-7171-2884-9, p.194

(5) *Every Day's Intelligence.* 24–31 Jan, 1651

(6) O'Ciardha, E. O., *Toryism in Cromwellian Ireland (1650–1660).* The Irish Sword, Vol. 19, 1995–6, p.294

(7) McNeill, C. (Ed.), *The Tanner Letters.* Stationery Office, Dublin, 1943, p.347

(8) Letter from Colonel Hewson. TT. E. 626 (11)

(9) Eason, D. M. R., *The Curse of Cromwell.* London, 1971, pp.147, 148

(10) Gilbert, J. T., *A History of the City of Dublin*, Vol. I, 1978, p.41, 0-7171-0942-9

(11) McNeill, C. (Ed.), *The Tanner Letters.* Stationery Office, Dublin, 1943, p.338

(12) Seymour, Revd. J. D., *The Puritans in Ireland 1647-1661*, Oxford University Press, 1921, p.58

(13) McNeill, C. (Ed.), *The Tanner Letters.* Stationery Office, Dublin, 1943, p.337

(14) Prendergast, J. F. ,*The Cromwellian Settlement of Ireland.* London, 1870, p.78

(15) Severall Proceedings in Parliament, from 26 of June to 3rd day of July, 1651

(16) Mc Neill, C. (Ed.), *The Tanner Letters.* Stationery Office, Dublin, 1943, p.339

(17) Gilbert, J. T., *A Contemporary History of Affairs in Ireland, 1641–52.* Part III, 1880, p.248

(18) Gilbert, J.T., *A Contemporary History of Affairs in Ireland, 1641–52*. Part III, p.251, 1880.

(19) Bagwell, R., *Ireland under the Stuarts*. Vol. II 1642–60, London 1909, p.269

(20) Dunlop, R., *Ireland under the Commonwealth*. Manchester University Press, 1913, pp.34–5

(21) Dunlop, R., *Ireland under the Commonwealth*. Manchester University Press, 1913, p.38

(22) Dunlop, R., *Ireland under the Commonwealth*. Manchester University Press, 1913, p.42

(23) Dunlop, R., *Ireland under the Commonwealth*. Manchester University Press, 1913, p.48

(24) Mayer, J. 1860/1, *Transactions of the Historic Society of Lancashire and Cheshire*. Vol.13. N.S.1, p.189. "Inedited letters of Cromwell, Col. Jones, Bradshaw and other regicides."

(25) Barnard, T. C., *Cromwellian Ireland*, Oxford University Press, 1975, p.99

(26) Dunlop, R., *Ireland under the Commonwealth*. Manchester University Press, 1913, p.71

(27) Dunlop, R., *Ireland under the Commonwealth*. Manchester University Press, 1913, p.75

(28) Dunlop, R. *Ireland under the Commonwealth*. Manchester University Press, 1913, p.88. f.f.224–7

(29) Dunlop, R., *Ireland under the Commonwealth*. Manchester University Press, 1913, p.114

(30) Temple, R. K. G., *The English Regicides*. Unpublished thesis for M.Phil. February 1988

(31) Hewetson, J., *Memoirs of the House of Hewetson or Hewson*. London, 1901, p.205

(32) Barnard, T. C., *Cromwellian Ireland*. Oxford University Press, 1975, p.103

(33) Dunlop, R., *Ireland under the Commonwealth*. Manchester University Press, 1913, p.129

(34) Venetian Ambassador's letters, *The English Civil War*. Caliban Books. 1996, p.84. ISBN 1-85066-0344

(35) O'Ciardha, E. O., *Toryism in Cromwellian Ireland 1650–60*. The Irish Sword, Vol.19, 1995–6, p.295

(36) Madge, S., *The Domesday of Crown Lands*. London, 1938, pp.223, 384N, 396.

(37) Dunlop, R., *Ireland under the Commonwealth"*. Manchester University Press, 1913, p.162

(38) Mc Neill, C. (Ed.), *The Tanner Letters*. Stationery Office, Dublin, 1943, pp.354–6.

(39) Mc Neill, C. (Ed.), *The Tanner Letters*. Stationery Office, Dublin, 1943, p359

(40) Petty, W. Cited by Raymond Gillespie, *Irish Economy at War, 1641–1652*. Possibly Dublin in 1927, p.160

References Chapter 8

(1) Mc Neill, C. (Ed.), *The Tanner Letters*. Stationery Office, Dublin, 1943. p.366

(2) Dunlop, R., *Ireland under the Commonwealth*. Manchester University Press, 1913, p.217. f.f. 156–7

(3) Mc Neill, C. (Ed.), *The Tanner Letters*. Stationery Office, Dublin, 1943, p.374

(4) Dunlop, R., *Ireland under the Commonwealth*. Manchester University Press, 1913, p.194/5. M.S. 844 f.128

(5) Dunlop, R., *Ireland under the Commonwealth*. Manchester University Press, 1913, p.230

(6) Mc Neill, C. (Ed.), *The Tanner Letters*. Stationery Office, Dublin, 1943, p.377

(7) Seymour, J. D. *The Puritans in Ireland, 1647–61*. Oxford University Press, 1921, p.58

(8) Moran, P. F., *Historical sketch of the persecutions suffered by the Catholics of Ireland*. Dublin, 1907, p.242 footnote

(9) Moran, P.F., *Historical sketch of the persecutions suffered by the Catholics of Ireland*. Dublin, 1907, p.242 footnote

(10) Mayer, J., Transactions of the Historic Society of Lancashire and Cheshire. (1860) Vol. 13. N.S. 1. p.212. Published 1861 at Liverpool. *Inedited letters of Cromwell, Col. Jones, Bradshaw and other regicides.*

(11) Seymour, J. D., *The Puritans in Ireland, 1647–61.* Open University Press, 1921, pp.78–9

(12) Dunlop, R., *Ireland under the Commonwealth.* Manchester University Press, 1913, p.307

(13) Wheeler, J. S., *Cromwell in Ireland.* 1999. ISBN 0-7171-2884-9 p.228

(14) Dunlop, R., *Ireland under the Commonwealth.* Manchester University Press, 1913, p.309

(15) Prendergast, J. P., *The Cromwellian Settlement of Ireland.* London, 1870, p.327

(16) Ashley, M., *Oliver Cromwell, the conservative dictator.* Jonathan Cape, 1937, p.188

(17) Barnard, T. C., *Cromwellian Ireland.* Open University Press, 1975, p.103 note

(18) Seymour, St. J., *The Puritans in Ireland'* 1921. O.U.P. p.214

References Chapter 9

(1) Woolrych, A., *Commonwealth to Protectorate.* Clarendon Press, 1982, p.418

(2) Temple, R. K. G., *The English Regicides.* Unpublished thesis. Feb. 1988

(3) Glass, H. A., *The Barebones Parliament.* London, 1899, p.91

(4) Rutt, J. T. (Ed.), *Diary of Thomas Burton.* London, 1828. Page (ii) in the Introduction

(5) Woolrych, A., *Commonwealth to Protectorate.* Clarendon Press, 1982, p.318

(6) Woolrych, A., *Commonwealth to Protectorate.* 1 Clarendon Press, 1982, pp.418–19

(7) Hainsworth, R., *The Swordsmen in Power.* 1997. ISBN 0-7509-0571-9, p.153

(8) Prendergast, J. P., *The Cromwellian Settlement of Ireland.* Manchester University Press, 1913, p.404

(9) Temple, R. K. G., *The English Regicides.* Unpublished thesis. Feb. 1988

(10) Rutt, J. T. (Ed.), *Diary of Thomas Burton.* 1828, reprinted 1972. Vol. II, p.60

(11) Ramsey, R. W., *Henry Cromwell.* Longmans Green 7 Co., London, 1933, p.42

(12) Hewetson, J., *Memoirs of the House of Hewetson or Hewson of Ireland.* London, 1901. p.205

(13) Ellis, P. B., *Hell or Connaught.* Belfast. Blackstaff Press, 1988, p.115

(14) D'Alton, J., *The History of the County of Dublin.* Hodges and Smith. British Library 13478168, Dublin, 1838, p.42

(15) Esson, D. M. R., *The Curse of Cromwell.* London, 1971, p.183

(16) Gardiner, S. R., *History of the Commonwealth and Protectorate.* Vol. III, London, 1903, p.271

(17) Ludlow, E., *Memoirs.* Vol. I. Clarendon Press, 1894, p.401

(18) Prendergast, J. P., *The Cromwellian Settlement of Ireland.* London, 1870, p.108

References Chapter 10

(1) Dunlop, R., *Ireland under the Commonwealth.* Manchester University Press, 1913, p.451–2

(2) Dunlop, R., *Ireland under the Commonwealth*, 1913, Manchester University Press, p.452

(3) Dunlop, R., *Ireland under the Commonwealth*, 1913, Manchester University Press, p.454

(4) Dunlop, R., *Ireland under the Commonwealth*, 1913, Manchester University Press, p.462

(5) Dunlop, R., *Ireland under the Commonwealth*, 1913, Manchester University Press, p.464

(6) Dunlop, R., *Ireland under the Commonwealth*, 1913, Manchester University Press, p.473

(7)   Ludlow, E., *Memoirs*. Vol. I. Clarendon Press, 1894, p.402

(8)   Kaplan, L., *Oliver Cromwell*. 1986. ISBN 0-245-60107-4, p.96

(9)   Buchan, J., *Cromwell*. 1934 (Sphere Books reprint in September 1971) p.457

(10) Dictionary of National Biography, 1921 Edition, p.702

(11) Dunlop, R., *Ireland under the Commonwealth*. Manchester University Press, 1913, p.475

(12) Calendar of State Papers, Domestic, 1655-6, of 12 February, 1655.

(13) Dunlop, R., *Ireland under the Commonwealth*. Manchester University Press, 1913, p.486

(14) Gardiner, S. R., *History of the Commonwealth and Protectorate. 1649–1656*. Vol. IV (1655–56). London, 1903, p.103

(15) Dunlop, R., *Ireland under the Commonwealth*. Manchester University Press, 1913, p.489

(16) Dunlop, R., *Ireland under the Commonwealth*. Manchester University Press, 1913, p.499

(17) Dunlop, R., *Ireland under the Commonwealth*. Manchester University Press, 1913, p.544

(18) Esson, D. M. R., *The Curse of Cromwell*. London, 1971, p.178

(19) General Orders A/5, 5, f.188

(20) Ellis, P. B., *Hell or Connaught*. Belfast, 1988, p.106

(21) Curtis, E., *A History of Ireland*. London, 1936, p.256 of the 6th Edition, 1950.

(22) Dunlop, R., *Ireland under the Commonwealth"*. Manchester University Press, 1913, pp.536 and 538

(23) Dunlop, R., *Ireland under the Commonwealth*. Manchester University Press, 1913, p.544

(24) *Publick Intelligencer* of 29 Oct.–5 Nov., 1655

(25) Ellis, P. B., *Hell or Connaught*. Belfast, 1988, p.161

(26) Firth, C. H., *The Last Years of the Protectorate*. London, 1909. Vol. II pp.126, 127

(27) Brown, L. F., *"Baptist and Fifth Monarchy Men*. Oxford University Press, 1912, p.139.

(28) Noble, Revd. M., *Lives of the Regicides*. London, 1798, Vol. I. p.353

(29) Davies, G., *The Restoration of Charles II*. Oxford University Press, 1969, p.241

(30) Dunlop, R., *Ireland under the Commonwealth*. Manchester University Press, 1913, p.571

(31) Seymour, Revd. J. D., *The Puritans in Ireland*. Oxford Univesity Press, 1921, pp.118–19

(32) Ramsey, R. W., *Henry Cromwell*. London, 1913, p.133. The original letter of 12 August 1656 is in Lansdowne MSS. 821, held in the British Library.

(33) English Civil War Times. No. 52. Partizan Press. p.12

References Chapter 11

(1) Hainsworth, R., *The Swordsmen in Power*. 1997. ISBN 0-7509-0571-9. p.230

(2) Hainsworth, R., T*he Swordsmen in Power*. 1997. ISBN 0-7509-0571-9. p.183

(3) Smith, J. E., *The Parliamentary Representation of Surrey*. London, 1927, pp.26, 85.

(4) Smith, J. E., *The Parliamentary Representation of Surrey*. London, 1927, p.26.

(5) Woolrych, A., *Commonwealth to Protectorate*. Clarendon Press, 1982, p.419

(6) Thurloe, V. 423, 657, 714; calendar, 1656-7, pp.128,133–9.

(7) Hewetson, J., *Memoirs of the House of Hewetson or Hewson of Ireland*. London, 1901, p.205.

(8) Rutt, J. T. (Ed.), *Diary of Thomas Burton*. London, 1828, Vol. I. p.164

(9) Rutt, J. T. (Ed.), *Diary of Thomas Burton*. London, 1828. Vol. I. p.150

(10) Rutt, J. T. (Ed.), *Diary of Thomas Burton*. London, 1828. Vol. I. p.178

(11) Rutt, J. T. (Ed.), *Diary of Thomas Burton.* London, 1828. Vol. I. p.230

(12) Rutt, J. T. (Ed.), *Diary of Thomas Burton.* London, 1828, Vol. I. p.236

(13) Rutt, J. T. (Ed.), *Diary of Thomas Burton.* London, 1828, Vol. I. p.246

(14) Rutt, J. T. (Ed.), *Diary of Thomas Burton.* London, 1828, Vol. I. pp.246–7

(15) Aylmer, G. E., *The Interregnum.* 1972. London. p.163 (Article by Ivan Roots)

(16) Rutt, J. T. (Ed.), *Diary of Thomas Burton.* London, 1828, Vol. I. p.296

(17) Brown, L. F., *The Political Activities of the Baptists and Fifth Monarchy Men.* London and Oxford, 1912. Footnote p.149. Possibly relevant is Thurloe, IV, 422. same to same, n.d., Rawlinson MSS., A5, fol. 249, .

(18) Firth, C. H., *Cromwell and the Crown.* English Historical Review, 1903, Vol. XVIII. p.54.

(19) The letter from Anthony Morgan is apparently recorded in the Lansdowne M.S. 821. f. 294 in the British Library.

(20) Buchan, J., *Cromwell.* 1934. Sphere Books 1971 edition, p.470

(21) Firth, C. H., *The Last Years of the Protectorate 1656–1658.* Vol. I London, 1909, p.151

(22) Ramsey, R. W., *Henry Cromwell.* London, 1933, p.161

(23) Firth, C. H., *The Last Years of the Protectorate 1656–1658.* Vol. I 1909. London. p.168

(24) Temple, R. K. G., Unpublished thesis, *The English Regicides.* 1988

(25) Pender, S., *A Census of Ireland, c. 1659.* Dublin Stationery Office, 1939, p.391

(26) Brown, L. F., *The Political Activities of the Baptists and Fifth Monarchy Men in England.* Oxford University Press, 1912, p.165. Also see Henry Cromwell's letter to Thurloe of 4 March 1657.

(27) Fraser, A., *Cromwell, Our Chief of Men.* London, 1973, p.609

(28) Brown, L. F., *The Political Activities of the Baptists and Fifth Monarchy Men in England*. London and Oxford, 1912, p.166

(29) Razzell, E. & P., *The English Civil War. A contemporary account. 1657–1675*. Vol. 5 ISBN 1-85066-0352, p.48

(30) Carlyle, T., *Cromwell's Letters and Speeches*.

(31) Sherwood, R., "*Oliver Cromwell, King in all but name*. ISBN 0-7509-1066-6, p.119

(32) Fraser, A., *Cromwell, Our Chief of Men*. London, 1973, p.645

(33) Firth, C. H., *The House of Lords during the Civil War*. 1910. Reprinted 1974. ISBN 0-416-80960X. p.255

(34) Journal of the [Protectorate] House of Lords. Hist. MSS. Comm. The MSS of the House of Lords (New Series), iv. 508

References Chapter 12

(1) Thurloe, VII, 374

(2) Thurloe, VII, 386

(3) Davies, G., *The Restoration of Charles II*. Oxford University Press, 1969, p.8

(4) Berry and Lee, *A Cromwellian Major-General*. Clarendon Press, 1938, p.209

(5) A list of the Colonels of the Irish regiments at the time of Richard Cromwell's assumption of the Protectorate on 3 September 1658. Public Records Office document, S.P. 18 Vol. 183 No. 117. under date 17 November, 1658, in Calendar of State Papers Domestic 1658/9 (p.188).

(6) Berry and Lee, *A Cromwellian Major-General*. Clarendon Press, 1938, pp.211–12

References Chapter 13

(1) Raikes, G. A., *The History of the Honourable Artillery Company*. 1878.

(2) Lansdowne MSS. 823

(3) Ramsey, R. W., *Henry Cromwell*. Longmans, London, 1933, p.326

(4) Firth, C. H., *The Regimental History of Cromwell's Army*. Oxford University Press, 1940, pp.412, 682, 684.

(5) Clark, A., *Prelude to Restoration in Ireland*. 1999, ISBN 0-521-65061-5. p.52

(6) Dunlop, R., *Ireland under the Commonwealth*. Manchester University Press, 1913, p.697. Orders A/17. 17. f.4.

(7) Davies, G., *The Restoration of Charles II*. Oxford University Press, 1969, pp.139–40.

(8) Old Parliamentary History, XXI. 444.

(9) Davies, G., *The Restoration of Charles II*. Oxford University Press, 1969, p.147

(10) Carte, *Original Letters*. Ii. 266; Ludlow, ii. 138–40

(11) Roots, I., *The Great Rebellion 1642-1660*. London, 1966, p.247

(12) Ludlow, E., *Memoirs*. Vol. II. 1894. Oxford Clarendon Press, 1894, p.149

References Chapter 14

(1) Davies, G., *The Restoration of Charles II*. Oxford University Press, 1969, p.182

(2) Davies, G., *The Restoration of Charles II*. Oxford University Press, 1969, p.182

(3) Firth, C. H., *The Regimental History of Cromwell's Army*. Oxford University Press, 1940, p.415

(4) Firth, C. H., *The Regimental History of Cromwell's Army*. Oxford University Press, 1940, p.415

(5) Common's Journals, vii. 804

References Chapter 15

(1) Woolrych, A., *Milton*. p.196

(2) Firth, C. H., *The Regimental History of Cromwell's Army*. Oxford University Press, 1940, p.416

(3) Ludlow, E., *Memoirs*. Vol. II, Clarendon Press, 1894, p.269

(4) Granger, J., *A Biographical History of England*. (5th edn. 6 vols). London. 1824; the account of Hewson appears in Vol. IV.

(5) Ludlow, E., *Memoirs*. Vol. II, Clarendon Press, 1894, p.267

References Chapter 16

(1) Pepy's *"Diary"*. Entry for 26 January 1661; Evelyn's *"Diary"*. Entry for 17 October 1660.

(2) The letter was probably addressed to Clarendon. See Firth, C.H; also Ludlow, E. *Memoirs*. 2 Vols. Oxford U. P. 1894. Vol. II, p.330. footnote.

(3) Cited in L. Stephen & S. Lee (Eds.), *Dictionary of National Biography* (22 Vols, London, 1908-9); the biography of Hewson, by C.H. Firth, appears in vol. IX, pp.762–3.

(4) Noble, Revd. M. *Lives of the English Regicides* (2 Vols.) London. 1798. I. 352 and Granger, J. *Biographical History*, IV, 3. 1824.

(5) Catterail, R. C. H. *Sir George Downing and the Regicides*. 1912. *American Historical Review*, Vol. 12. pp.268–89.

(6) Ludlow, E. *Memoirs*. (ed.) Firth Vol. II. p.392 footnote

(7) Muddiman, J. G. (ed.), *Trial of Charles the First*. Edinburgh and London, 1928, p.185

(8) Dictionary of National Biography (1922), IX, 763.

(9) Benham, W. G. *Playing Cards*. London, 1931, p.37

References Chapter 17

(1) Firth, C. H., *Cromwell's Army*. 1992 ISBN 1-85367-120-7

(2) Seymour, J. D., *The Puritans in Ireland, 1647-1661*. Oxford University Press, 1921, p.22

(3) Ohlmeyer, J. H., *Ireland from Independence to Occupation, 1641–1660*. Cambridge University Press, 1995, p.210

(4) Ohlmeyer, J. H., *Ireland from Independence to Occupation, 1641-1660*. Cambridge University Press, 1995, pp.210–11

(5) Brown, L. F., *Baptists and Fifth Monarchymen*. Oxford University Press, 1912, p.136

(6) Fraser, A., *Cromwell, Our Chief of Men*. 1973, p.646

(7) *A Publike Conference betwixt the Six Presbyterian Ministers and some Independent Commanders*. P.R.O. E363/4 and 363/6

(8) Brown, L. F., *Baptists and Fifth Monarchy Men*. Oxford University Press, 1912, pp.160–1

(9) Ramsey, R.W., *Henry Cromwell*. London, 1933, p.133. The original letter of 12 August, 1656, is in Lansdowne MSS.821, at the British Library.

(10) Ellis, P. B., *Hell or Connaught*. Belfast, 1988, p.106

References Chapter 18

(1) Temple, R. K. G. Unpublished M. Phil Thesis, *The English Regicides*. Feb. 1988

(2) Hewetson, J., *Memoirs of the House of Hewetson or Hewson of Ireland*. London, 1901, pp.204–6

(3) Graves, Revd J. Article entitled *The Surrender of Ballysonan to the Parliamentary Forces*, printed in "The Kilkenny Archaeological Journal" for 1856, page 110, covers this event.

(4) Temple, R. K. G. Unpublished M. Phil Thesis *The English Regicides*. Feb. 1988 pp.A-27, 28.

(5) Ashley, M., *Oliver Cromwell. The conservative dictator*. 1937. Jonathan Cape, 1937, p.188

(6) Aitkin, J., *General Biography on Lives*. 1802. Vol. III London. Entry under "Cromwell".

(7) Noble, Revd. M., *Lives of the English Regicides*. London, 1798, Vol. I p.354

(8) Ridley, J., *The Roundheads*. Constable. London, 1976. Chapter 15.

(9) Ashley, M., *Cromwell's Generals*. Jonathan Cape. London, 1954, p.188

References Chapter 19

(1) Temple, R. K. G. Unpublished M. Phil Thesis *The English Regicides*. Feb. 1988 p.A-27.

(2) Burke, *The General Armory*. London, 1884

(3) Hewetson, J., *Memoirs of the House of Hewetson or Hewson of Ireland*. London, 1901, pp.204–6

(4) Rutt, J. T. (Ed.), *Diary of Thomas Burton*. 1828. Vol. III. p.535n.

(5) Rutt, J. T. (Ed.), D*iary of Thomas Burton*. 1828. Vol. III. p.535n.

(6) Burke, *The General Armory*. London, 1884, p.486

(7) Burke, *The General Armory*. London, 1884, p.486

References Chapter 20

(1) Temple, R. K. G. Unpublished M. Phil Thesis, *The English Regicides*. Feb. 1988 p.A-27.

(2) Rutt, J. T. (Ed.), *Diary of Thomas Burton*. 1828. Vol. II. p.60 footnote.

(3) Prendergast, J. P., *The Cromwellian Settlement of Ireland*. London, 1870, Longmans, p.340.

(4) Ludlow, E., *Memoirs*. Clarendon Press, 1894, Oxford. Vol. I. p.401

(5) Prendergast, J. P., *The Cromwellian Settlement of Ireland*. London. 1870, Longmans, p.108

(6) Prendergast, J. P., *The Cromwellian Settlement of Ireland*. London, 1870, Longmans, p.108

(7) Pender, S., *A Census of Ireland, c. 1659*. Hardinge MSS. Dublin Stationery Office, 1939, p.391.

(8) Pender, S., *A Census of Ireland, c. 1659*. Hardinge MSS. Dublin Stationery Office, 1939, p.391.

(9) Public Records Office Class LR2 provides a list of the regicides' estates forfeited to the Crown in 1660, showing in which counties they were situated, and their value. Class E 178 (Special Commissioners of the Exchequer) surveys property of the regicides under the Act of Indemnity and Oblivion.

(10) Hewetson, J. *Memoirs of the House of Hewetson or Hewson of Ireland*. London, 1901

(11) The Carte Manuscripts, Vols. 41, 42 and 43. Bodleian Library.

(12) 14 & 15 Chas. II. Chap.2. sec. 188

(13) Moody et al., *New History of Ireland*. Vol. III. p.373. Clarendon Press, Oxford, 1976

(14) Petty, *Political Anatomy*. p.152

(15) Further information on this issue may result from the research of
      Kevin McKenny in compiling a land record (computer profile)
      for the whole of Ireland. He lectured in Irish Studies at Queen's
      College, City University of New York.

(16) The original letter held in the Bodleian Library is catalogued
      under Carte Calendar Volume 31, January – May 1661. MS. Carte
      41, fol (S), 550.

BIBLIOGRAPHY

In preparing this account of the life of Colonel Hewson the information presented has been gleaned from a wide ranging trawl through numerous books and articles published during the last four centuries.

The following list of publications perused is not exhaustive, but is intended to assist research into particular issues.

Abbott, W. C., (Ed.) *Writings and Speeches of Oliver Cromwell 1599–1649*, Vol. I Cambridge, Mass, 1937; Clarendon Press Oxford, 1989.

Abell, H. F., *Kent and the Great Civil War.* Ashford: Kentish Express (Igglesden & Co.) Ltd., 1901

Adamson, J. H. & Folland, H. F., *Sir Harry Vane, His Life and Times*, London: The Bodley Head, 1973.

Aikin, J., Morgan, T. Mr. Nicholson *General Biography or Lives of the Most Eminent Persons.* London, 1802 (Vol. III) other Vols. have various dates. Printed for J. Johnson, St. Pauls' Churchyard.

Airy, O., (Ed.) *Burnet's History of my own time*, Oxford: Clarendon Press, 1897.

Aphorismical Discovery of Treasonable Faction I. 772 II. Refer to Gilbert, J. T.

Arnold, L. J., *The Cromwellian Settlement of Co. Dublin 1652–1660.* Journal, Royal Society of Antiquities of Ireland. 1971 Vol. 101

Ashley, M., *Oliver Cromwell: the Conservative Dictator.* London: Jonathan Cape Ltd., 1937.

Ashley, M., *Oliver Cromwell and his World.* London: Thames & Hudson, 1972.

Ashley, M., *The English Civil War*, Stroud, Glos.: Alan Sutton Publishing Ltd, 1974, 1990. British Library Catalogue Title 942.06 '2

Ashley, M., *Cromwell's Generals*, London: Jonathan Cape, 1954.

Attenborough, J., *Destiny our Choice*, London: Hodder & Stoughton Ltd, 1987. Charnwood, Jan 1988.

Aylmer, G. E. (Ed.) *The Interregnum: The Quest for Settlement 1646–1660*. London: Macmillan Press Ltd., 1972 "Focus Series".

Bagwell, R., *Ireland under the Stuarts*. Vol. II. 1642–60. London: Longmans Green & Co., 1909.

Barbary, J., *Puritan & Cavalier*. London: Victor Gollanez Ltd., 1977.

Barham, P., *Maidstone Fight 1648*. Kent: Smiling Roundhead Press, 1996.

Barnard, T. C. ,*Cromwellian Ireland. English Government and Reform in Ireland 1649–1660*. Oxford: Oxford University Press, 1975.

Barnard, T. C., *Planters and Policies in Cromwellian Ireland*. Journal: Past & Present magazine No. 61 (1973).

Barnard, T. C., *The English Republic 1649-1660*. Seminar Studies in History. London: Longmans, 1982.

Bayley, A. R., *The Great Civil War in Dorset, 1642-1660*. Taunton: Barnicott & Pearce, The Wessex Press, 1910.

Berry, Sir James & Lee, S. G., *A Cromwellian Major General: The career of Colonel James Berry*. Oxford: Clarendon Press, 1938.

Boate, G., *Ireland's Natural History* London: 1652.

Borlase. *History of the Execrable Irish Rebellion*, London: 1680.

Bowle, J., *Charles the First*. London: Weidenfeld & Nicholson, 1975.

Bradley, K., Article in *English Civil War, Notes & Queries*. Issue No. 6. Partizan Press, Leigh-on-Sea.

Brewer, *Beauties of Ireland* Vol.II

Briggs, A., *A Social History of England*. Penguin, 1985.

Brown, L. F., *The Political Activities of the Baptists and Fifth Monarchy Men in England during the Interregnum*. London: Henry Frowde, Oxford: Oxford University Press, 1912.

Bruodin *Propug* p.684

Bryant, A., *Freedom's Own Island*. Vol. II, 1986.

Buchan, J., *Cromwell*. London: Hodder & Stoughton, 1934; London: Sphere Books editions 1970 & 1971.

Burke, Sir Bernard, *The General Armory of England, Scotland, Ireland and Wales*. London: Burkes Peerage Ltd, 1884.

Burton, T., (Ed: Rutt, J. T.) *Diary of Thomas Burton, with Introduction from Parliamentary Journal of Guibon Goddard of 1654*. 4 Vols. London: Henry Colburn, Reprinted 1972. New York & London: Johnson Reprint Corporation (Vol II), 1974.

Calendar of State Papers: Domestic C.S.P.D.

1 Year 1655
2 Year 1656–57
3 Year 1654
4 Year 1659–60
5 Year 1657–58

Carlin, N., *The Levellers and the Conquest of Ireland in 1649*. Historical Journal, 30 No. 2. (1987), pp 269–88 (page 283 refers).

Carlton, C., *Going to the Wars*. London: 1992.

Carlyle, T., *Cromwell's Letters and Speeches*. (ed. Lomas) 3 Vols., 1904. Letters CV, CVI; Common's Journals, vii.

Carte Papers or Collection.

XVI Carte Papers, XXV, p.25.

Carte 'Original Letters', II.

Papers or collection held in Bodleian Library. Include Ormonde papers. Catalogued in part by Rev. Dr. C. W. Russell and J. P. Prendergast, HMSO, London 1871.

Carte Collection or Carte Papers: *'A Collection of Original Letters and Papers, concerning the Affairs of England, from the year 1641 to 1660'* 2 Vols by A. Millar, London, 1739.

Cary, H., *Memorials of the Great Civil War in England from 1646 to 1652*. Vol II Published by Henry Colburn, 1842. British Library W5-2494 15563406.

Castlehaven, Lord, *Memoirs of the Engagement and Carriage of the Civil War of Ireland from 1642 to 1651*. Pub. 1680; 2nd Edn.1685.

Catterall, R. C. H., *Sir George Downing and the Regicides*. American

Historical Review Vol. 17 (1912). British Library Shelf-mark 0818.500000.

Clarendon, Edward, Earl of. *The History of the Rebellion and Civil Wars in England begun in the year 1641*. Ed: W. Dunn Macray in six volumes. Oxford: Clarendon Press First Edn 1888. Reprints 1958, 1969.

Clarke, A. *Prelude to Restorations in Ireland The end of the Commonwealth, 1659–1660*. Cambridge: Cambridge University Press, 1999.

Clarke, Sir William; Firth, C. H. Edited by Firth, C. H. *The Clarke papers: selections from the papers of William Clarke*. USA: Offices of the Royal Historical Society, 1992. London.

Clode, C. M. (Ed.) *London during the Great Rebellion* being Memoir of Sir Abraham Reynardson, Lord Mayor of London. London: Harrison and Sons, 1892.

Coonan, T. L. *The Irish Catholic Confederacy and the Puritan Revolution*. London: Burns Oates & Washbourne Ltd., 1954.

Crawford, P. *Denzil Holles 1598–1680*. London: Royal Historical Society, 1979.

Cromwell, H. Letter dated 19.12.1655, to Secretary Thurloe

Curtis, E. *A History of Ireland*. London. Methuen & Co. 6th Edn, 1950.

D'Alton, J. *The History of the County of Dublin*. Dublin: Hodges & Smith, 1838. British Library 13478168.

Davies, G. *The Parliamentary Army under the Earl of Essex, 1642–45*. English Historical Review, Vol. 49 Edn. 1934, pp.32–54.

Davies, G. *The Army of the Eastern Association, 1644–5*. English Historical Review, Vol. 46 Edn. 1931 p.p.88–96.

Davies, G. *The Restoration of Charles II, 1658-1660*. California: Huntingdon Library, 1955. Reprinted Oxford University Press, 1969.

Dawson, W. H. *Cromwell's Understudy: The Life and Times of General John Lambert*. London, Edinburgh, Glasgow: William Hodge & Co. Ltd., 1938.

Denton, B. *The Crisis in the Army, 1647*. Essex: Partizan Press, 1984.

Dictionary of National Biography, 1921 Edition. pp. 702–703.

Dunlop, D (or possibly R. T.) *Cromwell in Ireland.* Dublin: M.H. Gill & Sons, 1883.

Dunlop, R. T. *Ireland under the Commonwealth*, Vol. I; Vol. II. Manchester University Press, 1913.

Ellis, P. B. *Hell or Connaught! The Cromwellian Colonisation of Ireland.* Hamish Hamilton Ltd., 1975. Belfast: Blackstaff Press, 1988.

Emberton, W. *Love Loyalty.*

England's New Chains. Sig.B., E. 545, 27. Public Record Office.

English Civil War – Notes and Queries. Essex: Caliver Books/Partizan Press.

English Civil War Times. Essex: Partizan Press.

Esson, D. M. R. *The Curse of Cromwell.* London: Leo Cooper Ltd., 1971.

Evelyn, J., *The Diary of John Evelyn.* ed. John Bowles. Oxford: Oxford Unversity Press, 1983.

Everitt, A. M. *The Community of Kent and the Great Rebellion 1640–1660.* 1st Edition, Leicester: Leicester University Press, 1966. 2nd Edition, Leicester: Leicester University Press, 1973.

Fairfax, *Correspondence.*

Fellowe, *Fellowe's Historical Sketches.* Pamphlet. London c.1660.

Firth, C. H. *Cromwell and the Crown.* English Historical Review, vol. XVII pp. 429–42, 1902.

Firth, C. H. *Cromwell and the Crown.* English Historical Review, vol. XVIII pp. 52–80, 1903.

Firth, C. H., *Cromwell's Army.* London: Greenhill Books, 1902 & 1992.

Firth, C. H., *The Regimental History of Cromwell's Army.* Revised by Godfrey Davies, Oxford: Clarendon press, 1940.

Firth, C. H., *The House of Lords during the Civil War.* Methuen & Co., London, 1910, reprinted 1974.

Firth, C. H., *The Narrative of General Venables.* London: Longmans, Green & Co., 1900.

Firth, C. H., *The Last Years of the Protectorate 1656–1658.* vols. I & II. London: Longmans, Green & Co., 1909.

Fitzmaurice, Lord E. *Life of Sir William Petty, 1623–1687*. London: John Murray, 1895.

Fitzpatrick, S. A. O. *Dublin, a historical and topographical account*. London: Methuen & Co., 1907.

Fletcher, C. R. L. & Butler, H. B. *Historical Portraits 1600–1700*. Oxford: Oxford Clarendon Press, 1911.

Foard, G. *Colonel John Pickering's Regiment of Foot 1644–1645*. Kent: Pryor Publications, 1994.

Foard, G. *Naseby: The Decisive Campaign*. Kent: Pryor Publications, 1995.

Fraser, A. *Cromwell, Our Chief of Men*. London: Weidenfeld & Nicholson, 1973.

Gardiner, S. R. *History of the Commonwealth and Protectorate, 1649–1656*, in Four Volumes. London: Longmans, Green & Co. 1903.

Gardiner, S. R. *History of the Great Civil War, 1642-1649*. London: Longmans, Green & Co. 1894.

Gaunt, P. *The Cromwellian Gazetter*. Alan Sutton & The Cromwell Association: 1992.

Gentles, I. J. *The New Model Army in England, Scotland, 1645–1653*. Oxford: Blackwell, 1992; reprinted 1994.

Gilbert, J. T. *A Contemporary History of Affairs in Ireland from 1641 to 1652*. (Also referred to as "Aphorismical Discovery of Treasonable Faction") Dublin: The Irish Archaeological & Celtic Society Vol. II, 1879 or 1880.

Gilbert, J. T. *A History of the City of Dublin*. Vol. I, II & III. Dublin: Gill & Macmillan Ltd.,1978. (First published, Dublin 1854–9. Republished: The Sackville Library Edn. Irish Academic Press.) 0-7171-0942-9 (3 vols.).

Glass, H. A. *The Barbone Parliament*. London: James Clarke & Co., 1899.

Goodwin, T. *Dorset in the Civil War 1625–1665*. Dorset: Dorset Books, 1996.

Granger, J. *A Biographical History of England, Vol. IV. p.3* from Egbert the Great to the Revolution. London: William Heineman Ltd, 1824.

Graves, Revd. J. "History of St. Canice's Cathedral". Kilvenny.

Graves, Revd. J. *"The Surrender, in March, 1649–50, of Ballysonan, in the County of Kildare, to the Parliamentary Forces."* Article in Journal of the Kilkenny & South East of Ireland Archaeological Society. Vol. I, New Series, 1856–7. Page 110 onwards.

Greaves, R. L. & Zaller, R. *Biographical Dictionary of British Radicals in the Seventeenth Century*. Vol. I. Brighton: The Harvester Press, 1982.

Greaves, R. L. & Zaller, R. *Biographical Dictionary of British Radicals in the Seventeenth Century*. Vol. II. Brighton: The Harvester Press, 1983.

Green, E. *The Siege of Bridgwater, July 1645*. Bath: George Gregory, 5 Argyle Street, Bath, 1905.

Gregg, P. *Free-Born John*. London: George G. Harrap & Co. Ltd., 1961.

Gregg, P. *King Charles I*. London: J. M.Dent & Sons Ltd., 1981.

Gurney Benham, W. *Playing Cards*. London: Ward, Lock & Co. Ltd., 1931.

Hainsworth, R. *The Swordsmen in Power*. Gloucester: Sutton Publishing Ltd., 1997. ISBN 0-7509-0571-9.

Hall, "Ireland" Vol (ii).

Hardiman, "History of Galway" 18XX.

Hewetson, J. *Memoirs of the House of Hewetson or Hewson of Ireland*. London: Mitchell & Hughes, 1901.

Hewson, John Letter to Speaker Lenthall of 03.3.1649-50.
Letter to Speaker Lenthall of 14.3.1651.
Letter to Speaker Lenthall of 05.6.1651.
Letter to Parliamentary Commissioners 19.6.1651.

Hill, C. *God's Englishman*. London: Weidenfeld & Nicholson, 1970.

Hobbes, T. *"Behemoth"*.

Holles. *"Memoirs"*.

Hollick, C. Article in *"English Civil War, Notes & Queries."* Issue No.8. Leigh-on-Sea: Partizan Press.

Holmes, C. *The Eastern Association in the English Civil War*. Cambridge: Cambridge University Press, 1974, 1897.

Indictment of the Regicides, London: 1724.

Jordan, D. and Walsh. "The King's Revenge". Little, Brown, 2012.

Jackson, R.W. *The Story of Kilkenny*. Dublin & Cork: The Mercia Press, 1974.

Jubbes, J. tract entitled *"Humble Remonstrance and desires of divers officers and soldiers in the Army under Colonel Hewson"*. Dated 9 Nov. 1647.

Kaplan, L. *Cromwell*. London: Harrap's "World Leaders" Series, 1986.

Kennedy, J. *"Old Kilkenny Review"* 1984 Issue.

Keogh, J. *"The Normans in Rathvilly"* Tullow Historical Society. http://www.rtc-carlow.ie/Carlow/normans.html, 1998.

Kerr, A. W. M. *An Ironside of Ireland: The Remarkable Career of Lieut-General Michael Jones*. London: Heath Cranton Ltd., 1923.

King, D. W. *The Succession of Colonels in the Army of Ireland 1658–9*. Journal of the Society for Army Historical Research, Spring 1977, Vol.55

Kingston, A. *Hertfordshire During the Great Civil War and the Long Parliament*. London: Elliot Stock, 1894.

Kingston, A. *East Anglia and the Great Civil War*. London: Elliot Stock, 1897.

Kinross, J. *Walking & Exploring the Battlefields of Britain*. David & Charles London & Newton Abbott, 1933 & 1988.

Kishlansky, M. A. *The Rise of the New Model Army*. Cambridge University Press, 1979.

Kishlansky, M. A. (article) *Past and Present*, LXXXI (1978) pp. 51–74

Koch, H.W. *History of Warfare*, London: Bison Books Ltd, 1987.

Laker, J. *History of Deal* 2nd Edition. Deal: T.F.Pain & Sons, 1921.

Lambert, Lord *Letter to the Speaker.*

Lansdowne, M. S. At British Library.

Latimer, J. *The Annals of Bristol in the Seventeenth Century*. Bristol, 1900. Kingsmead Reprints, 1970.

Lecky, Stated to be biased against Cromwell

(The) *Legal Fundamental Liberties*. 2nd Edition, E. 561. Public Record Office.

Leland, Rev. Dr. *History of Ireland* Dublin or London 1773.

Leyborne – Popham M.S.S.

Lister, S. (article) *English Civil War, Notes & Queries*. Issue No. 44 Partizan Press, Leigh-on-Sea.

Lucas Phillips, C.E. *Cromwell's Captains*. London: William Heinemann Ltd., 1938.

Ludlow, E. *Memoirs of Edmund Ludlow 1625–1672* (2 vols.) Ed: C. H. Firth, Oxford: Clarendon Press, 1894.

Ludlow, E. *Letters from Ludlow.*

Macken, W. *Seek the Fair Land*. London: Pan Books, 1974, 1988.

Macmillan's magazine, London, November 1893.

Madge, S. J. *The Domesday of Crown Lands*. London: 1938.

Malden, H. E. *English Historical Review*. Edn. 1892 (7) pp. 533–6.

Manning, B. *The Crisis of the English Revolution*. London: Bookmarks, 1992.

Markham, Sir C. R. *A Life of the Great Lord Fairfax*. London: Macmillan & Co. 1870.

Matthews, A. G. *Calamy Revised*. Oxford: 1934.

Mayer, J. (article) "Inedited Letters of Cromwell, Colonel Jones, Bradshaw and other Regicides" in *Transactions of the Historic Society of Lancashire and Cheshire*. Vol.13, New Series, pp. 177–300. Session 1860-61. Published 1861, Liverpool.

McKeiver, P. *A New History of Cromwell's Irish Campaign*. Advance Press, Didsbury, Manchester 2007.

Mercurius Prag. No. 38 (12–19 Dec 1648) [B.M.] E 476, 35 Historical Collections. Public Record Office.

(The) Moderate 24 April–1 May 1649. Public Record Office.

Modest Narrative E. 547, 9. Public Record Office.

Moody, T.W., Martin, Byrne. *A New History of Ireland* Vol.III 1534–1691. Oxford: Clarendon Press, 1976.

Moran, Rev. P. F. *Historical Sketch of the persecutions suffered by the Catholics of Ireland under the rule of Cromwell and the Puritans*. Dublin: M. H. Gill & Son, Ltd. 1907.

Morgan, A. Letter to Henry Cromwell of 24.2.1657/8.

Morison, W. *Johnston of Warriston*, in the series "Famous Scots". Edinburgh: 1901.

Morrah, D. Book concerning the Restoration. 1960.

Morrill, J. S. *Past & Present*. Vol. 56, pp. 50–51. August 1972.

Muddiman, J. G. *Trial of King Charles the First*. London & Edinburgh: William Hodge & Co. Ltd., 1928.

Murphy, Revd. D. S. J. *Cromwell in Ireland* (p.75 Footnote[2]). Dublin: M. H. Gill & Son, 1883.

Murphy, Carrier, Sparey. *Britain, 1558–1689*. Collins, 2002.

Neely, W. G. *Kilkenny: An Urban History, 1391–1843*. Institute of Irish Studies, The Queen's University of Belfast, 1989.

Newman, P. R. *Companion to the English Civil Wars*. Oxford: Facts on File Ltd., 1990.

Noble, Revd. M. *The Lives of the English Regicides*, Vol. 1. London: 1798.

O'Cahan, T. S. *Owen Roe O'Neill*. London: T. Joseph Keane & Co., 1968.

O'Ciardha, E. *Toryism in Cromwellian Ireland (1650–60)*. The Irish Sword, vol. 19, 1995–6.

O'Connell *Memoir of Ireland.*

Ohlmeyer, J. H. *Civil War and Restoration in the Three Stuart Kingdoms*. Cambridge University Press, 1993.

Ohlmeyer, J. H. *Ireland from Independence to Occupation 1641–60*. Cambridge University Press, 1995.

Ollard, R. *This War Without an Enemy*. London: Hodder & Stoughton, 1976.

O'Meagher, Casimir. *Diary of Dr. Jones, Scout-Master-General to the Army of the Commonwealth, from 13th March 1649–50, to July, 1650*. Journal of the Royal Society of the Antiquaries of Ireland, 5th Series, 1893. Vol. 3 pages 44–54.

Ormonde Papers. These are held in Bodleian Library as part of the Carte, Thomas (Ed.), Collection. The Ormonde Papers, public and private, connected with the Government of Ireland 1641–1650, and 1660–1688. In various parts, including Letters (King's Letters) under Sign

Manual and Privy Seal. Vols 41, 42 and 43 of Carte Papers.

Paper Scattered about the Streets E.551, 21. Public Record Office.

Parry, R. H., ed., *The English Civil War and After 164–1658*. London: Macmillan & Co. Ltd., 1970.

Partridge, B. (article) "The Execution of Charles I", *English Civil War Times*, Issue No. 55 Partizan Press, Essex.

Peachey, S. & Turton, A. *Old Robin's Foot*, 1987. Partizan Press, Essex.

Pender, S. (Ed.) *A Census of Ireland, circa 1659* Dublin: Stationery Office for Irish Historical Manuscripts Commission, 1939.

Pepys, S. *Diary* Edition edited by Wheatley, Henry. Vol. I. London: G. Bell & Sons, 1917.

Perfect Diurnal. No. 158, August 3–10, 1646, E. 511 (29) Public Record Office.

Letter from Col. Hewson published 4.4.1650.

Also April 23 to 30th 1649.

Perfect Occurrences, E. 533, 15. Public Record Office.

(The) Perfect Weekly Account, E. 552, 2. Public Record Office.

Pine, L. G. *A Dictionary of Mottoes*. London: Routledge & Kegan Paul, 1983.

Pinnell, H. *A Word of Prophesy.*

Prendergast, J. P. (article) "The Clearing of Kilkenny, anno 1654", in *The Journal of the Kilkenny and South East of Ireland Archaeological Society*. New Series, 1860/61.

Prendergast, J. P. *The Cromwellian Settlement of Ireland*. London: Longmans, Green, Reader & Dyer, 1870.

Prestedge, J. Article in *English Civil War, Notes & Queries* Issue No. 44. Partizan Press, Leigh-on-Sea.

Public Record Office: State papers in P.R.O., folio 356, 252A, Part 1; The Certificate Book, folio 71, 253A Certificate Book B, No. 186.

Raikes, G. A. *The History of the Honourable Artillery Company*, 1878.

Ramsey, R. W. *Henry Cromwell*. London: Longmans Green & Co., 1933

Ray, P. (article) *English Civil War, Notes & Queries* Issue No. 50. Partizan Press, Leigh-On-Sea.

Razzell, E. & P. (Eds.) *The English Civil War: A Contemporary Account.*

Vol.5, 1657–1675. London: Caliban Press, 1996.

Reid, S. (article) "Street Fighting in the 17th Century" in *English Civil War, Notes & Queries* Issue No. 14. Partizan Press, Essex.

Reilly, T. *Cromwell at Drogheda*. Drogheda: Broin Print Ltd., 1993.

Ridley, J. *The Roundheads*. London: Constable & Co. Ltd., 1976.

Roots, I. *The Great Rebellion 1642–1660*. London: B.T. Batsford, 1966.

Rowse, A. L. *The Regicides and the Puritan Revolution*. London: Gerald Duckworth & Co. Ltd., 1994.

Rushworth, Rushworth vii, vi.

Russell, C.W. & Prendergast, J. P. *The Carte Manuscripts in the Bodleian Library, Oxford; a report*. London: Eyre & Spottiswoode for Her Majesty's Stationery Office, 1871.

Russell, Rev. Dr. catalogued part of Ormonde Papers.

Scott, W. R. (article) "Members for Ireland in the Parliaments of the Protectorate" in *Journal of the Royal Society of Antiquaries of Ireland*. Edn: 5th Series, Vol. III. 1893. p. 488.6.1.

Several Proceedings in Parliament E, 777.22. Public Record Office.

Seymour, Rev. St. J. D. *The Puritans in Ireland 1647–1661*. Oxford: Clarendon Press, 1921.

Shaw, H. *The Levellers*. Seminar Studies in History. Longmans, 1968.

Sherwood, R. *Oliver Cromwell: King in All But Name*. Stroud: Sutton Publishing Ltd, 1997.

Sherwood, R. *The Court of Oliver Cromwell*. London & New York: Croom Helm Ltd. 1997.

Slingsby, Sir H. *The Diary of Sir Henry Slingsby*. Edited by Parson. London: Longmans, 1836.

Smith, J. E. *The Parliamentary Representation of Surrey from 1290 to 1924*. London: Wightman & Co. Ltd., 1927.

Solt, L. F. *Saints in Arms: Puritanism and Democracy in Cromwell's Army*. Stanford & London: Oxford University Press, 1959.

Sprigge, J. *Anglia Rediviva*; 1648 Ed. 1854, p. 329, Oxford.

Sutton, J. (article) "Poets at War", in *Cromwelliana*, 1992.

Taft, B. "Voting Lists of the Council of Officers, December 1648." *Bulletin of the Institute of Historical Research*, pages 138–154. Lii

(1979) British Library Document Supply Centre.

Taft, B. (article) "The Council of Officer's Agreement of the People" in *The Historical Journal.* Vol. XXVIII, 1985, pp 170–171.

Tanner, Letters (ed. Charles McNeill), Dublin: Stationery Office, 1943.

Temple, R. K G. *The English Regicides*. Unpublished thesis for M. Phil, Feb 1988.

The Dictionary of National Biography, 1921, Edn.

Thoms, W. J. (article) "The Death Warrant of Charles the First". *Notes & Queries,* Fourth series, Vol. X. 1872 July–Dec. Copy examined in the Berkeley Library of Trinity College, Dublin.

Tibbutt, H. G. *Colonel John Okey, 1606–1662.* Bedfordshire: Bedfordshire Historical Record Society, XXXV (35) Luton 1955.

Tolmie, M. *The Triumph of the Saints. The separate churches of London 1616–1649.* Cambridge University Press, 1977.

Underdown, D. E. *Pride's Purge*. Oxford: Clarendon Press. 1971.

Varley, F. J (Compiled) *Mercurius Aulicus.* Oxford: Blackwell, 1948.

Venetian Ambassadors *The English Civil War: A Contemporary Account.* London: Caliban Books, 1996.

Walton, C. *History of the British Standing Army 1660–1700.* 1894.

Warner, F.*The History of the Rebellion and Civil-War in Ireland, 1641–60.* Dublin: 1768. London: 1767.

Warton, N. *Letters of Nehimiah Warton* Ed. By S. Ede–Borret. *Archaeologia*, XXXV. 326.

Wedgewood, C. V. *The King's War 1641–1647*. London: Collins, 1958.

Wenham, P. *The Great and Close Siege of York... 1644*. Kineton: The Roundwood Press, 1970.

Wheatley, H. B. (Ed.) *The Diary of Samuel Pepys, Vol. 1.* London: G. Bell & Sons, 1917.

Wheeler, J. S. *Cromwell in Ireland.* Dublin: Gill & Macmillan, 1999.

Whitebrook, J. C. (Ed.) *London Citizens in 1651* being a transcript of Harleian. MS.4778. London: Hutchings & Romer, 1910.

Williamson, H. R. *Four Stuart Portraits*. London: Evans Brothers Ltd., 1949.

Willis, B. *Notitia Parliamentaria*, Vol. II. London: 1715.

Wills *Prerogative Court of Canterbury*. P.C.C. 95 Rivers. (see note at "Wood" below).

Wilshire, J. & Green, S. *The Siege of Leicester – 1645*. Leicester: Leicester Research Dept, Chamberlain Music & Books, 1970 & 1984.

Wilson, J. *Fairfax*. London: John Murray, 1985.

Wood. *Annals of the University*, Oxford.

Wood, *"Fasti"*, 1649. P.C.C. 95 Rivers (Wills proved in the Prerogative Court of Canterbury, now in the Public Record Office. Distinguishing name of the volume being preceded by the follation of the Will in question.).

Woodhouse, A. S. P. *Puritanism & Liberty. 3rd Edition*. London: J.M. Dent & Sons Ltd. Everymans Library, 1992.

Woolrych, A. H. *Soldiers and Statesmen: The General Council of the Army and its Debates 1647–1648*. Oxford: Clarendon Press, 1987.

Woolrych, A. H. *England without a King 1649–1660*. (Lancaster pamphlets). London: Methuen & Co. Ltd.,1983.

Woolrych, A. H. C *Commonwealth to Protectorate*, pp. 182–183. Oxford: Clarendon Press, 1982.

Young. *Chronicles of the First Planters of the Colony of Massachusetts Bay*, p. 46. 1846.

Young, Brig. P. *Naseby 1645 – The Campaign and Battle*. Century Publishing Co., 1985.

Young, Brig. P. *Marston Moor 1644, Battle of.* Warwick: Roundwood Press, 1970.

Young, P. & Emberton, W. *Sieges of the Great Civil War, 1642–1646*. London: Bell & Hyman Ltd., 1978.

Young, P. & Holmes, R. *The English Civil War: A Military History of the Three Civil Wars 1642 – 1651*. London: Eyre Methuen, 1974.

INDEX